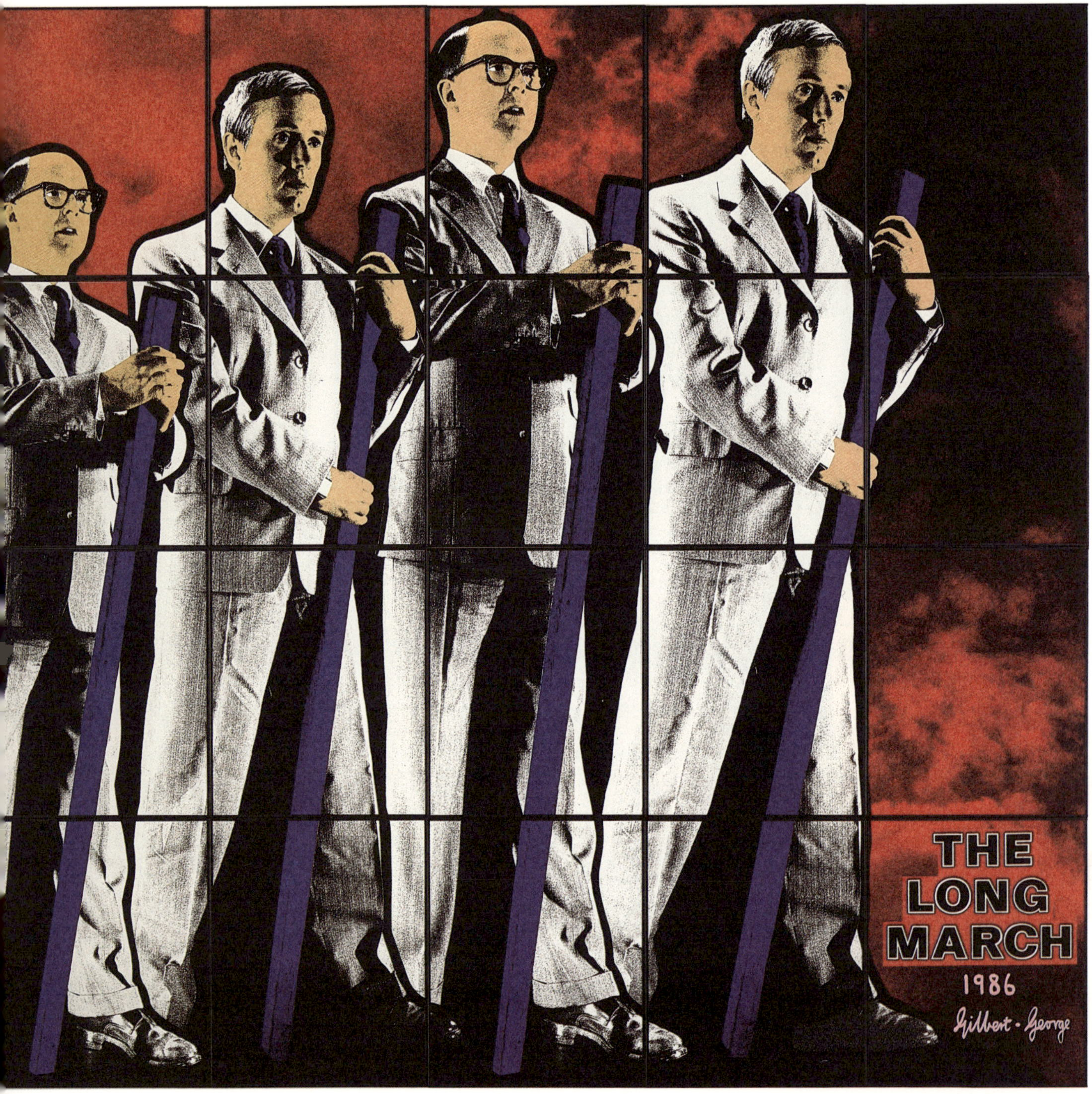

GILBERT & GEORGE, THE LONG MARCH / DER LANGE MARSCH, 1986, *95 x 199"* / 242 x 505 cm

COLLABORATION GILBERT & GEORGE

JEDE NUMMER DER ZEITSCHRIFT ENTSTEHT IN COLLABORATION MIT EINEM KÜNSTLER, DER EIGENS FÜR DIE LESER VON PARKETT EINEN ORIGINALBEITRAG GESTALTET. DIESES WERK IST IN DER GESAMTEN AUFLAGE ABGEBILDET UND ZUSÄTZLICH IN EINER LIMITIERTEN UND SIGNIERTEN VORZUGSAUSGABE ERHÄLTLICH. FÜR DIESE NUMMER HABEN GILBERT & GEORGE EINE DOPPELSEITIGE PHOTO-EDITION GESCHAFFEN, AUF KARTON AUFGEZOGEN UND IN DER MITTE FALTBAR. AUFLAGE 200 EXEMPLARE, 25,5 x 42 cm, SIGNIERT UND NUMERIERT. PREIS SFR. 440.–.

PARKETT NUMMER 15 ENTSTEHT IN COLLABORATION MIT MARIO MERZ.

EACH ISSUE OF THE MAGAZINE IS CREATED IN COLLABORATION WITH AN ARTIST, WHO CONTRIBUTES AN ORIGINAL WORK SPECIALLY MADE FOR THE READERS OF PARKETT. THE WORK IS REPRODUCED IN THE REGULAR EDITION. IT IS ALSO AVAILABLE IN A SIGNED AND LIMITED DELUXE EDITION. FOR THIS ISSUE GILBERT & GEORGE CREATED A PHOTOEDITION ON A DOUBLE PAGE MOUNTED ON CARDBOARD AND FOLDED IN THE MIDDLE. EDITION 200, 10 x 16½", SIGNED AND NUMBERED. PRICE $ 300.00.

MARIO MERZ WILL BE COLLABORATING ON PARKETT ISSUE NO. 15.

PARKETT

SCHWEIZER KUNSTZEITSCHRIFT IN DEUTSCHER UND ENGLISCHER SPRACHE ERSCHEINT VIERTELJÄHRLICH / *SWISS ART MAGAZINE IN ENGLISH AND GERMAN PUBLISHED QUARTERLY*. ADRESSE / *ADDRESS:* PARKETT-VERLAG AG, QUELLENSTRASSE 27, CH-8005 ZÜRICH, TEL. 01/42 81 40 / *NEW YORK OFFICE PARKETT: 14 WEST 10TH STREET, NEW YORK, NY 10011, PHONE 212/475-0227.*

HERAUSGEBER/*PUBLISHER*
PETER BLUM
JACQUELINE BURCKHARDT
BICE CURIGER
DIETER VON GRAFFENRIED
WALTER KELLER

CHEFREDAKTION/*EDITOR*
BICE CURIGER
GRAPHIK/*DESIGN*
TRIX WETTER
VERLAGSASSISTENZ/
PUBLISHER'S ASSISTANT
ELEONORE VON GRAFFENRIED

REDAKTIONSASSISTENZ USA/
ASSOCIATE EDITOR USA
KAREN MARTA
ENGLISCHES LEKTORAT/
EDITORIAL ASSISTANT FOR ENGLISH
CATHERINE SCHELBERT
KORREKTORIN/PROOF READING
CLAUDIA MENEGHINI
SATZ/*COPY*
ENGLERSATZ AG, ZÜRICH
LITHOS/*LITHOGRAPHIE*
LITHO AG, AARAU
DRUCK/*PRINTING*
BUCHDRUCKEREI STÄFA

INSERATE/*ADVERTISEMENTS:* «PARKETT»-VERLAG AG, ZÜRICH
JAHRESABONNEMENT / *ANNUAL SUBSCRIPTION:* SFR. 80.–/DM 98,–/*$ 63.00 (AIR MAIL POSTAGE INCLUDED)*

SPECIAL THANKS TO ANTHONY D'OFFAY GALLERY AND JUDY ADAM, LONDON

PRINTED IN SWITZERLAND ISSN 0256-0917

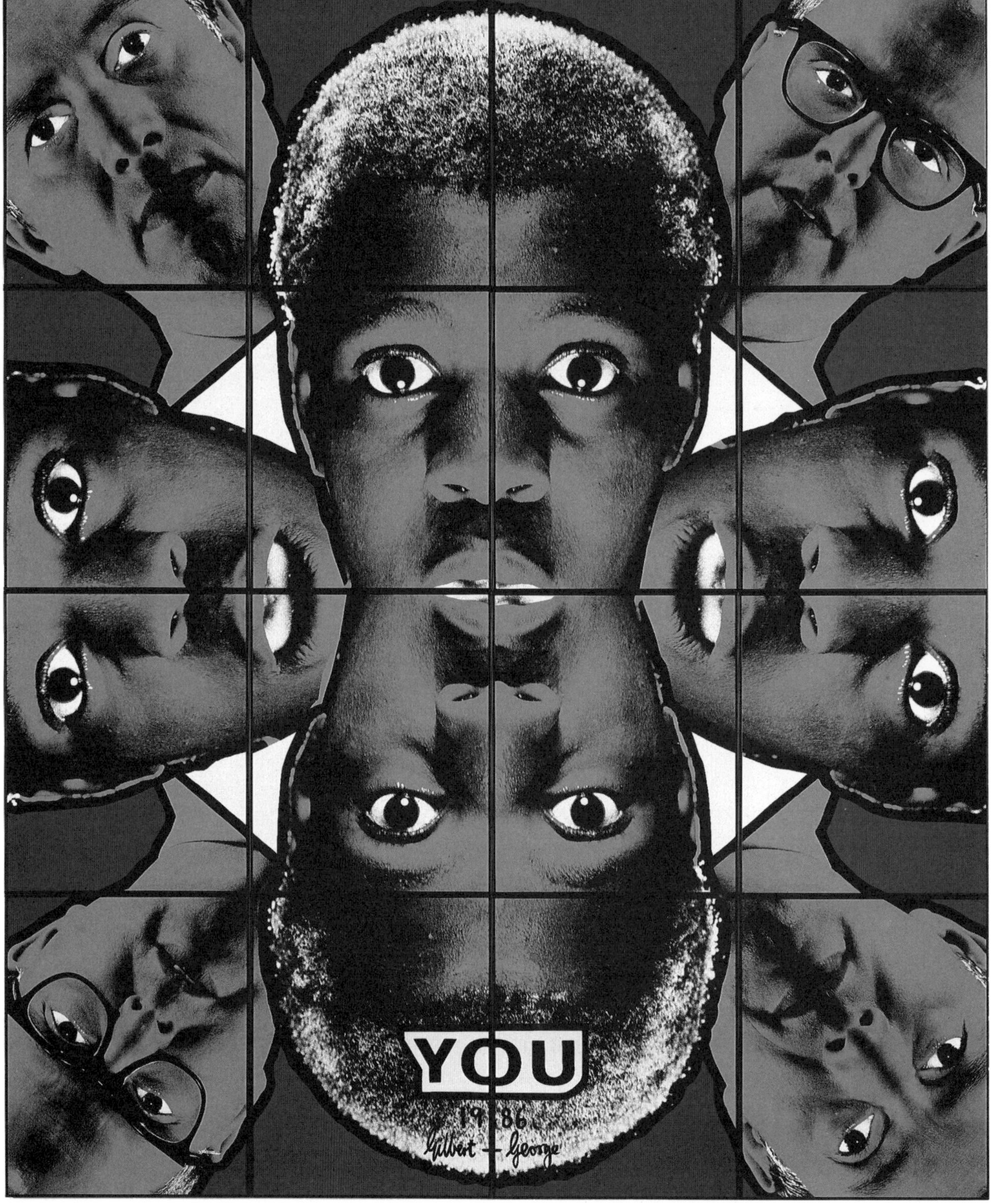

GILBERT & GEORGE, YOU / DU – IHR, 1986, *95 x 79½"* / 242 x 202 cm

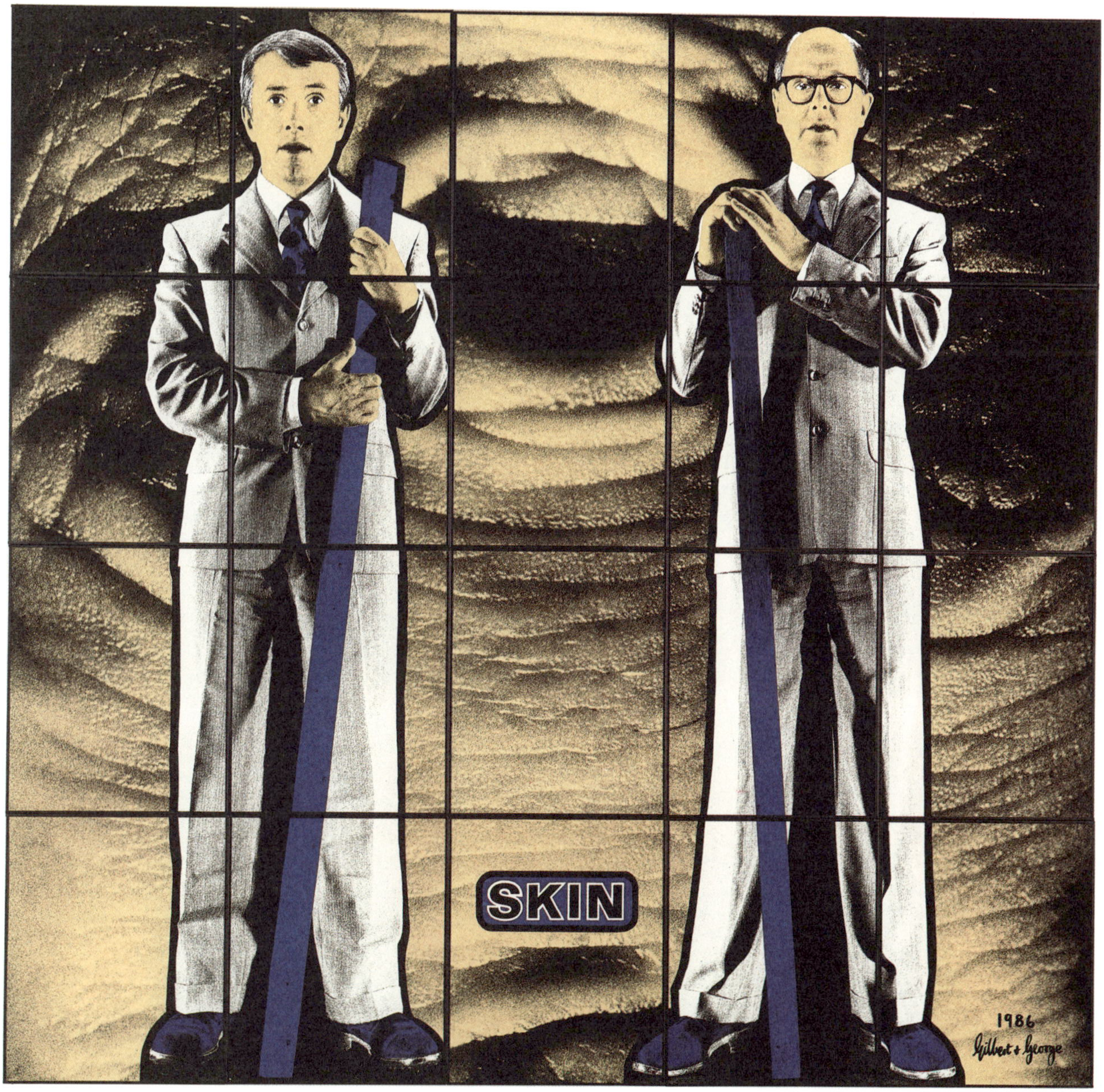

GILBERT & GEORGE, SKIN / HAUT, 1986,

95 x 99½" / 242 x 253 cm.

INHALT / *CONTENT*

Peripheral . Visions .

ROBERT STORR

Increasingly, Postmodernism in New York has become the affair of fainthearted suicides. Perched on every available ledge in a city of skyscrapers – to the ablest climbers go the most visible – they proclaim the nullity of contemporary life and the end of art. Yet somehow these avatars of ennui just can't bring themselves to take the definitive step. And while they contemplate the abyss in a state of dramatized inertia, we watch them from below with rapt indifference. This reciprocal fixation is called "closure." No one, it seems, has sufficient sense, or pity, to yell "Jump!"

Yet it is action we crave, and a release from numbed voyeurism. And, outside the closed circle of this static spectacle, things are moving. Regardless of the prevailing assumption that our "fin de siècle" is an epoch of ceaseless repetition, there are growing signs of change. Not for the better, in all likelihood, but change nonetheless. For few at the top or bottom of society have the luxury of standing still. A senescent president muffs his lines but delegates his powers to mercenaries. Anticolonial wars of liberation become national wars of attrition which the "Big Powers" seek to manage. The combatants, however, remain murderously unmanageable. Meanwhile, with economic "booms" having a proven tendency to convert themselves into "busts" the speculative euphoria of the early 1980s dissipates. Already, giddiness has set in. Soon more resolute sky-divers may be crowding access to the highest windows.

Despite ourselves we are about to be thrust back into "history." The question is what – if any – art can respond to the dislocations that are destined, and what art is ample or savvy enough to convincingly instruct those who mistook sloganeering and publicity for analysis, and T.V. time for their own uncertain lifespan. Not many come to mind. Of those who do, curiously enough, there are several already relegated to the purgatory of the immediate past. Chief among them is the painter-collagist Nancy Spero. Known as a "feminist" – which she most certainly is but which label has become a primary means of isolating and so disregarding her achievement – Spero, now in her 60s, is notable for her stamina and her stubborn refusal to be boxed in by stylistic, ideological or generational labels. All these factors would seem to suggest an eccentric, perhaps intractable art. Instead, Spero's work distinguishes itself by its openness and dynamism. That dynamism is of a unique variety.

Choosing her subject matter from the writings of Antonin Artaud – a genuine modernist who, to use his words, was all but "suicided by society" –,

---

ROBERT STORR is a painter and critic who lives in New York.

from grisly press reports of the persecution of political activists in the Third World, and from the mythic conflicts of the Gods, Spero strews her tableaux with episodes of extreme violence and anguish. Often, and most especially in her work of the 1970s, these images are rendered in a graphic manner of incomparable emotional urgency. Her gesture is sharp and concise, her surfaces sore with abrasions, her colors a peculiar range of bruised ochres and black. For all that, however, her pictures do not preach to us from the position of a secure and earnest "humanism" – to choose the malignant and often misogynistic writings of Artaud as her text raises many of the same issues and ambivalences as Simone de Beauvoir's perversely pioneering feminist essay, "Must We Burn Sade?" Much less, for all its expressivity, is Spero's work, in the conventional sense of the term, "Neo-Expressionist."

Quite the opposite. Much of the new Expressionist work either implicitly or explicitly reinvokes the romantic cult of the painter as hero living out freedoms lesser men and women have been obliged to forswear. The subject of these paintings are the acts of individuals, their scale a metaphor for the grandiosity of the artist's vision, their heft and "value" a promise of permanence. Everything in Spero's work contradicts these expectations. Spero has rendered the fat of Expressionism and preserved the sinew and the skin. Thus, though vigorous figures animate her work, and touch informs it, Spero's paintings, drawings and collages are remarkable for their almost ephemeral physical presence. Cut like monstrous paper-dolls or stamped with brittle contours on otherwise denuded sheets of paper joined end to end in scrolls, the very delicacy of her often tiny images heightens our awareness of the extreme situations to which they allude. And while heroes – or rather heroines – do appear from time to time, never does their maker intrude as a principal protagonist. What enthralls us is not the drama of the artistic creation but the political, historical and sexual dramas to which Spero, like us, is witness.

It is a drama of carnal torment, rebellion and celebration. In it women struggle against the violence done to them, parade their vitality and mock the authorities that would confine them to their rhetorical "place." In NOTES IN TIME ON WOMEN, for example, a nude female figure, legs spread, is catapulted over the quotation from Derrida, "there is no essence of woman, there is no truth about women, feminist women ... are men ..." Such critical counterpoint between text and image is essential to Spero's enterprise, and, it should be added, it has been characteristic of her work since long before the advent of currently fashionable forms of appropriation and deconstruction. The constant slippage from one representational code (pictures) to another (words), and often their jarring confrontation, results in a fully realized dialectic between perceptual apprehension and conceptual inquiry. Images do not exist merely as talking heads for a more important critical soundtrack, nor do words merely caption visual scenarios. Each sign, whether graphic or verbal, is both felt and thought. Each discourse is interrupted and answered by its contrary. Tidiness is inimical to her purpose.

To accommodate such a multiplicity of voices and languages, Spero has improvised a new pictorial format. Stretching the standard rectangle into long ribbons over which are distributed a wealth of disparate incidents, Spero has arrived at the perfect structure for a discursive as opposed to a narrative art, an unframed, uncompartmentalized version of the "bande-dessinée." (The English term comic strip, emphasizes content over form and is, for that reason, less useful here.) Hung in disjunctive groupings, some of these segments are positioned vertically and others horizontally. As in the case of the CODEX ARTAUD, the measurements of each distinct section may run from twenty inches in width to sixteen to thirty feet in length or height. On several occasions, moreover, Spero has overstepped the edge of her paper support and printed images directly on the wall, in a Lascaux-like dispersion of phantom-silhouttes. What Spero has done is to explode the conventional pictorial grid and permit its axes to extend at will in all directions. To follow the complex detail and grasp the complex syntax of a given series of these pictorial fragments one must constantly readjust one's gaze,

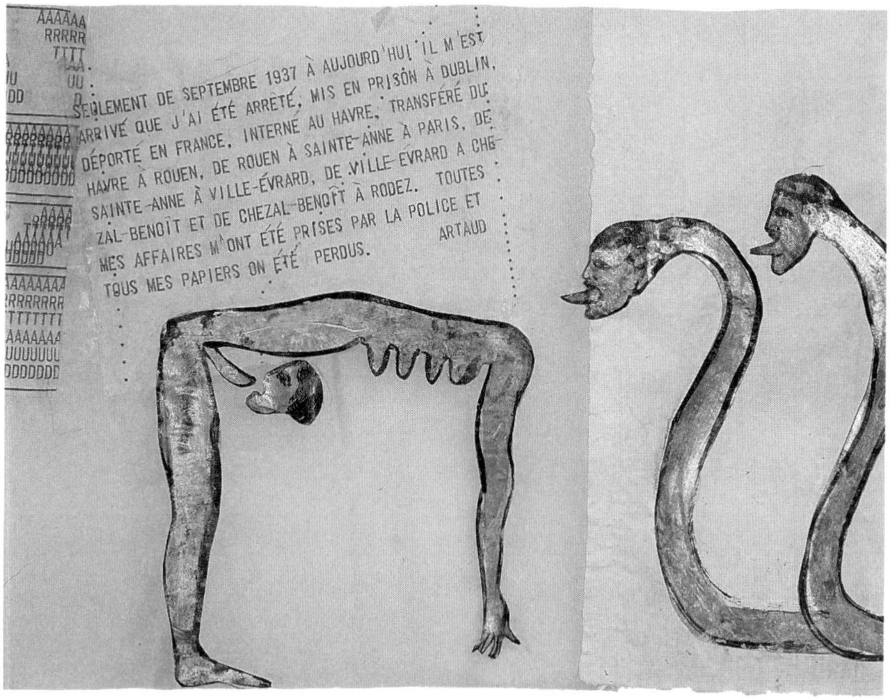

NANCY SPERO, DETAIL: CODEX ARTAUD (VI) 1971,
PAINTING AND TYPEWRITER, COLLAGE ON PAPER / MALEREI UND SCHREIBMASCHINENSCHRIFT, COLLAGE AUF PAPIER,
20½ x 124½" / 52 x 316,3 cm *(Photo: David Reynolds)*

jumping from one extreme of vision to another and then back to images too hastily scanned in the process.

In this respect, "reading" a work by Spero is akin to reading stanzas of shaped verse projected on a mural scale. And as with the best of concrete poetry, one experiences a uniquely active visual and intellectual engagement. Contradictions, digressions and ruptures in the flow of the line do not engender the sense of confusion and stasis that is evident in much recent work using the closed framing of the traditional easel painting as a means to impose an absolute relativism on a host of incommensurable symbols and modes of address. Rather, the notion of dynamic simultaneity, which was the hallmark of early modernism, returns within a new and expansive structure. The key lies with the viewer's capacity to exploit peripheral vision as a way of encompassing a whole that is always about to exceed one's scope, while at the same time using focused vision as a way to take full account of each of the dense images and phrases which flash within that field.

This, then, is the formal structure of a new "history painting." For that is what Spero has been up to for the past twenty years. Cross-referencing icons from the past with documents and emblems that invoke current events, her codices – contemporary hieroglyphic chronicles – depict a syn-

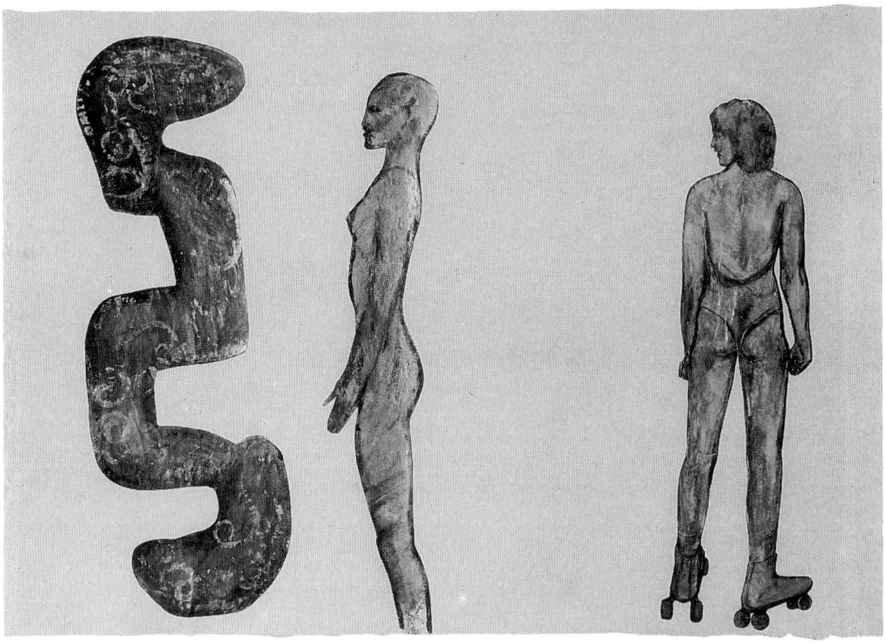

NANCY SPERO, 2 DETAILS: THE FIRST LANGUAGE / DIE ERSTE SPRACHE, 1981,
PAINTING, COLLAGE, HANDPRINTING ON PAPER / MALEREI, COLLAGE, HANDDRUCK AUF PAPIER,
20" x 190 ft. / 0,50 x 57,91 m.

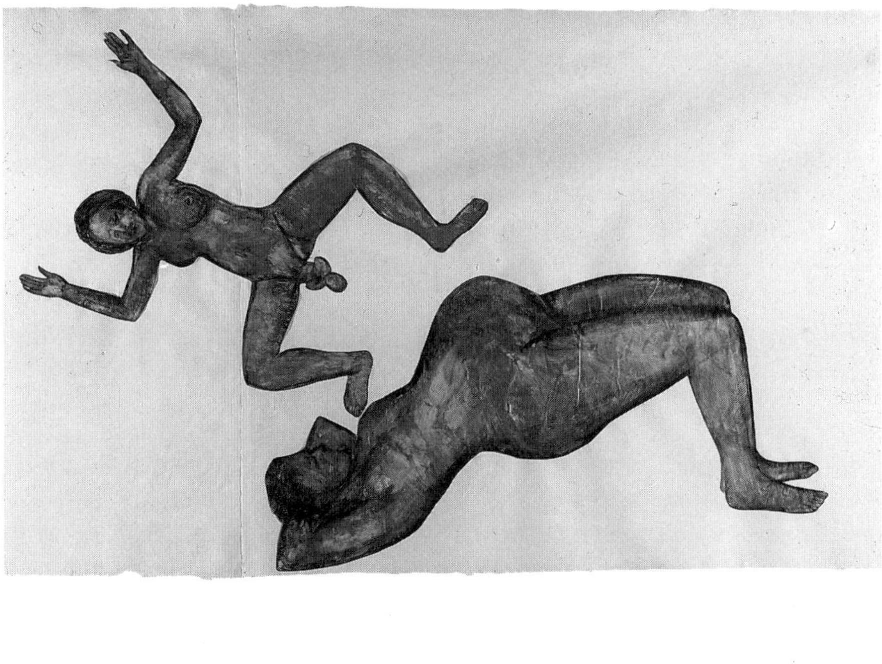

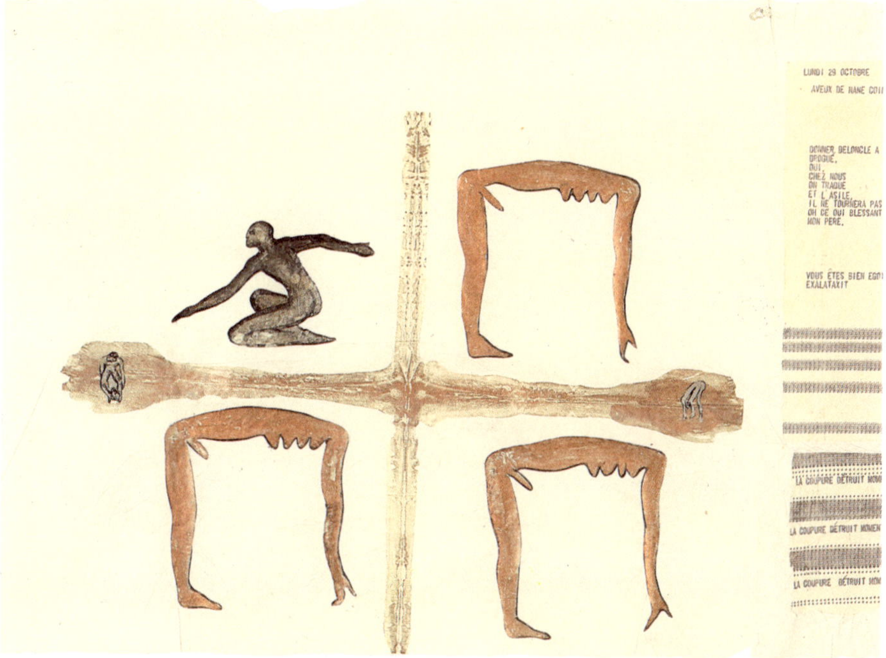

NANCY SPERO, DETAIL: CODEX ARTAUD (XXV), 1971,
PAINTING AND TYPEWRITER, COLLAGE ON PAPER / MALEREI UND SCHREIBMASCHINENSCHRIFT, COLLAGE AUF PAPIER,
20½ x 124½" / 52 x 316,3 cm *(Photo: David Reynolds)*

chronous and thoroughly modern sense of time. No "mainstream" obtains; the sequencing of images is dispersed and channeled by numerous currents, tributaries and deltas. None of the "great narratives" circumscribes the range of her interests – neither that of Freud nor Marx nor any of the more recent theorists – yet all find a place within the spacious framework of her work, which also incorporates the generally ignored stories of the sexual, cultural and economic "Other." Nor is any apocalypse foreseen, any halt to the challenges of perpetual flux. To grasp meaning thus requires a temporal equivalent to peripheral vision, a full acknowledgement of our involuntary and discomforting capacity for simultaneously looking back and thinking forward. "History is a nightmare from which I am trying to awake," wrote Joyce at the beginning of the modernist age. Perhaps the most radical and truthful admission at the end of the modern epoch is that there is no "end," and that we have been awake all along. The idea of finality, it turns out, has been a weary daydream. Hence, in the last analysis post-modernism demonstrates that we cannot outrun, reenact or stop history – though we may at any point put a stop to ourselves – but must live in it as fully conscious of our circumstances as curiosity and tolerance will allow. Spero is one of a small contingent of artists who make that alternative seem not only conceivable, but in brief moments, hopeful.

Periphere . Visionen .

ROBERT STORR

Die New Yorker Postmoderne ist zu einer Angelegenheit verzagter Selbstmörder geworden. In einer Stadt der Wolkenkratzer verkünden sie, von allen erreichbaren Fenstersimsen herab – die weit herum sichtbarsten sind den fähigsten Kletterern vorbehalten –, die Nichtigkeit des zeitgenössischen Lebens und das Ende der Kunst. Trotzdem bringen diese Inkarnationen der Langeweile es irgendwie nicht fertig, den endgültigen Schritt zu tun. Und indem sie in einem Zustand dramatisierter Trägheit den Abgrund beschauen, betrachten wir sie mit gespannter Gleichgültigkeit von unten. Diese reziproke Fixierung wird «geschlossener Zustand» genannt. Niemand hat genügend Verstand oder Mitleid, wie es scheint, «Spring!» zu schreien.

Trotzdem ist es Action, nach der wir verlangen, und eine Erlösung von stumpfem Voyeurismus. Und ausserhalb dieses geschlossenen Kreises sind Dinge in Bewegung. Ungeachtet der herrschenden Annahme, dass unser Fin de siècle eine Epoche unaufhörlicher Wiederholungen sei, gibt es wachsende Anzeichen der Veränderung. Aller Wahrscheinlichkeit nach nicht zum Besseren, aber trotzdem Veränderung. Denn wenige an der Spitze oder auf dem Grund der Gesellschaft beherrschen den Luxus stillzustehen. Ein alternder Präsident bringt seine Texte durcheinander, aber er delegiert seine Macht an Söldnertruppen. Antikoloniale Befreiungskriege werden zu nationalen Zermürbungskriegen, welche die «Grossmächte» in die Hand zu nehmen suchen. Die Kombattanten bleiben jedoch auf mörderische Weise schwer zu handhaben. Angesichts der nachweislichen Tendenz wirtschaftlicher «Booms», sich selbst in «Pleiten» umzuwandeln, löst sich die spekulative Euphorie der frühen achtziger Jahre mittlerweile in nichts auf. Schon setzt Schwindelgefühl ein. Möglicherweise werden bald resolutere Himmelstaucher die Zugänge zu den höchsten Fenstern verstopfen.

Ohne es zu wollen, sind wir im Begriff, in die «Geschichte» zurückgeworfen zu werden. Die Frage lautet, welche Kunst – wenn überhaupt eine – vermag auf die Verschiebungen, die vorausbestimmt sind, Antworten zu geben? Und welche Kunst ist umfassend genug oder hat Köpfchen genug, um auf überzeugende Art diejenigen zu belehren, die Phrasendrescherei und Propaganda mit kritischer Analyse verwechseln und «TV-Time» als ihre eigene ungewisse Lebensdauer missdeuten? Viel fällt einem dabei nicht ein. Und von den Künstlern, an die man denkt, sind merkwürdigerweise einige bereits an das Fegefeuer der unmittelbaren Vergangenheit verwiesen. Die wichtigste unter ihnen ist die Malerin/Collagistin Nancy Spero. Bekannt als «Feministin» – was sie ganz gewiss ist, welches Aushängeschildchen aber ein pri-

---

ROBERT STORR ist Künstler und Kunstkritiker. Er lebt in New York.

märes Mittel geworden ist, um das von ihr Geleistete zu isolieren und somit zu übergehen – ist die mittlerweile über sechzigjährige Spero berüchtigt für ihre Zähigkeit und ihre halsstarrige Weigerung, mittels stilistischer, ideologischer oder die Generation betreffender Aushängeschildchen in Schubladen gepackt zu werden. Alle diese Faktoren sollten auf eine exzentrische, vielleicht eigensinnige Kunst schliessen lassen. Statt dessen zeichnet sich das Werk der Spero durch Offenheit und Dynamik aus. Diese Dynamik ist von einer einzigartigen Vielfalt.

Dadurch, dass sie ihre Inhalte aus den Schriften Antonin Artauds bezieht – einem unverfälschten Modernen, der, um seine Worte zu benutzen, beinahe «von der Gesellschaft selbstgemordet» worden wäre –, aus schauerlichen Presseberichten über die Verfolgung politischer Aktivisten in der Dritten Welt und aus den mythischen Auseinandersetzungen der Götter, sind die Bilder der Spero mit Episoden extremer Gewalt und Pein übersät. Diese Bilder sind häufig, und ganz besonders in ihrem Werk der siebziger Jahre, in einer graphischen Manier von emotionaler Dringlichkeit dargestellt. Ihre Gestik ist scharf und bündig, ihre Oberflächen sind wund von Abschürfungen, ihre Farben eine eigentümliche Auswahl von zerstossenem Ocker und Schwarz. Trotz alledem predigen uns ihre Bilder nicht vom Standpunkt eines sicheren und ernsthaften «Humanismus» her – und indem sie die gehässigen und oft weiberfeindlichen Werke Artauds als Ausgangspunkt wählt, schneidet sie eine Vielzahl der gleichen Sachverhalte und Ambivalenzen an wie Simone de Beauvoirs in eigensinniger Weise bahnbrechender feministischer Essay «Müssen wir Sade verbrennen?» Auch ist das Werk Speros, angesichts all seiner Expressivität, keineswegs im konventionellen Sinn des Wortes «neoexpressionistisch».

Ganz im Gegenteil. Viele der neuen expressionistischen Arbeiten beschwören, stillschweigend oder ausdrücklich, den romantischen Kult des Malers als eines Helden, der Freiheiten auslebt, denen geringere Männer und Frauen entsagen mussten. Thema dieser Bilder ist das Tun und Handeln von Einzelmenschen, ihr Format eine Metapher für die Grossartigkeit der Vision des Künstlers, ihre Bedeutung und ihr «Wert» eine Verheissung von Dauerhaftigkeit. Diesen Erwartungen widerspricht im Werk der Spero alles. Sie hat das Fett des Expressionismus ausgeschmolzen und die Sehnen und die Haut bewahrt. So sind ihre Gemälde, Zeichnungen und Collagen, obwohl kraftvolle Figuren ihr Werk beleben und Berührung sie beseelt, auffallend wegen ihrer beinahe ephemeren physischen Präsenz. Wie riesenhafte Papierpuppen geschnitten oder auf sonst entblössten, an den Enden rollenförmig verbundenen Papierbögen mit zerbrechlichen Konturen gestanzt, steigert die blosse Zartheit ihrer vielfach winzigen bildlichen Darstellungen unsere Bewusstheit der extremen Situationen, auf die sie anspielen. Und indem von Zeit zu Zeit tatsächlich Helden – oder vielmehr Heldinnen – auftreten, drängt sich die Macherin niemals als hauptsächliche Trägerin der Handlung auf. Was uns bezaubert, ist nicht das erregende Geschehen der künstlerischen Schöpfung, sondern sind die dramatischen politischen, historischen und sexuellen Vorgänge, deren Zeuge Spero ist, wie auch wir es sind.

Es ist ein Drama fleischlicher Qual, Rebellion und Zelebrierung. Darin kämpfen Frauen gegen die ihnen zugefügte Gewalt, stellen ihre Vitalität zur Schau und verspotten die Autoritäten, die sie auf ihren schönrednerischen «Platz» zu verbannen pflegen. In NOTES IN TIME ON WOMEN (Rechtzeitige Anmerkungen zu Frauen), zum Beispiel, wird eine nackte Frauenfigur, die Beine gespreizt, über ein Derrida-Zitat katapultiert, « ... es gibt kein absolutes Sein der Frau, es gibt keine die Frauen betreffende Wahrheit, feministische Frauen ... sind Männer ...» Ein solcher kritischer Kontrapunkt zwischen Text und Bild ist wichtig für das Unterfangen der Spero und war, das sollte hinzugefügt werden, für ihr Werk charakteristisch lange vor der Ankunft der gegenwärtig modischen Spielarten der «Aneignung» und «Dekonstruktion». Das fortwährende Überleiten von einem gegenständlichen Code (Bilder) zu einem anderen (Wörter), und deren häufig aufreibende Konfrontation, mündet in eine vollständig verwirklichte Dialektik zwischen wahrnehmungsmässigem Erfassen und konzeptuellem Untersuchen. Bilder existieren nicht nur als sprechende Köpfe für eine wichtigere kritische Tonspur, noch sind Wörter bloss dazu da, visuelle Szenarien mit einer Legende zu versehen. Jedes Zeichen, ob graphisch oder verbal, wird sowohl gefühlt wie gedacht. Jeder Gedankengang wird unterbrochen

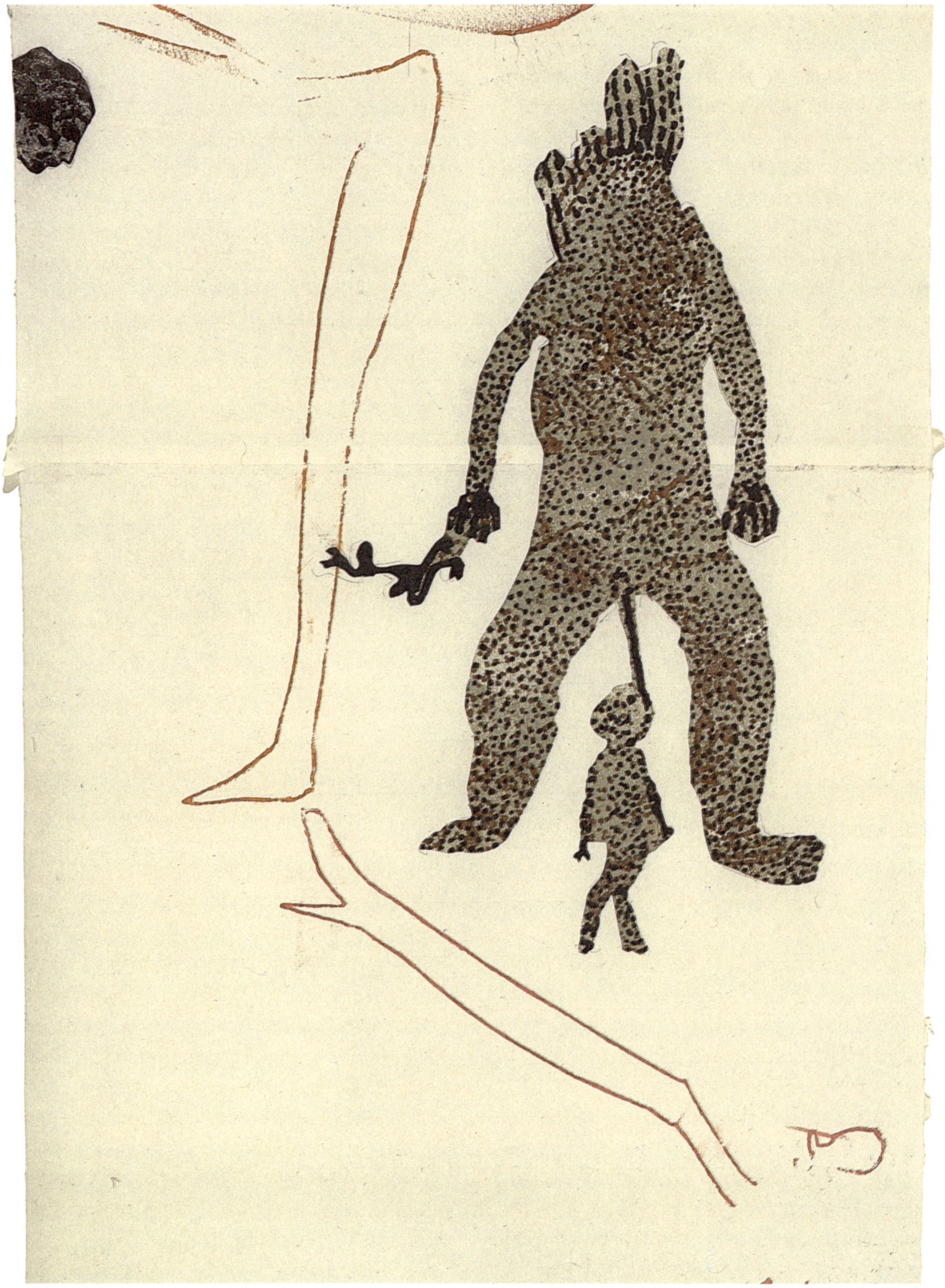

NANCY SPERO, DETAIL: SKY GODDESS, DIPTYCH II / HIMMELSGÖTTIN, DIPTYCHON II, 1986,

HANDPRINTING AND COLLAGE ON PAPER / HANDDRUCK UND COLLAGE AUF PAPIER, *110 x 54"* / 279,4 x 137,2 cm

(Photo: David Reynolds)

und von seinem Gegenteil erwidert. Nettigkeit steht ihren Absichten entgegen.

Um eine solche Mannigfaltigkeit von Stimmen und Ausdrucksweisen unterzubringen, hat Spero ein neues Bildformat improvisiert. Indem sie das normale Rechteck zu langen Bändern dehnt, über die eine Fülle ungleichartiger Ereignisse verteilt sind, ist Spero bei der perfekten Struktur einer diskursiven Kunst angelangt – verstanden im Gegensatz zur narrativen Kunst –, bei einer ungerahmten, nicht in Bildfelder eingeteilten Version der bandes dessinées (der englische zudehnen. Um dem komplizierten Detail zu folgen und die komplizierte Syntax einer bestimmten Serie dieser Bildfragmente zu begreifen, muss man seinen Blick fortwährend wieder neu einstellen, indem man von einer extremen Vision zur anderen springt und dann zurück zu Bildern, die man dabei zu hastig überflogen hat.

In dieser Hinsicht ist das «Lesen» einer Arbeit von Nancy Spero verwandt mit dem Lesen gestalteter und auf eine Mauer projizierter Verszeilen. Und wie bei der Lektüre eines guten Beispiels konkreter Poesie erlebt

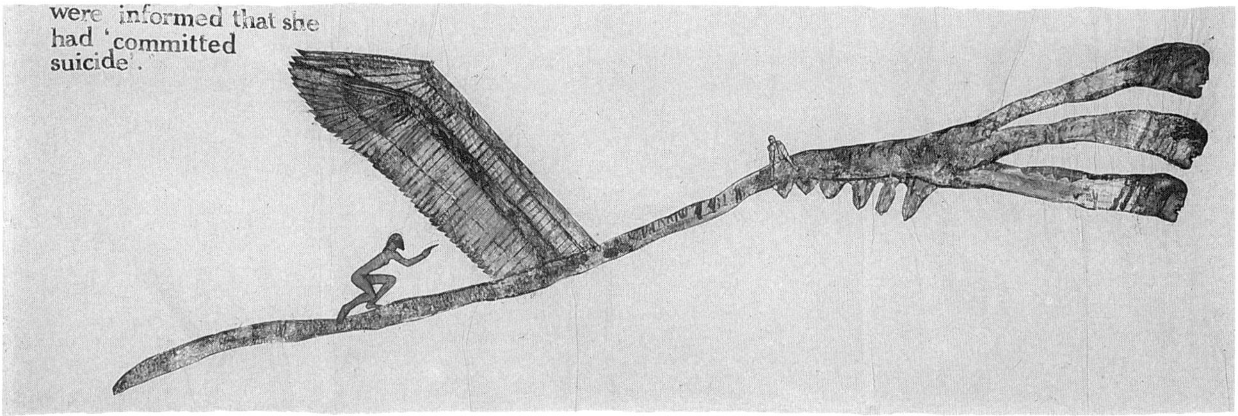

NANCY SPERO, DETAIL: TORTURE OF WOMEN (XI) / GEWALTTÄTIGKEIT AN FRAUEN (XI), 1976,
HANDPRINTING AND TYPEWRITER, COLLAGE ON PAPER / HANDDRUCK UND SCHREIBMASCHINENSCHRIFT, COLLAGE AUF PAPIER,
20" x 125 ft. / 0,50 x 38,1 m *(Photo: David Reynolds)*

Begriff «comic strip» erhebt den Inhalt über die Form und ist hier deshalb weniger angebracht). In unterscheidenden Gruppierungen gehängt, sind einige dieser Segmente vertikal und andere horizontal an den rechten Platz gebracht. Wie im Fall des CODEX ARTAUD können die Masse jedes einzelnen Teilstücks sich von fünfzig Zentimetern Breite bis zu Längen zwischen knapp fünf Metern und etwas über neun Metern bewegen. Darüber hinaus hat Spero bei verschiedenen Gelegenheiten die Begrenzung ihres papierenen Trägermaterials überschritten und Bilder in einer Lascaux-ähnlichen Verteilung von Bildsilhouetten direkt auf die Wand gedruckt. Spero hat damit das konventionelle Bildgitter gesprengt und seinen Achsen gestattet, sich nach Belieben in alle Richtungen aus- *man ein einzigartig aktives visuelles und intellektuelles Involviertsein. Widersprüche, Abschweifungen und Brüche im Fluss der Zeile rufen nicht jenes Gefühl von Verwirrung und Stauung hervor, das in der neueren Malerei oft augenscheinlich ist. Dort wird die abschliessende Einrahmung der traditionellen Staffeleimalerei als ein Mittel eingesetzt, um inkommensurablen Symbolen und Methoden des Ausdrucks einen absoluten Relativismus aufzudrängen. Bei Spero verhält es sich vielmehr so, dass der Begriff einer dynamischen Gleichzeitigkeit, der das Kennzeichen der frühen Moderne war, innerhalb einer neuen und expansiven Struktur wiederkehrt. Der Schlüssel liegt beim Betrachter und seiner Fähigkeit, peripheres Sehvermögen als eine Methode zu benutzen, ein Ganzes zu*

umfassen, das stets im Begriff ist, seinen Horizont zu überschreiten, während er zur gleichen Zeit konzentriertes Sehvermögen als eine Methode benutzt, um jedes der dicht aneinandergereihten Bilder und alle Sätze, die innerhalb dieses Sichtfeldes aufblitzen, vollständig zu berücksichtigen.

Dies ist also die formale Struktur einer neuen «Geschichtsmalerei». Denn das ist es, was Spero über die vergangenen zwanzig Jahre hinweg im Schilde führte. Querverweise herzustellen zwischen Bildern aus der Vergangenheit und Dokumenten und Emblemen, die gegenwärtige Ereignisse heraufbeschwören; ihre Codizes – zeitgenössische hieroglyphische Chroniken – veranschaulichen synchrones und durch und durch modernes Zeitempfinden. Kein «Hauptstrom» herrscht vor; das Aufeinanderfolgen-Lassen der Bilder ist zerstreut und wird durchfurcht von zahlreichen Strömungen, Zuflüssen und Deltas. Keine der «grossen Erzählungen» vermag ihre Interessen voll abzudecken – weder die von Freud noch die von Marx, auch keine irgendeines der neueren Theoretiker. Trotzdem finden alle einen Platz innerhalb des ausgedehnten Systems ihrer Arbeit, welches auch die gemeinhin nicht beachteten des sexuell, kulturell und wirtschaftlich «Anderen» in sich enthält. Auch ist keinerlei Apokalypse zu sehen, keinerlei Unterbruch im stets herausfordernden, unaufhörlichen Fliessen. Bedeutung erfassen erfordert also eine zeitliche Entsprechung zur peripheren Vision, ein vollständiges Eingeständnis unserer unfreiwilligen und beunruhigenden Fähigkeit, gleichzeitig zurückzublicken und vorauszudenken. «Geschichte ist ein Alptraum, aus dem ich zu erwachen suche», schrieb Joyce zu Beginn des modernen Zeitalters. Vielleicht ist am Ende der modernen Epoche das radikalste und wahrste Eingeständnis das, dass es kein «Ende» gibt und dass wir die ganze Zeit wach gewesen sind. Die Vorstellung von Finalität, so stellt sich heraus, ist ein ermüdender Tagtraum gewesen. Daher demonstriert die Postmoderne, in der abschliessenden Analyse, dass wir Geschichte nicht überrunden, wiederholen oder anhalten können – obwohl wir an jedem beliebigen Punkt uns selbst ein Ende machen können –, sondern in ihr leben müssen, und zwar in einem so vollen Bewusstsein unserer Lage, wie Neugier und Toleranz es zulassen. Nancy Spero ist eine aus einem kleinen Kontingent von Künstlern, die diese Alternative nicht nur vorstellbar erscheinen lassen, sondern, in kurzen Augenblicken, als zu erhoffende.

(Übersetzung: Udo Breger)

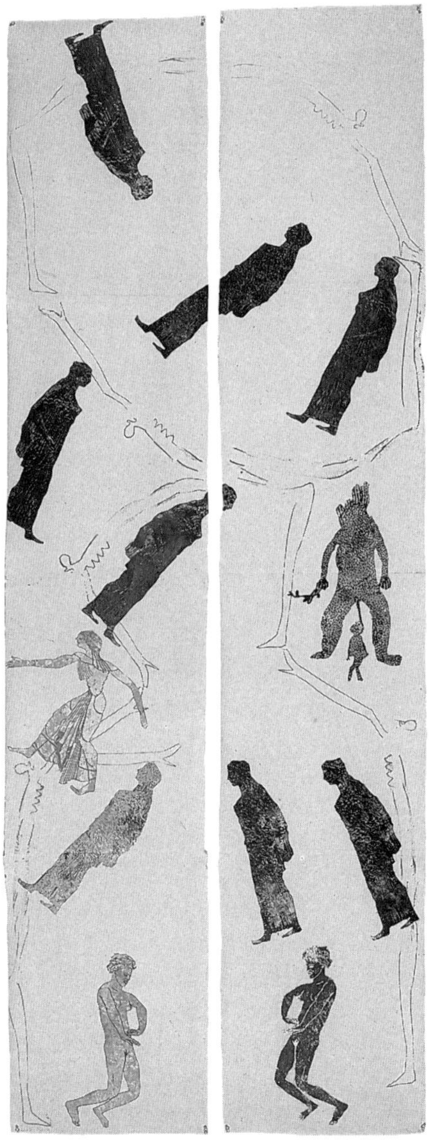

NANCY SPERO, DETAIL: SKY GODDESS, DIPTYCH II / HIMMELSGÖTTIN, DIPTYCHON II, 1986, *HANDPRINTING AND COLLAGE ON PAPER* / HANDDRUCK UND COLLAGE AUF PAPIER, *110 x 54"* / 279,4 x 137,2 cm

(Photo: David Reynolds)

HAIM STEINBACH

JOY OF TAPPING OUR FEET

"A pornography of all functions and objects in their readability, their fluidity, their availability, in their forced signification, in their performativity, in their branching, in their polyvalence, in their free expression." Jean Baudrillard, THE ECSTASY OF COMMUNICATION

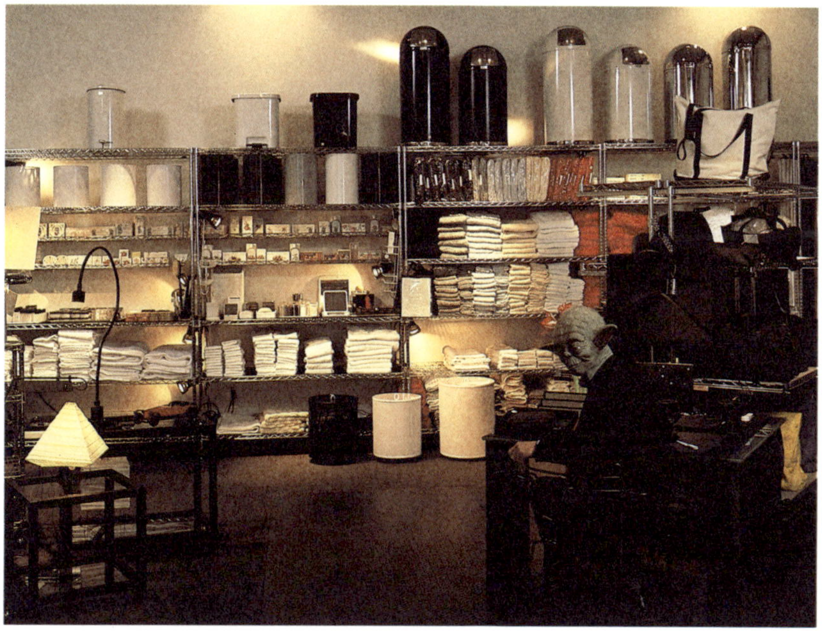

HAIM STEINBACH 1987 AT D.F. SAUNDERS ON WESTBROADWAY /
HAIM STEINBACH 1987 IM GESCHÄFT D.F. SAUNDERS AM WESTBROADWAY. *(Photo: David Lubarsky)*

A pornography of all images and objects, of speech and gesture, of the movies and television, of slogans and advertisement, of science and architecture. Pornography orders everything; the contour of every form, object, thing perceived, the surface of everything touched (even the keys of technological instruments), the taste of everything meeting the tongue.
The word "pornography" generally means the prostitution of a body, just as the word "kitsch" connotes the prostitution of an object. The targeting of functions, subjects and objects with these words most often implies a pose of moralizing, condescension and contempt. However, in a culture where all functions and objects are equivalent, pornography and sublimity as well as kitsch and high art become interchangeable. How, for instance, does the function of a significant work of art becomes «pornographic" and "kitsch"? It does so because the very notions of pornography and kitsch have lost the basis of their historical significations, they too have come to be available, fluid and readable. Pornography and kitsch along with transcendence and sanctification have been denuded of their originality. One may conclude that

a subject may no longer be a prostitute of another anymore than an object be the prostitute of another object. While the use of hierarchical structures continues, this practice is constantly contradicted by the simultaneous exposure of its mechanisms through subversive and equalizing activities.
All "free expression" of functions is defunct, for only self-conscious expression remains, and it is convincing to the point of unbelievability.
Pornography is seductive, it is comprised of formal elements designed, manipulated and registered to attain high states of stimulation. We may no longer entertain utopian notions of state-of-the-art objects free of pornographic expression and content, nor imagine ourselves standing apart, distanced or removed from it. We live in a culture of "pornography," we are engulfed by it, contained in it.
At this point in the timeline of the history of "progress" we have arrived at what is often referred to as the condition of the nullity of meaning. Faced with this situation, artists are asking themselves how they are still able to take pleasure in making art, finding amusement in the panorama of visual and material information generated by a social system that produces computerized technology, nuclear power plants and Music Television.
To some of us, this very moment in which experience has reached a level of simulation, in which unreality has become an everyday make-believe of reality, is pregnant with the possibility of meaning. If this state of things is "pornographic" we must look at it and ask ourselves how we partake in it.
On an emotional level we are recognizing our extreme state of ambivalence, feeling fascination and revulsion at the same time. Also, we are aware that this "pornography of all functions" is our cultural reality. Hence we choose to allow ourselves this entertainment while taking into account that our problematic situation has to do with the fact that this "pornography" is our pleasure. Furthermore, we accept this production to be ours, not that of others. We mark our place in no-man's-land, our loss of ideology. Playing the games of the culture of the spectacle we use devices of contradiction, subversion and inversion in order to frustrate the seamless appearance of its signs, messages, and surfaces.
Imagine that "progress," a twentieth-century cultural myth, is pornographic, and it is in the shape and form of a spaceship set on a fixed and predetermined course. Rather than shoot it down from above, we choose to usurp the captain's seat and try to reset its course from within. This means we are going to enjoy the ride to somewhere or nowhere while it lasts. Fastened to our seats in a state of inertia, suspended in a false reality and heading on in a false spirit, we choose to engage our vehicle by playing its computer game. Aware that our culture is excessively artificial and even meaningless, we nonetheless choose to live in it. In the process, because of this both pleasurable and disturbing condition, we will at times use irony, mimicry, and even mockery in order to identify the position we are in. We will jam and rearrange the computer to reconstruct our course of travel.

HAIM STEINBACH, born 1944, is an artist living in New York. He taught design and home decoration in the 1970s and first exhibited an installation with objects at Artist's Space in 1979.

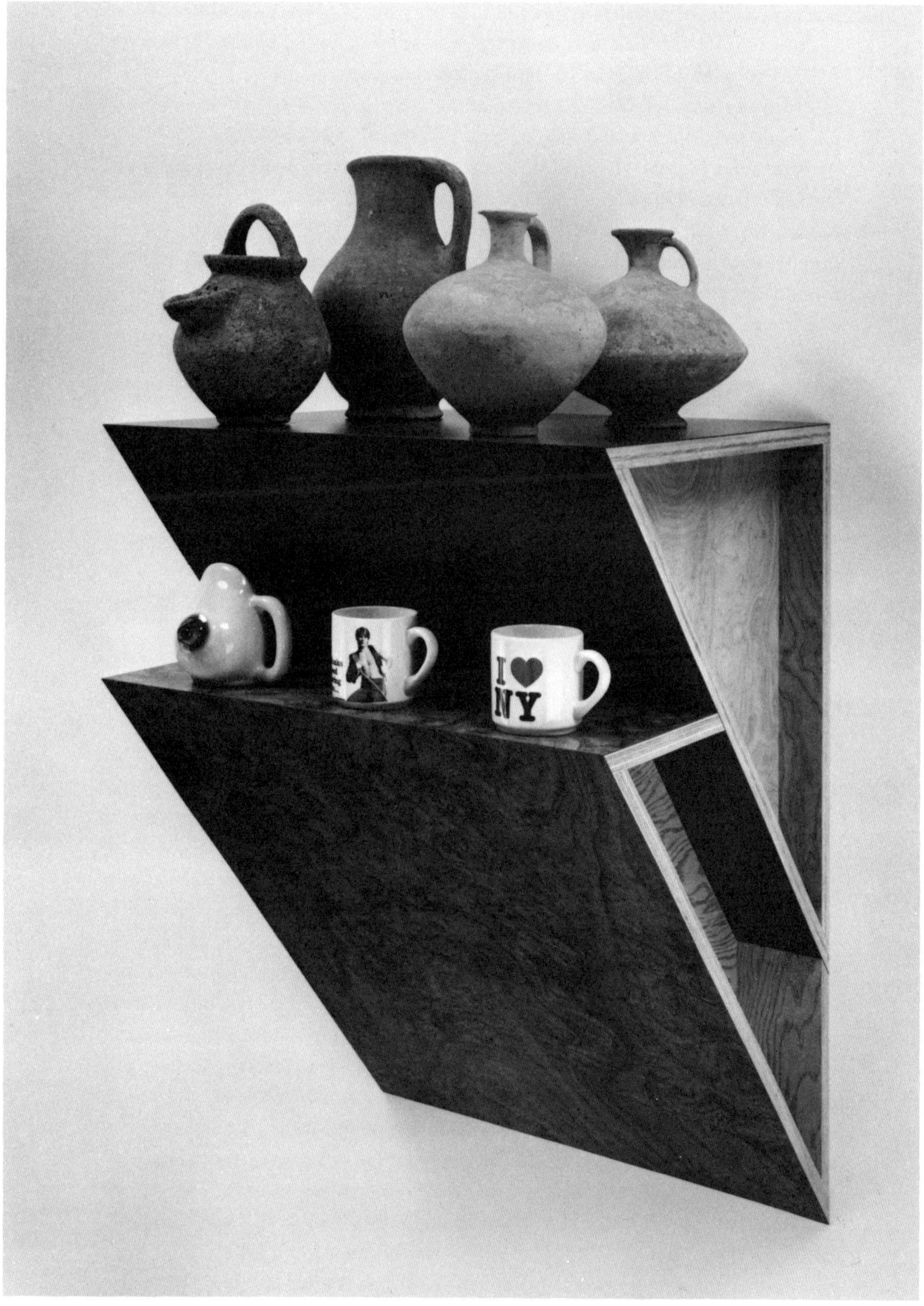

HAIM STEINBACH, UNTITLED (JUGS, MUGS) # 1 / OHNE TITEL (KRÜGE, BECHER) # 1, 1987,

MIXED MEDIA CONSTRUCTION, 43¾ x 23¾ x 19" / 111,1 x 60,3 x 48,3 cm

(Photo: David Lubarsky)

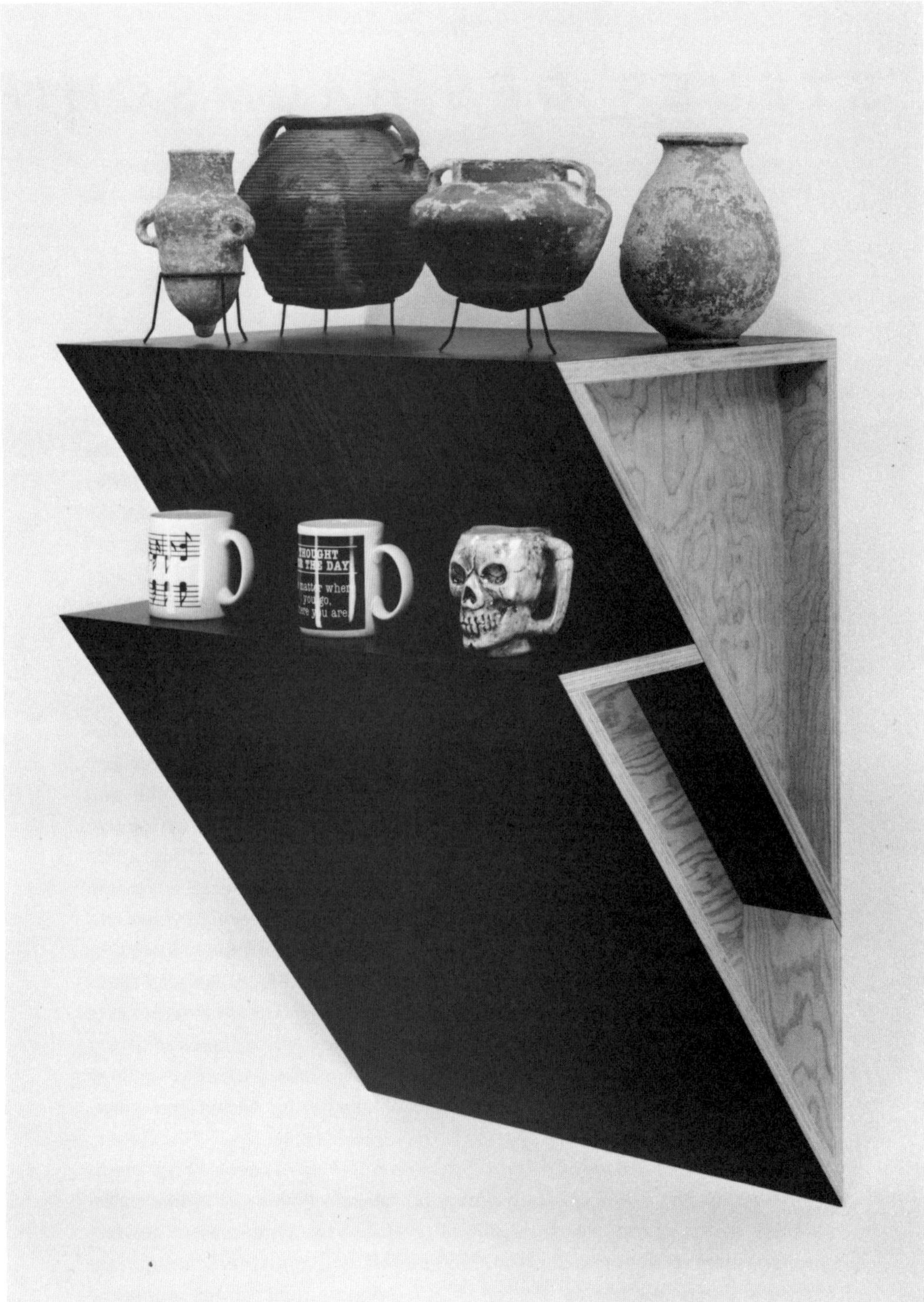

HAIM STEINBACH, UNTITLED (JUGS, MUGS) # 2 / OHNE TITEL (KRÜGE, BECHER) # 2, 1987,

MIXED MEDIA CONSTRUCTION, 41¾ x 23¾ x 19" / 106 x 60,3 x 48,3 cm

(Photo: David Lubarsky)

HAIM STEINBACH

AM STEUER DES RAUMSCHIFFS

«Eine Pornographie aller Funktionen und Objekte in ihrer Lesbarkeit, ihrer Geläufigkeit, ihrer Verfügbarkeit, in ihrer erzwungenen Bedeutung, in ihrer Aufführbarkeit, in ihrer Verästelung, in ihrer Mehrwertigkeit, in ihrem freien Ausdruck.»
Jean Baudrillard, *DIE EKSTASE DER KOMMUNIKATION*

Eine Pornographie aller Bilder und Objekte, von Sprache und Gestik, von Kino und Fernsehen, der Slogans und Anzeigen, der Wissenschaft und Architektur. Pornographie beeinflusst alles; die Kontur jeder Form, jedes Objekts, alles Wahrgenommenen, die Oberfläche alles Berührten (sogar die Tasten technologischer Instrumente), den Geschmack all dessen, was mit der Zunge in Berührung kommt.

Das Wort «Pornographie» kennzeichnet generell die Prostitution eines Körpers, so wie das Wort «Kitsch» die Prostitution eines Objekts bedeutet. Das Zur-Zielscheibe-Machen von Funktionen, Subjekten und Objekten mit diesen Wörtern impliziert meist eine Pose des Moralisierens, der Herablassung und der Geringschätzung. In einer Kultur jedoch, wo alle Funktionen und Objekte gleichwertig sind, werden Pornographie und Erhabenheit ebenso wie Kitsch und hohe Kunst untereinander austauschbar. Wie zum Beispiel wird die Funktion eines bedeutenden Kunstwerks «pornographisch» und «kitschig»? Eben dadurch, dass die Begriffe Pornographie und Kitsch die Grundlage ihrer historischen Bedeutungen verloren haben; auch sie sind verfügbar, geläufig und lesbar geworden. Pornographie und Kitsch wurden, im Verein mit Transzendez und Sanktifizierung, ihrer Originalität entblösst. Man mag folgern, dass ein Subjekt nicht länger Prostituierte eines anderen sein kann, ebensowenig wie ein Objekt Prostituierte eines anderen Objekts. Während die Verwendung hierarchischer Strukturen anhält, wird dieser Praxis durch die simultane Aufdeckung ihrer Mechanismen mittels subversiver und gleichmachender Aktivitäten unaufhörlich widersprochen.

Jeglicher «freier Ausdruck» von Funktionen ist erloschen, übrig bleibt selbstbewusster Ausdruck, und dieser ist bis zum Punkt der Unglaubwürdigkeit überzeugend. Pornographie ist verführerisch, sie besteht aus formalen Elementen, zugeschnitten, manipuliert und registriert, um heftige Stimulierungszustände zu erreichen. Wir können nicht länger utopische Vorstellungen vom «Zustand der Kunst»-Objekte aufrechterhalten, frei von pornographischem Ausdruck und Gehalt, noch uns selbst abseits stehend, davon getrennt oder entfernt denken. Wir leben in einer Kultur der «Pornographie», wir werden verschlungen von ihr, sind enthalten in ihr.

An diesem Punkt auf der Zeitspur der Geschichte des «Fortschritts» sind wir bei dem häufig zitierten Zustand der Nichtigkeit jeglicher Bedeutung angelangt. Angesichts dieser Situation stellen Künstler sich selbst die Frage, wie es ihnen immer noch möglich sein soll, Vergnügen am Kunst-Machen zu finden, da man sich doch im Panorama visueller und materieller Information vergnügen kann, welches von einem Gesellschaftssystem generiert wird, das Computer-Technologie, Kernkraftwerke und Music-Television produziert.
Für manchen von uns ist genau dieser Zustand, in dem Erfahrung ein Niveau der Simulation erreicht hat, in dem Unwirklichkeit ein alltägliches Scheinbild der Wirklichkeit geworden ist, aufgeladen mit neuen Möglichkeiten von Bedeutung. Wenn dieser Stand der Dinge «pornographisch» ist, müssen wir ihn betrachten und uns fragen, wie wir uns darin zu verhalten gedenken. Auf emotionaler Ebene erkennen wir unseren extremen Zustand der Ambivalenz und verspüren gleichzeitig Faszination und Abscheu. Auch ist uns bewusst, dass diese «Pornographie aller Funktionen» unsere kulturelle Wirklichkeit ist. Daher ziehen wir es vor, uns Spass zu gewähren und gleichzeitig zu berücksichtigen, dass unsere problematische Situation mit eben der Tatsache zu tun hat, dass diese «Pornographie» unser Vergnügen ist. Überdies erkennen wir diesen Vorgang als eigenen, nicht als den anderer an. Wir markieren unseren Platz im Niemandsland, unseren Verlust von Ideologie. Und indem wir das Spiel der Kultur des Spektakels spielen, verwenden wir Sinnbilder des Widerspruchs, der Subversion und der Umkehrung, um das nahtlose Auftreten ihrer Zeichen, Botschaften und Oberflächen zu vereiteln.
Man stelle sich vor, dass «Fortschritt», ein kultureller Mythos des zwanzigsten Jahrhunderts, pornographisch sei und die Gestalt und die Form eines auf einen festgelegten und vorbestimmten Kurs geschickten Raumschiffs habe. Anstatt es von oben abzuschiessen, ziehen wir es vor, den Platz des Kommandanten an uns zu reissen. Wir versuchen, den Kurs von innen her neu festzulegen. Das heisst, wir werden die Reise nach Irgendwo oder Nirgendwo geniessen, solange sie dauert. In einem Zustand der Trägheit an unsere Sitze geschnallt, in falscher Wirklichkeit schwebend und in falschem Geist dahinsteuernd, ziehen wir es vor, unser Gefährt in unseren Dienst zu nehmen, indem wir sein Computerspiel spielen. Im Bewusstsein dessen, dass unsere Kultur übertrieben künstlich und sogar bedeutungslos ist, ziehen wir es trotzdem vor, in ihr zu leben. Wegen dieses sowohl angenehmen wie auch beunruhigenden Zustands werden wir Ironie einsetzen, Nachäffung und sogar Possenspiel, um die Position zu bestimmen, in der wir uns befinden. Wir werden den Computer blockieren und neu arrangieren, um den Kurs unserer Reise zu rekonstruieren.

HAIM STEINBACH, geb. 1944, ist Künstler in New York. In den siebziger Jahren lehrte er Design und Innenarchitektur. 1979 stellte er erstmals eine Installation mit verschiedenen Objekten in «Artist's Space» aus.

Collaboration

Gilbert & George

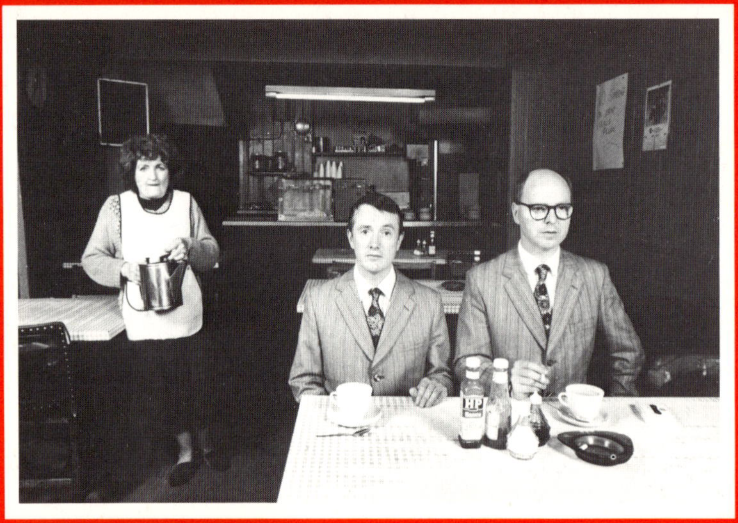

HERBIE KNOTT, GILBERT & GEORGE AT THE MARKET CAFÉ, LONDON 1987

Gilbert AND George TALKED TO/ WRITTEN ON

DUNCAN FALLOWELL

LONDON. The pictures begin in this city.
"London is the only up-to-date place in the world," says George, lighting a cigarette. He smokes a great deal. "London is raw, it's animal. But we don't go out much. Sometimes 6 months go by and we haven't been into the West End."
"When we visit Europe," says Gilbert (who doesn't smoke), "or New York, those places seem so provincial."
"In London everyone can have an opinion," says George.

ENGLAND. Gilbert: "England has the most multiracial society in Europe, and the young people of England are the most visually-orientated people in the world."

HOME. They share an early 18th century house in the East End of London. The house is honey wood inside – floorboards, panelled walls, wooden staircase – and creaks like an old ship as you move around in it. The rooms are filled with 19th century gothic furniture, and cupboards and horizontal surfaces are crammed with collections of Victorian pottery of an extreme, almost Martian weirdness.

GILBERT. Born in the Dolomites of North Italy, 1943. Physically looser than George and less studied in manner. He speaks with a continental accent which is noticeable but not intrusive.

GEORGE. Born Devon, England, 1942. Speaks in a voice whose composure and fineness of tone are at first rather startling. "Unfortunately I had elocution lessons when I was young," he says. Schoolmasterly.

DUNCAN FALLOWELL is a novelist based in London. This is a non-fiction piece.

Their Differences. "I'm small, he's big; he has glasses, I don't. Inside there are differences too. But it's not a good idea to ask us about those," says Gilbert.
"We don't think about them," says George.
"We are 2 complete individuals. That's part of our strength," says Gilbert.
"That's what «we» is," says George.
"When was your last row?"
"We never stop rowing in a sense," says George.

Living Sculptures. They adopt a pose for hours or perform a task repeatedly.
"Do you have to make sure you have a pee beforehand?"
"No," says Gilbert. "We just get up on the platform and do it. Then after 8 hours we stop and come down."
"A policeman is a kind of living sculpture," says George, "or a guardsman at Buckingham Palace."
Living sculptures/dead people. They haven't done these lately.

Selves. They are shy men. They often include photographs of themselves in their pictures. Why?
"Because," says George, "we want the viewers to be always reminded that we are speaking to them."
But it is the picture that speaks. Obsession with self hides behind a robotic streamlining of the personality. The obverse of shyness is exhibitionism.

Art. "We want people to bring their life to our exhibitions, not their knowledge of art," says George. "True art has to overcome and speak across the barriers of knowledge. We are opposed to art that is about art. A load of string stuck on a wall isn't art – it's a trick. We believe that art has a real function to advance civilisation." Art talk... Meanwhile their pictures flower forth into fundamental splendour.

Their Relationship. George says "It is such an idiotic idea that an artist has to be 1. In other aspects of life it is 2 – or more."
"Have you ever been tempted, since you came together, to work apart?"
"No. We are interested in what we dread, what we think, as opposed to what Gilbert fears and what I fear. It is like issuing a statement from a Board of Governors."
"Are you lovers?"
"We don't want to tell journalists what we do or don't do with our dicks, gobs, bums and hands, either with each other or with anybody else."

Shopping. George: "We don't do shopping. We order things over the phone."
Gilbert: "In bulk. We don't need to buy food. We don't eat here. Ever. We eat in the local café. 2 meals a day. Breakfast and lunch. And we might eat in a restaurant in the evening if we are still hungry."
They demonstrate their kitchen, full of wood and outlandish pottery like the other rooms, except that in the corner, like a naughty boy, are sink and draining board, electric kettle and carton of longlife milk. That's it. Nothing else. Not even a fridge. But they are not anti-modern. Their studio has the latest equipment. And there is a television upstairs. George

finds the News soothing. Gilbert likes English soap operas, not American ones.

ALCOHOL. George drinks more than Gilbert.

MONEY. Gilbert pours tea and George says "Compared to many of our contemporaries, we are quite rich... We've always lived from our work. We've had to."

SUNSHINE. George: "It's too cheerful for us. We're very interested in misery."

SEX. Gilbert: "Yes, we're very interested in sex. And in sexy art."
Often their pictures confront us with the animal aspect of our nature. The animal in us must not be rejected. It must be understood. Truth is never sordid. Only lies are sordid. The visceral hit is something they have in common with Francis Bacon – after seeing those works one likewise emerges in a state of sexual aliveness. Such artists try to go deep to where we are uncooked, unprepared, new. Other contemporary artists seem effete.

LOVE. Burning Love. Love. Naked Love. Various Loves, Coloured Loves... Love Lake... Death on Hope with Love...

GILBERT & GEORGE. They both come from "poor country families" in George's words. They both wear the same clothes (but different colours). And wear the same style of clothes every day. George: "It means we don't have to think about what to wear. It saves time."

DEATH. George: "We're very conscious of having limited time. There's urgency."

HOW TO MAKE A PICTURE. Gilbert: "First you do your living. And the suffering. Amazing feelings of unhappiness inside. Then you search for the pictures to visualise that."
George: "We make a lot of notes and sketches round the table in the beginning. By the time we go into the studio, it's all set.
The form is cool (technological); the content is warm (human)."

SUCCESS. Gilbert & George run forward without permission.

THE ENGLISH COUNTRYSIDE. "We're never there," says George.
"If we want landscape, we go to Kew Gardens," says Gilbert.
"Do you drive?"
"No," says Gilbert.
"Luckily," says George.
"Bus. Walk," says Gilbert.
"Taxi," says George.

HOME CONTINUED. "We've been here almost 20 years," says George. "When we first came it was completely Jewish and very run down. Then it was completely Maltese. Then it was completely Indian. Now it's getting a bit trendy, but we don't mind, we're not snobbish."

The house is in beautiful condition after years of painstaking repair. It is sparklingly clean. A man comes once a week to clean it.
"If it caught fire, what would you grab on the way out?"
"Nothing," says Gilbert. "We'd just start again somewhere else."

MAN. Gilbert: "Some artists use landscape to say what they want. Or fruit. We use men and boys. There's a lot of work to be done on men. It's a Greek idea to concentrate on the man."
George: "We find them around here. We've got a young friend who brings his friends. Or we see someone in the street and say «Have you got an hour to spare?»."
Gilbert: "We pay them all! That's important. They are just human beings. That's what we like. They shouldn't have an image."

WOMAN. George: "If you are on a train and talk to the person opposite and say you are an artist, they always think you paint naked ladies – and shag them afterwards. The image of the woman is very abused – not only in art but also in advertising – and used-up in a way."
Gilbert: "We have a lot of women followers. Women get very sexed-up by our art. We like that."

FEAR AND LONELINESS. "What frightens you?"
"Everything frightens us," says George, lighting a cigarette.
"Does death frighten you?"
"No," says George.
"Life frightens us," says Gilbert. "That's why we collect things – as a buffer against that. We think everyone is afraid."
"Do you experience loneliness?"
"Of course," says George. "We have many works on that subject."
"What makes you happy?"
"That's not one of our interests," says George. "What makes us scared? Being asked why we are happy!"

COLOUR. Gilbert: "People are shocked by our colour." People are frightened of being drenched.

RELIGION. The artist in his centre is free from all religions, all propaganda, all upholstery, all bits.

URBAN VIOLENCE (MADRID I). The Spanish Parliament is opening and the students are rioting: they roar like a football crowd: water cannon, tear gas, mounted police charge.

MADRID II. The American girl was unhappy in love and said "I think your pictures are C for cunt, R for rectum, A for anus, and P for prick." Then she went to her room and cried.
Later she said "I don't think Gilbert liked it. He just sat there rubbing his shoes together.

But you see, he asked me what I thought of them." The next day she said "I'm sorry about last night. But their pictures make me panicky."

MADRID III. Lady Mary Gordon-Lennox, the British Ambassador's wife, is burning brightly in a gas blue dress with a black & gold striped tiger at her throat. She says "Do you know what? I just said to Gilbert «Are you going to the Prado?» and he said «No, I hate old art.» How can he not be curious? God, it's quite a week! We've got Ben Nicholson on Friday."

MADRID IV. A fish restaurant. "Do you know that remark of Noël Coward's?" asks the Art Critic. "He'd been reading Wilenski's book on modern French painting and Coward said «Wilenski talks a lot about emotional force and constant functional forms etc. Then you turn to the illustration and find a square lay with 3 tits and a guitar up her crotch!»."
Georges says "It's much the best thing to be lower class about art."

MADRID V. Through the Parque del Retiro to the Palacio de Velazquez, an elegant iron and glass structure from the 19th century.
"It was built at the end of the last century to celebrate Spain's loss of the Philippines," says George, standing very erect in the centre of it, holding a cigarette between his 3rd and 4th fingers. On distant walls the vivid photopieces soak into the Spanish air. His eyes glint behind the spectacles and he says "How's that girl to-day? She deserves a kick up the bum."
One of Gilbert & George's assistants says "Her reaction was a good example of G & G bringing up what's inside you."

WORDS. Titles are important (poetry, the event). Manifestos are unimportant (justification after the event). The pictures are rich in meaning/content; the title is one crucial trigger for this.

VICES. Gilbert: "We probably have them all."
George: "We don't run away from the things inside ourselves."

CRYING. "Gilbert cries at films and soap operas. I cry at real things. That's the difference. I get moved to tears quite regularly."
"I cry at any film if it's romantic," says Gilbert.
"Would you describe yourselves as romantic?"
"Absolutely not," says Gilbert.
"It's a derogatory term," says George.
"Is classical a derogatory term?"
"No. We would use that of ourselves," says George.

ON THE CREST OF A WAVE. Gilbert: "We accept life as it is, we accept it all. We never dislike a piece of ours. It's just part of life."
George: "And we never have to decide what piece to do next. However we are, we do that. There's no choosing."

PENIS. George: "The art critic Edward Lucie-Smith was furious that one of our pieces had a penis in it. I took him to task on the phone – the only time we've ever resonded in this way – I said I was amazed because museums are filled with penises, the National Gallery, the British Museum, I said you can even find them in trousers. Panic immediately! A few years later he invited us to take part in a group show in Liverpool and wrote us a letter saying but no cocks please."
The desire for castration is a strange desire. The male is inescapable.

THE FEMININE. Gilbert & George bring out the feminine in the man, with flowers and plants, evocations of insecurity, tenderness, coquetry, dreaming...

THE FEMALE. The iris flower. The cleft tongue. Much female imagery. An anus is a rose is a vagina. Metaphors of parturition. The female is inescapable.

EVIL. "Who is the most evil person you've ever met?"
Gilbert tightens his mouth, picks up a teaspoon, and slides his eyes across to George. "Should I tell him?"
George buys several seconds' time by having a slow pull on his cigarette and then replies "Mmm, yes, absolutely," exhaling a cloud of smoke.
Gilbert turns back and says "The vicar. Our vicar. He did a big piece against us on television."
"He hurt us very much. We haven't really recovered," says George quietly. "He's not really our vicar. I'm Methodist and Gilbert is Catholic by upbringing. But he's the local vicar. Our neighbour for years. Always very polite – and his family even more so."
"More tea?" interposes Gilbert.
"Then, one day, a television team came here to make a documentary about us... We were watching the documentary on television," says George. "Suddenly the fucking vicar comes on the screen! We knew nothing about it. He said horrible things and ended up by saying we were sick, sad and serious – as in this is a serious matter."
"Well, we <u>are</u> serious," says Gilbert. "We did one piece called <u>Shitted</u> –"
"Shithead?"
"Shitted," repeats Gilbert. "He was devastated that we portrayed human shit."
"That hypocrisy. The way he pretended to be so neighbourly, but all the time... well, since then he hasn't been able to face us in the street," says George. "He always dodges us. We don't want to shock. We want to unshock."
"Why shouldn't shit be normal?" asks Gilbert.

DEATH CONTINUED. "Have you made a will?"
"We haven't thought about that," says George, lighting another cigarette.

THE CULT OF PERSONALITY. Images of self. Very romantic. The last ghetto to be escaped.

Gilbert UND George GESPROCHEN/ BESCHRIEBEN

DUNCAN FALLOWELL

LONDON. *Die Bilder beginnen in dieser Stadt.*
«London ist die einzig wirklich moderne Stadt der Welt», meint George, während er sich eine Zigarette anzündet. Er raucht ziemlich viel. «London ist roh, es ist animalisch. Aber wir gehen nicht sehr viel aus. Manchmal verstreichen sechs Monate, ohne dass wir im West End gewesen wären.»
«Immer wenn wir den Kontinent besuchen», fährt Gilbert fort (der nicht raucht), «oder New York, dann erscheinen uns diese Orte so provinziell.»
«In London kann jeder seine Meinung haben», meint George.

ENGLAND. *Gilbert: «England verfügt über die rassenmässig am stärksten durchmischte Gesellschaft Europas, und die englischen Jugendlichen sind die am stärksten visuell orientierten Menschen auf der Welt.»*

ZUHAUSE. *Gilbert und George teilen ein Haus aus dem frühen 18. Jahrhundert im Londoner East End. Innen ist das Haus mit honigfarbenem Holz ausgekleidet: Riemenböden, getäfelte Wände, Holztreppe. Und es knirscht wie ein altes Boot, wenn man sich darin bewegt. Die Zimmer sind voll von neugotischen Möbeln aus dem 19. Jahrhundert. Schränke und Ablageflächen sind vollgestellt mit viktorianischer Keramik von bizarrer Fremdheit.*

GILBERT. *Geboren in den Dolomiten, Norditalien, 1943. Physisch lockerer als George und weniger einstudierte Manieren. Er spricht mit einem kontinentalen Akzent, der erkennbar, keineswegs aber aufdringlich ist.*

DUNCAN FALLOWELL ist Schriftsteller und lebt in London. Dieser Text ist nicht fiktiv.

CECIL BEATON, PORTRAIT OF GILBERT & GEORGE, 1974

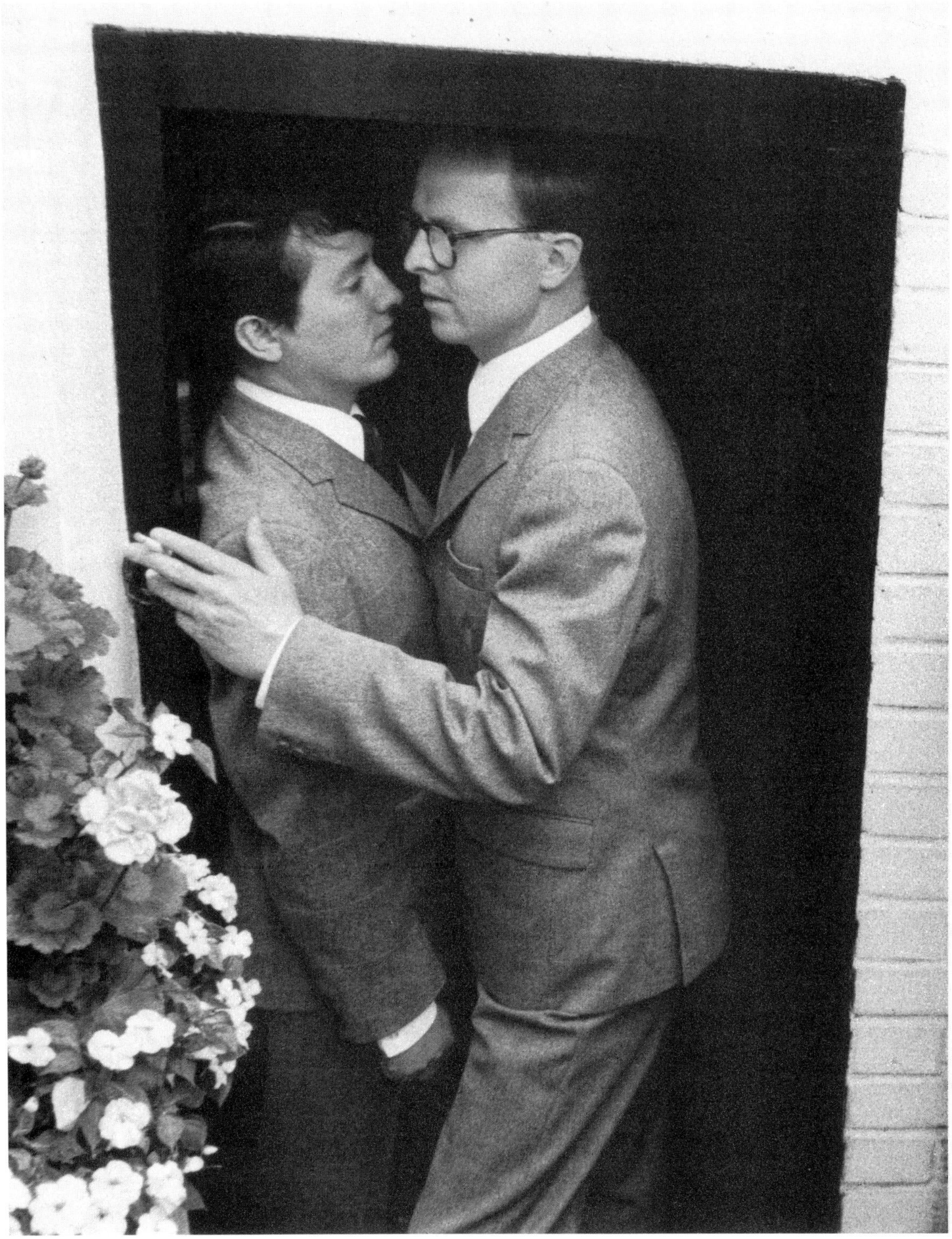

George. *Geboren in Devon, England, 1942. Spricht mit einer Stimme, deren Gelassenheit und Feinheit im ersten Augenblick leicht verwundert. «Ich hatte leider Sprechunterricht, als ich jung war», erzählt er. Schulmeisterlich.*

Ihre Unterschiede. *«Ich bin schwarzhaarig, er ist blond; ich bin klein, er ist gross; er trägt eine Brille, ich nicht. Auch im Inneren gibt es Unterschiede. Aber es ist besser, wenn Sie uns darüber nicht fragen», meint Gilbert.*
«Wir denken nicht darüber nach», meint George.
«Wir sind zwei vollständige Individuen. Das ist Teil unserer Stärke», meint Gilbert.
«Das ist es, was das „Wir" ausmacht», fügt George hinzu.
«Wann habt Ihr Euch zum letzten Mal gestritten?»
«Wir hören in gewissem Sinne nie zu streiten auf», meint George.

Lebende Skulpturen. *Sie nehmen eine Pose während Stunden ein oder führen immer und immer wieder dieselbe Tätigkeit aus.*
«Müsst Ihr jeweils daran denken, im voraus zu pinkeln?» «Nein», antwortet Gilbert. «Wir betreten einfach die Bühne und beginnen. Nach acht Stunden hören wir dann wieder auf und kommen runter.»
«Ein Polizist ist auch eine Art lebende Skulptur», ergreift George das Wort, «oder eine Wache vor dem Buckingham Palace.»
Lebende Skulpturen/tote Leute. Sie haben dies schon eine Weile nicht mehr aufgeführt.

Sie selbst. *Sie sind schüchtern. Oft verwenden sie in ihren Bildern Photographien von sich selbst. Warum das? «Weil», meint George, «wir wollen, dass der Zuschauer stets daran erinnert wird, dass wir zu ihm sprechen.»*
Aber es ist das Bild, das spricht. Die Besessenheit mit dem Selbst versteckt sich hinter einer roboterhaften Gleichrichtung der Persönlichkeit. Kehrseite der Schüchternheit ist der Exhibitionismus.

Kunst. *«Wir wollen, dass die Leute ihr Leben in unsere Ausstellungen mitbringen, nicht ihr Wissen über Kunst», meint George. «Wahre Kunst muss die Barrieren des Wissens überwinden und über diese hinwegsprechen. Wir sind gegen die Kunst über Kunst. Ein Haufen Schnüre, die an einer Wand befestigt werden, sind keine Kunst: Das ist ein Trick. Wir glauben, dass die Kunst die Aufgabe hat, die Zivilisation vorwärtszubringen.» Kunst-Gerede ... Inzwischen blühen ihre Bilder auf zu fundamentaler Pracht.*

Ihr Verhältnis. *George: «Welch eine idiotische Idee ist es doch, dass ein Künstler 1 sein soll. In anderen Bereichen des Lebens sind es 2, oder mehr.»*
«Habt Ihr, seit Ihr Euch zusammentatet, je Lust verspürt, getrennt zu arbeiten?»
«Nein. Wir interessieren uns für das, was wir fürchten, was wir denken, im Gegensatz zu dem, was Gilbert fürchtet und was ich selbst fürchte. Das ist, wie wenn ein Gouverneursrat eine offizielle Verkündung herausgibt.»
«Seid Ihr ein Liebespaar?»
«Wir wollen Journalisten keine Auskunft geben darüber, was wir mit unseren Schwänzen, Hintern und Händen machen, weder untereinander noch mit anderen.»

EINKAUFEN. *George: «Wir gehen nicht einkaufen. Wir geben telefonische Bestellungen auf.»*
Gilbert: «Mengenbestellungen. Wir brauchen keine Lebensmittel zu kaufen. Wir essen nicht hier. Nie. Wir essen im nahegelegenen Kaffeehaus. Zwei Mahlzeiten pro Tag. Frühstück und Mittagessen. Manchmal essen wir am Abend in einem Restaurant, falls wir immer noch Hunger haben.»
Sie führen ihre Küche vor, die voll ist von Möbeln und fremdartiger Keramik, ähnlich den übrigen Zimmern, ausser dass in der Ecke wie ein unfolgsames Kind der Spülstein, das Abtropfbrett, der Elektrokocher und ein Karton mit uperisierter Milch stehen. Das ist alles. Nichts weiter. Nicht einmal ein Kühlschrank. Aber sie sind nicht gegen das Moderne. Ihr Studio ist mit den neusten Geräten ausgestattet. Und im oberen Stockwerk steht ein Fernseher. George empfindet die Nachrichten als wohltuend, während Gilbert englische Seifenopern liebt. Nicht amerikanische.

ALKOHOL. *George trinkt mehr als Gilbert.*

GELD. *Gilbert schenkt Tee aus und George sagt: «Im Vergleich zu vielen unserer Zeitgenossen sind wir ziemlich reich ... Wir haben immer von unserer Arbeit gelebt. Wir waren dazu gezwungen.»*

SONNENSCHEIN. *George: «Die Sonne ist zu heiter für uns. Wir interessieren uns für das Leiden.»*

SEX. *Gilbert: «Ja, wir interessieren uns sehr für Sex. Und für sexy Kunst.» Ihre Bilder konfrontieren uns oft mit dem animalischen Aspekt unserer Natur. Das Tier in uns darf nicht abgelehnt, sondern muss verstanden werden. Die Wahrheit ist nie schmutzig. Nur Lügen sind schmutzig. Das von den Eingeweiden Ausgehende ist etwas, das sie mit Francis Bacon gemeinsam haben. Nach dem Betrachten seiner Werke befindet man sich ebenso in einem Zustand sexueller Bewusstheit. Diese Art Künstler versucht, sehr tief vorzudringen, wo wir sozusagen ungekocht, nicht vorbereitet, neu sind. Andere Künstler erscheinen daneben oft kraftlos.*

LIEBE. *Glühende Liebe. Liebe. Nackte Liebe. Verschiedene Lieben, farbige Lieben ... Liebes-See ... Tod auf Hoffnung mit Liebe ...*

GILBERT UND GEORGE. *Sie beide stammen nach Georges Worten aus «armen Familien auf dem Lande». Sie beide tragen dieselben Kleider (aber verschiedene Farben). Und sie tragen jeden Tag denselben Kleiderstil. George: «So brauchen wir nicht darüber nachzudenken, was wir anziehen sollen. Das spart Zeit.»*

TOD. *George: «Wir sind uns sehr bewusst, dass unsere Zeit beschränkt ist. Wir müssen uns beeilen.»*

WIE MAN EIN BILD MACHT. *Gilbert: «Zuerst gibst du dich dem Leben hin. Und dem Leiden. Erstaunliche Gefühle des Unglücklichseins in deinem Innern. Dann suchst du nach Bildern, um dies zu visualisieren.»*
George: «Am Anfang haben wir immer den Tisch voller Notizen und Skizzen. Wenn wir das

Studio dann betreten, ist alles klar.
Die Form ist kühl (technologisch), der Inhalt ist warm (menschlich).»

Erfolg. *Gilbert und George eilen ohne Erlaubnis vorwärts.*

Die englische Countryside. *«Wir sind nie dort», sagt George.*
«Wenn wir Landschaften sehen wollen, fahren wir nach Kew Gardens», meint Gilbert.
«Mit dem Wagen?»
«Nein», sagt Gilbert.
«Zum Glück», meint George.
«Bus. Zu Fuss», sagt Gilbert.
«Taxi», meint George.

Zuhause, Fortsetzung. *«Wir haben schon bald 20 Jahre hier gewohnt», erzählt George. «Als wir hierherkamen, war der Stadtteil ausschliesslich jüdisch und sehr heruntergekommen. Dann war er ausschliesslich maltesisch. Dann wurde er ausschliesslich indisch. Jetzt wird es langsam „in", aber das stört uns nicht, wir sind nicht snobistisch.»*
Das Haus ist nach jahrelangen sorgfältigen Ausbesserungen in einem hervorragenden Zustand. Es glänzt vor Sauberkeit. Einmal die Woche kommt ein Mann zum Putzen.
«Was würdet Ihr bei einem Brand auf der Flucht retten?»
«Nichts», meint Gilbert. «Wir würden ganz einfach woanders wieder anfangen.»

Mann. *Gilbert: «Gewisse Künstler benutzen Landschaften, um sich auszudrücken. Oder Früchte. Wir benutzen Männer und Jünglinge. Da ist vieles, was mit Männern zu machen wäre. Es ist eine Idee der Griechen, sich auf den Mann zu konzentrieren.»*
George: «Wir finden sie hier in der Gegend. Wir haben einen jungen Freund, der seine Freunde mitbringt. Oder dann sehen wir jemanden auf der Strasse und fragen ihn: „Haben Sie eine Stunde Zeit?"
Gilbert: «Wir bezahlen sie alle! Das ist wichtig. Sie sind schliesslich Menschen, und das ist es, was wir mögen. Sie sollten kein Image haben.»

Frau. *George: «Wenn du im Zug sitzt und mit der Person gegenüber sprichst, und du erzählst ihr, du seist Künstler, dann meinen die Leute immer, du würdest nackte Damen malen – und sie dann vögeln. Das Bild der Frau ist sehr abgenutzt – nicht nur in der Kunst, auch in der Werbung – und irgendwie auch aufgebraucht.»*
Gilbert: «Wir haben viele weibliche Bewunderer. Frauen werden von unserer Kunst sexuell erregt. Wir mögen das.»

Furcht und Einsamkeit. *«Wovor habt Ihr Angst?»*
«Alles macht uns Angst», antwortet George, indem er sich eine Zigarette anzündet.
«Fürchtet Ihr den Tod?»
«Nein», meint George.
«Wir fürchten das Leben», meint Gilbert. «Darum sammeln wir Dinge, als Puffer dagegen. Wir glauben, dass alle Menschen Angst haben.»
«Erlebt Ihr Einsamkeit?»
«Natürlich», meint George. «Wir haben viele Arbeiten zu diesem Thema gemacht.»

«Was macht Euch glücklich?»
«Das gehört nicht zu unseren Interessen», meint George.
«Was uns Angst macht? Gefragt zu werden, warum wir glücklich sind.»

FARBE. *Gilbert: «Unsere Farben schockieren die Leute.»*
Die Leute haben Angst, durchtränkt zu werden.

RELIGION. *Der Künstler ist in seinem Innersten frei von aller Religion, Propaganda, Polsterung, Einschränkungen.*

URBANE GEWALTTÄTIGKEIT (Madrid I). *Das spanische Parlament wird eröffnet, und unter den Studenten tritt Aufruhr auf. Sie toben wie ein Fussballstadion: Wasserwerfer, Tränengas, berittene Polizei.*

MADRID II. *Das amerikanische Mädchen war unglücklich verliebt und sagte: «Ich finde, Eure Bilder sind C für „cunt" (Möse), R für „rectum" (Darm), A für „anus" und P für „prick" (Schwanz) (= crap: engl. Mist, Scheisse). Dann ging sie auf ihr Zimmer und heulte. Später sagte sie: «Ich glaube nicht, dass Gilbert das mochte. Er sass einfach da und rieb seine Schuhe gegeneinander. Aber siehst du, er fragte mich, was ich darüber dachte.»*
Am nächsten Tag sagte sie: «Es tut mir leid wegen gestern nacht. Aber Ihre Bilder versetzen mich in Panik.»

MADRID III. *Lady Mary Gordon-Lennox, die Frau des britischen Botschafters, glüht hell in ihrem gasblauen Kleid mit schwarz-golden-gestreiftem Tiger am Hals. Sie sagt: «Wissen Sie was? Ich fragte soeben Gilbert: „Gehen Sie in den Prado?" Und er sagte: „Nein, ich hasse alte Kunst." Wie ist es möglich, dass er nicht einmal neugierig ist? Ach Gott, welch eine Woche, und wir haben Ben Nicholson am Freitag.»*

MADRID IV. *In einem Fischrestaurant: «Kennst Du jene Bemerkung Noël Cowards?» fragt der Kunstkritiker. «Er hatte Wilenskis Buch über moderne französische Malerei gelesen, und Coward sagte: „Wilenski spricht viel über die Kraft der Emotionen, über konstante, funktionale Formen usw. Dann nimmst du die Illustrationen hervor und siehst eine viereckige Dame mit drei Brüsten und einer Gitarre zwischen den Beinen!"*
George sagt: «Es ist wohl am besten, in bezug auf Kunst den Unterschichten anzugehören.»

MADRID V. *Durch den Parque del Retiro zum Palacio de Velasquez, einer eleganten Eisen- und Glasstruktur aus dem 19. Jahrhundert.*
«Er wurde Ende des letzten Jahrhunderts gebaut, um den spanischen Verlust der Philippinen zu feiern», erzählt George, während er kerzengerade im Zentrum desselben steht und eine Zigarette zwischen dem Mittel- und Ringfinger hält. Die lebhaften Bilder auf den entfernten Wänden vermischen sich mit der spanischen Luft. Seine Augen leuchten hinter der Brille, und er sagt: «Wie geht es dem Mädchen heute? Sie verdient einen Tritt in den Hintern.» Einer der Assistenten von Gilbert und George sagt: «Ihre Reaktion war ein typisches Beispiel dafür, wie G & G das herauslocken, was in uns drinsteckt.»

WÖRTER. *Titel sind wichtig (Poesie, das Ereignis). Manifeste sind unwichtig (Recht-*

fertigung nach dem Ereignis). Die Bilder sind reich an Bedeutung/Inhalt; der Titel ist ein entscheidender Auslöser hierfür.

LASTER. *Gilbert: «Wir haben sie vermutlich alle.»*
George: «Wir laufen den Dingen in unserem Innern nicht davon.»

WEINEN. *«Gilbert weint bei Filmen und Seifenopern. Ich hingegen weine bei realen Dingen. Das ist der Unterschied. Ich werde ziemlich regelmässig zu Tränen gerührt.»*
«Ich weine bei jedem Film, wenn er romantisch ist», erklärt Gilbert.
«Würdest Du Dich selbst als romantisch bezeichnen?»
«Auf keinen Fall», meint Gilbert.
«Es ist ein lächerlicher Ausdruck», meint George.
«Ist „klassisch" ein lächerlicher Ausdruck?»
«Nein. So könnten wir uns selbst bezeichnen», meint George.

AUF DEM KAMM EINER WELLE. *Gilbert: «Wir akzeptieren das Leben, so wie es ist, voll und ganz. Es kommt nie vor, dass wir eines unserer Werke nicht mögen. Es ist einfach Teil des Lebens.»*
George: «Und wir müssen nie entscheiden, welches Werk wir als nächstes machen sollen. Wie immer wir sind, so machen wir es. Da ist keine Wahl.»

PENIS. *George: «Der Kunstkritiker Edward Lucie-Smith war wütend darüber, dass auf einem unserer Werke ein Penis war. Ich stellte ihn am Telefon zur Rede – das einzige Mal, dass wir je auf diese Weise reagiert haben –, und ich sagte, ich sei erstaunt, denn die Museen seien doch voll von Penissen, die National Gallery, das British Museum ... Ich sagte, man könne sie sogar in Hosen finden. Unverzügliche Panik! Ein paar Jahre später lud er uns ein, an einer Gemeinschafts-Show in Liverpool teilzunehmen, und schrieb uns einen Brief, in dem er sagte, aber bitte keine Schwänze.»*
Das Kastrationsbedürfnis ist ein merkwürdiges Bedürfnis. Das Männliche bleibt unentrinnbar.

DAS FEMININE. *Gilbert und George lassen das Feminine im Mann hervortreten, mit Blumen und Pflanzen, mit der Evokation von Unsicherheiten, Zärtlichkeit, Koketterie, Träumen ...*

DAS WEIBLICHE. *Die Schwertlilie. Die gespaltene Zunge. Viel weibliche Symbolik. Ein After ist eine Rose ist eine Vagina. Metaphern des Gebärens. Das Weibliche bleibt unentrinnbar.*

DAS ÜBLE. *Wer ist die übelste Person, die Ihr je angetroffen habt?*
Gilbert spitzt den Mund, greift nach einem Teelöffel und richtet seine Augen auf George. «Soll ich es ihm sagen?» George versucht, einige Sekunden Zeit zu gewinnen, indem er langsam an seiner Zigarette zieht und dann «Mmm, ja, unbedingt» antwortet, während er eine Rauchwolke ausstösst. Gilbert wendet sich zurück und sagt: «Der Pfarrer. Unser Pfarrer. Er brachte ein grosses Ding gegen uns am Fernsehen.»
«Er hat uns sehr verletzt. Wir haben uns noch gar nicht richtig davon erholt», erzählt George mit ruhiger Stimme. «Er ist nicht wirklich unser Pfarrer. Ich bin Methodist und Gilbert ist

katholisch erzogen. Aber er ist der örtliche Pfarrer. Unser Nachbar seit Jahren. Immer sehr höflich – und seine Familie sogar noch mehr.»
«Noch etwas Tee?» wirft Gilbert dazwischen.
«Eines Tages kam ein Fernsehteam hierher, um einen Dokumentarfilm über uns zu drehen . . . Wir sahen den Film am Fernsehen», erzählt George. «Plötzlich erscheint der verdammte Pfarrer im Bild. Wir wussten nichts davon. Er sagte schreckliche Dinge und meinte zum Schluss, wir seien gestört, traurig und ernst.»
«Nun ja, wir sind ernst», meint Gilbert. «Wir machten ein Werk, genannt „Shitted“ (geschissen).»
«Shithead?» (Scheisskopf)
«Shitted», wiederholt Gilbert. «Er war verstört darüber, dass wir menschlichen Kot portraitierten.»
«Welche Scheinheiligkeit! Die Art, wie er vorgab, so nachbarlich zu sein, während er die ganze Zeit . . . Nun ja, seit damals hat er es noch nicht geschafft, uns auf der Strasse zu begegnen», meint George. «Er meidet uns ständig. Wir wollen nicht schockieren. Wir wollen „entschocken“.»
«Warum sollte Kot nicht normal sein?» fragt Gilbert.

TOD, FORTSETZUNG. *«Habt Ihr ein Testament aufgesetzt?» «Daran haben wir noch nicht gedacht», meint George, während er sich eine weitere Zigarette anzündet.*

PERSÖNLICHKEITSKULT. *Darstellungen des Selbst. Sehr romantisch. Das letzte Ghetto, in welches zu fliehen wäre.*

(Übersetzung: Anne Kammenhuber)

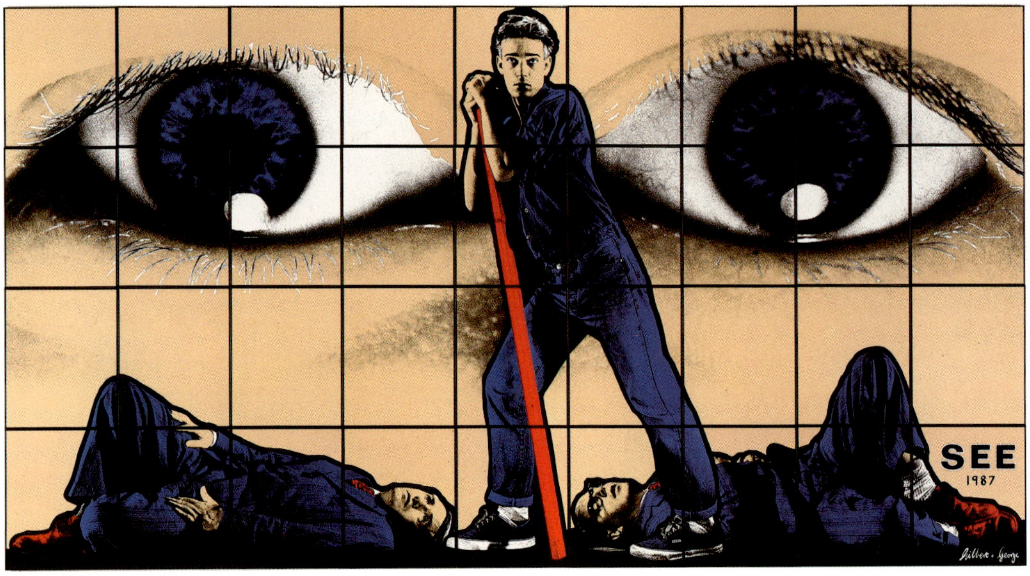

GILBERT & GEORGE, SEE / SEHEN, 1987

95 x 179" / 242 x 455 cm.

Gilbert & George

MARIO CODOGNATO

Human nature with the whole of its ambitions and failures, hopes and disillusions, dismays and daemons has always been the inexhaustible source of inspiration for the work of Gilbert & George.

They minutely dissect the human earthly adventure through several levels of representation which include the experiences and emotions of their own existence. These they integrate with the reality around them and the values that history has handed down to us. Through their works we should be able to reconstruct the vital forces which accompany the life of any individual. The gestures or the expressions of Gilbert & George, the images of the reality around them, their imaginary world aim at establishing an immediate relationship with the viewer.

All their efforts are turned to the creation of images and concepts which can be immediately understood by anybody without any sophisticated cultural or academic mediation, besides life itself, as a universal experience. Gilbert & George have brought the contents of life back into the artistic context. They have broken the barrier between art and life, not favouring one over the other, but making them coincide. They have recovered art in terms of life's progress and liberation. They have recovered life in terms of nourishing ambrosia for art.

The presence of their physical image in many of their works – particularly in very early and very recent ones – has given cause for many misunderstandings. It is a matter of primary importance to understand that their art is not autobiographical in a strict sense. They never represent themselves in situations that could not be immediately related to our life or to that of other individuals. Their fears are symbols, metaphors, representations, visions of our fears: their reasons for happiness or sorrow, love or hate, participation or isolation stand for ours. The essence of humanity is universal. Cultural and social conditions make us participate voluntarily or involuntarily in different contingent situations or states. Gilbert & George, as artists, aim at creating images that have universal values. As human beings they cannot escape a particular cultural and social position within the system and environment in which they live. Our duty as

MARIO CODOGNATO is studying art history at the University of East Anglia and writes for several art publications.

viewers is to recognize a universal reality and message through their representations, which are necessarily particular. It is not important to recognize ourselves directly in the images or situations they create; we must accept them as a sort of "contemporary" allegory of mankind, of the environment our species lives in and continuously tends to modify. The use of the photographic medium in their works emphasizes this wish to render the message as direct as possible and stresses the function of their art as a mirror of the individual and/or collective tragedy of human existence.

Gilbert & George consider themselves warriors "fighting for a total expression." They want to involve all our experiences, intellectual and physical, even the most dramatic, the most banal, the most shunned by social custom. Their daily struggle for artistic creative action becomes a metaphor of the unceasing desperate activity of man. If art is the highest means of communication, Gilbert & George reveal its compelling necessity, its greatness, but also the struggle, the doubt, the anguish of the action.

The first photopieces between 1972 and 1974 dramatically present the world of alcoholism. The tragic images of Gilbert & George intoxicated communicate a sense of total abandonment of the mind, of a human need or desire to escape reality, of perdition. There is a clear sense of self-denigration, of search for unpleasant situations. Life is taken to the brink of a precipice. In Gilbert & George one seems to see a taut string at the point of snapping. In HUMAN BONDAGE, 1974, alcoholism stands for all the slaveries of our time (such as the subjugation to heroin, to the rhythm of the assembly line, to consumer culture) and for the slaveries of our nature, of our caducity, of our egoism, of our ancestral bad habits, of our social conventions. The DARK SHADOW series, 1974, is an introspection accompanied by a silent shout. There is a sense of existential boredom, of vacuity, of flatness. There seems to be no difference between the flatness of the panels and the expressions of the two human beings.

Red with its violent archaic endless symbology permeates many of the works made between 1974 and 1978. The CHERRY BLOSSOMS, 1974, are the first ones to fade away. In Japan this word is used for the young soldiers who were the first to volunteer in case of danger for their fatherland, the first to be killed. The desperate red of BLOODY LIFE, 1975, is a haemoptysis from the soul. Gilbert & George act out that human feeling of denial of life, of weariness or boredom for this world, a feeling which undermines men's will to live. In different ways or frequencies, this feeling affects the life of every individual. The two artists invite us to consider it like

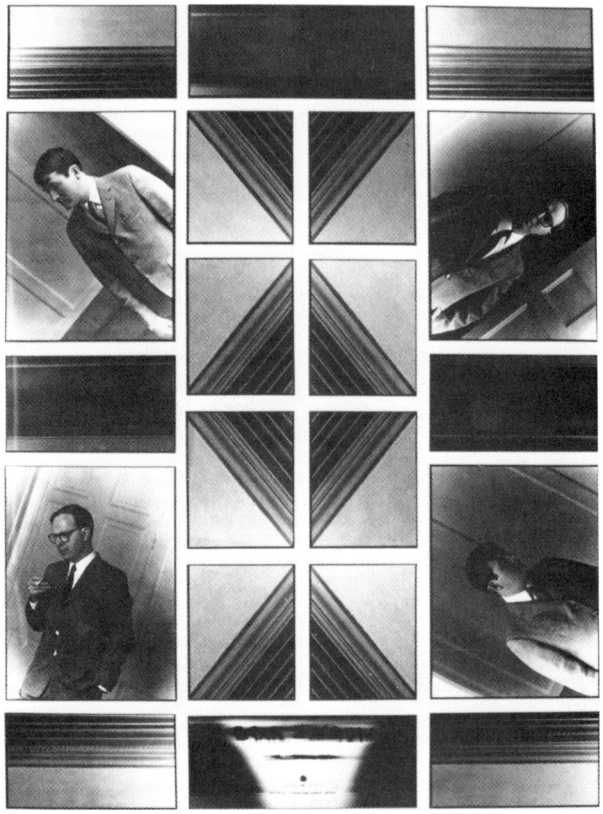

GILBERT & GEORGE, DARK SHADOW /
DUNKLER SCHATTEN, NO. 5, 1974,
83 x 62" / 211 x 156 cm.

a component of human nature. They give us the universality of this tragic but human feeling. The viewer recognizes his own desperation in the desperation of others. The pessimistic vision of life becomes a sympathetic feeling for other individuals. The BAD THOUGHTS series, 1975, acts as a flaming mirror. Always inscrutable, Gilbert &

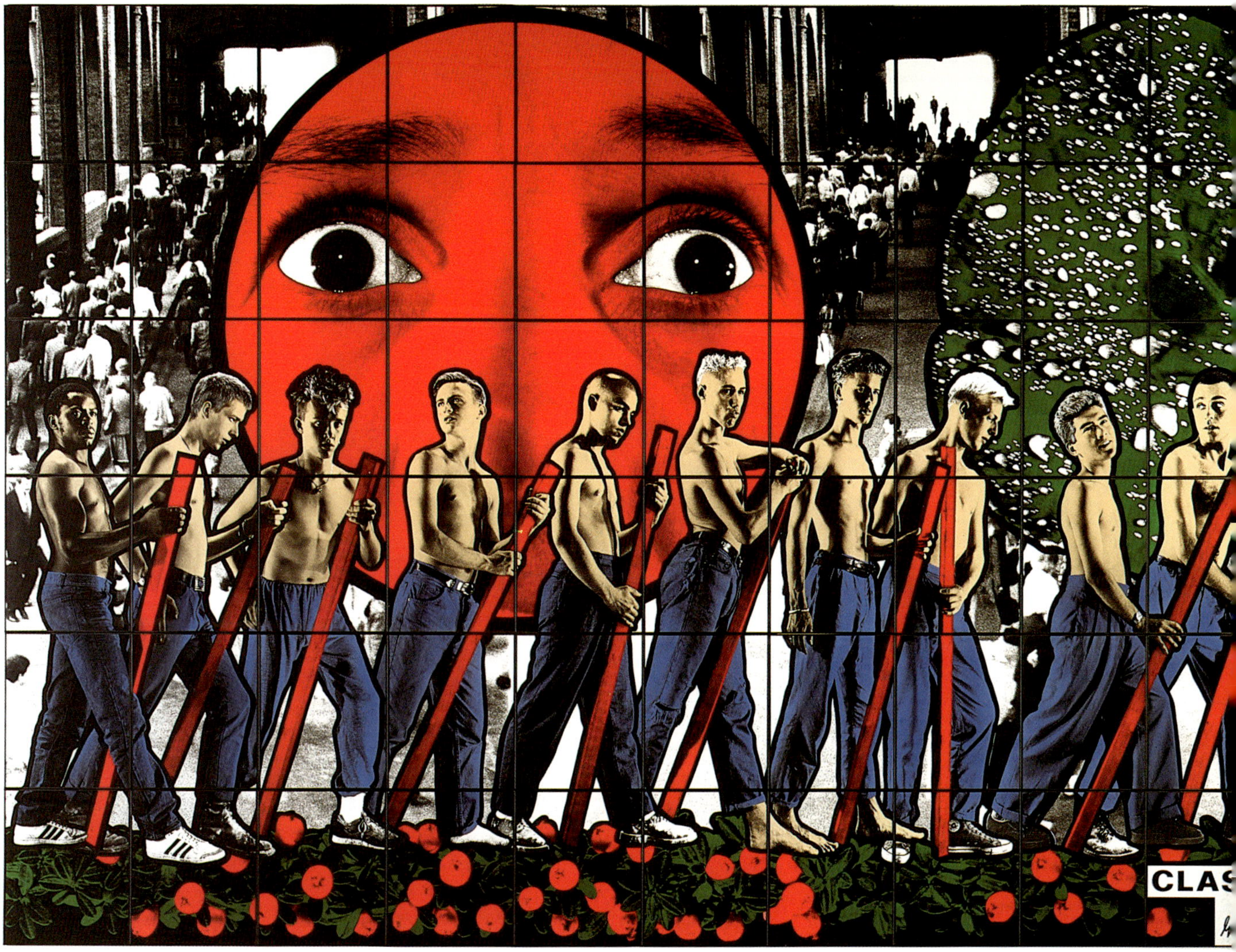

George's bad thoughts unpityingly force us to confront ours. Isolation is also the leit-motive of the desperate grey of DUSTY CORNERS, 1975, and DEAD BOARDS, 1976.

Life tends to expand in the cosmos, it tends to appropriate the universe. But it also tends to look for a place to shelter its essence. It tends to look for a lonely corner in which to find its own exclusive peace or damnation. MENTAL, 1976, in the colloquial meaning of mad, is the route to nowhere that the artists cover, marching isolated away from the natural world (flowers) and the world of men (the asphalt of the city). The alienation, the disaster, the vertigo, the violence, the degradation, the iniquity, the loneliness of modern city life "explode" in the RED MORNING and DIRTY WORDS series of 1977. Each of the words has a different title with a "negative" or "polemical" or "sexual" connotation attached to it. The dirty words of the graffiti become the "natural" caption for the atmosphere of doom in the metropolis. From that moment onwards, modern city life becomes a central theme in their work. In their opinion it is the most typical example of human behaviour. It contains, exalts,

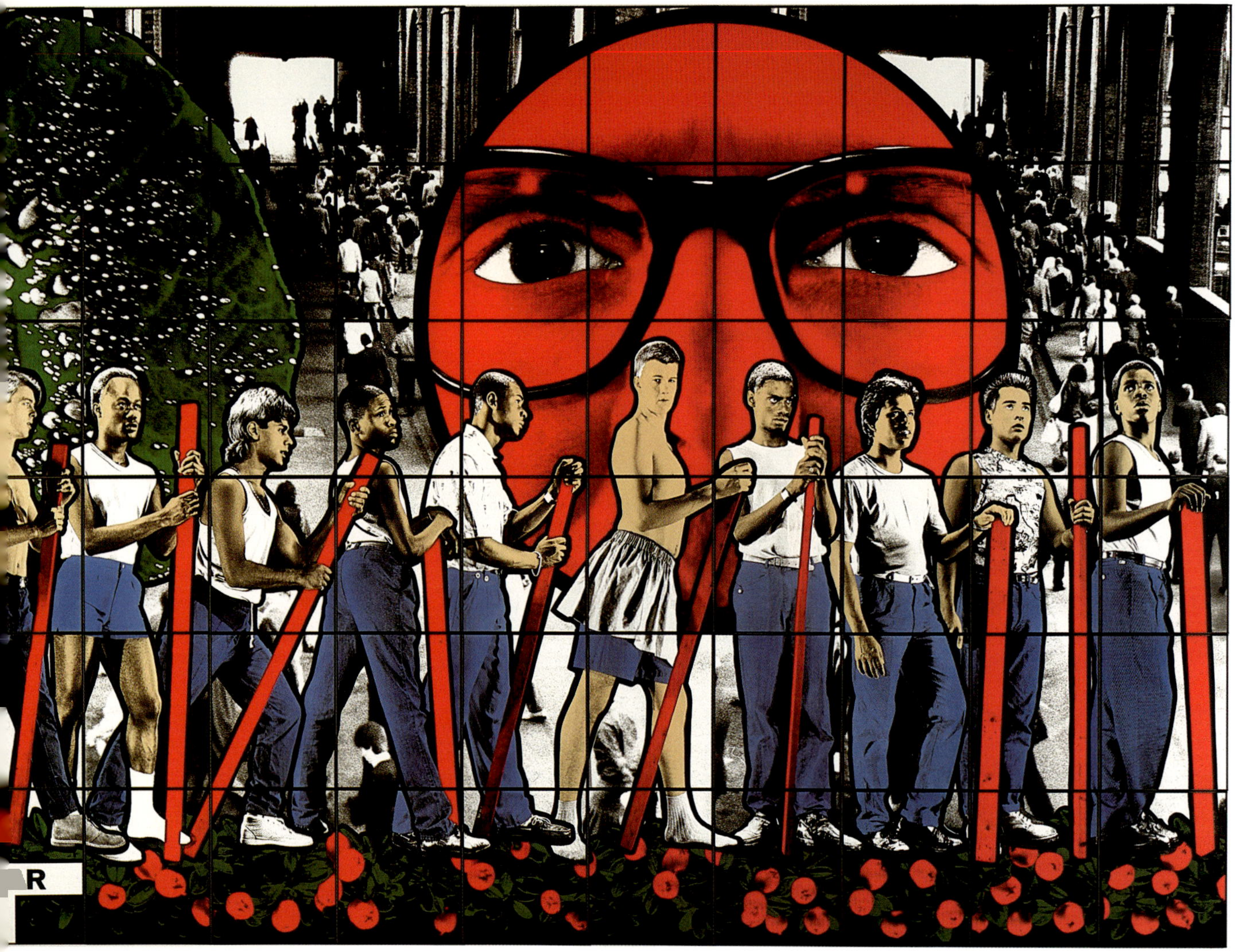

GILBERT & GEORGE, CLASS WAR / KLASSENKAMPF, 1986, *142 x 398"* / 363 x 1010 cm.

stresses the relationships and conflicts between human beings. It becomes a mirror and a metaphor of human conduct. In the works of 1978 the artists "break the wall" of their isolation and turn their attention to the surrounding reality. They seem to be spectators of a still dance in which men and natural phenomena, buildings and trees share the same tragic plastic ineluctable presence.

The works of the 1980s present a radical turning point. The images and the themes span all of reality. A contemporary version of medieval frescoes, they narrate and investigate the pain and the real or presumed essence of all human life, now with crude realism, now with symbolical transposition, now with a delirious vision. Like the images on the stained glass windows of a northern cathedral they tend to morally admonish, to exhort, they tend to act on the soul of those who look at them. The skin of animate beings or the textures of inanimate objects are rendered cruelly palpable. The blacks and whites petrify bodies and things into a statue-like state of sharp and irreverent beauty. The colours, of symbolic and emotional impact, become themselves a pure and stupifying element

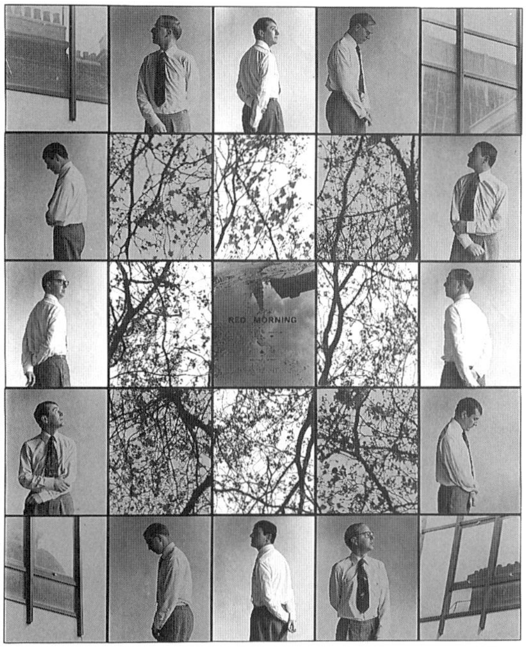

GILBERT & GEORGE, RED MORNING. ATTACK /
ROTER MORGEN. ATTACKE, 1977,
118 x 99" / 300 x 250 cm

of living reality. The ordinary places and people of the East End borough in which Gilbert & George live, become the inspiration of a visual parable.

An artistic practise which presupposes man's life as its leit-motive leads to the identification of the life forces which determine our being in the world. Gilbert & George believe that these forces are sex and religion. The representation and the understanding of the innumerable forms through which these two forces determine our existence are the basis of their art, because they are the basis of their and our lives. Despite its universal preponderant role, there is still a taboo attached to the word sex.

Civilizations and individuals all base morality upon their attitude towards sex, erecting a barrier against all unaccustomed sexual forms. The artists show us that each individual responds and reacts differently towards sex; they invite us to accept its role as a driving force, to abandon hypocrisy. Works such as SHIT or SPERM EATER, both 1982, show images that are normally embarrassing in our society, both for the receiver and the maker. Gilbert & George, presenting them in the art context, tend to un-shock us, to eliminate any mischievous attitude or at least to make us aware of it.

Often the works show naked bodies. They expose the fact that we still belong to a natural and instinctive world. They are always male bodies. For Gilbert & George that is a necessity since women's naked bodies inevitably have a pornographic connotation in our society, due to their exploitation by the mass media. The artists consider religion the other human driving force. They believe that all human beings are religious to a certain degree. The forces underlying this universal religious sense, whatever they may be, are another primary source of inspiration for their photopieces. They are a representation of the eternal existential revolution between the spiritual and physical world. In many works we can find crosses. They assume the meaning of symbols of a universal spiritual reality. Faith in something is deeply rooted in our nature; it is part of our existence. In SHIT FAITH, 1982, the daily natural act of defecating is associated with a religious symbology. Defecation – like sex – is universal but embarrassing in social life. The association with faith returns both to the level of the human natural world.

The vegetable world, plants, flowers, fruit, are a basic component in many of Gilbert & George's works. They have always appealed to human beings. Man has found in them analogies with his existence. Many times he gave them names which have a precise reference to his life. Every plant has a different appearance but is equal in essence to the other plants, as every human being "lives" different situations but is equal in essence to the others. The ephemeral beauty of flowers is an allegory for the ephemeral joys of life and its brevity. The evident degeneration of an old tree is an allegory for the physical and psychical decay in human ageing. A dry branch is an allegory for our cadaverous state after death. Plants also have a macroscopic sexual connotation. Their shapes remind us of our sexual organs. Their simple and spontaneous sexual life is an exemplification of ours. In SLEEPY, 1985, the sleep and the weight of the body (of life?) are rendered evident by the folly of the flowered branch as much as by the closed eyes of the young boy.

Gilbert & George

MARIO CODOGNATO

Für Gilbert & George ist schon immer die Natur des Menschen mit all ihrem Ehrgeiz und ihren Misserfolgen, mit ihren Hoffnungen und Enttäuschungen, Schrecken und Dämonen die unerschöpfliche Quelle der Inspiration ihres Werkes gewesen.

Peinlich genau zerlegen sie das irdische Abenteuer des Menschen. Sie verwenden dabei verschiedene Darstellungsebenen, die den Erfahrungen und Gemütsbewegungen ihres eigenen Lebens entsprechen, fügen diese mit der sie umgebenden Wirklichkeit und den uns von der Geschichte überlieferten Werten zu einem Ganzen zusammen. Mittels ihrer Arbeiten sollten wir imstande sein, die lebensnotwendigen Kräfte wiederherzustellen, die das Dasein eines jeden Einzelmenschen begleiten. Die Gebärden und Ausdrucksweisen Gilbert & Georges, die Bilder der sie umgebenden Wirklichkeit und ihrer Phantasiewelt zielen auf ein unvermitteltes In-Beziehung-Treten mit dem Betrachter hin.

Alle ihre Anstrengungen richten sich auf das Erschaffen von Bildern und Ideen, die, ohne differenzierte kulturelle oder akademische Vorbildung – ausser dem Leben selbst –, von jedermann unmittelbar als eine universelle Erfahrung verstanden werden können. Gilbert & George haben die Inhalte des Lebens in den künstlerischen Zusammenhang zurückgebracht. Sie haben die Schranken zwischen Kunst und Leben niedergerissen; wobei sie das eine dem anderen nicht vorziehen, sondern beides miteinander zur Deckung bringen. Sie haben sich die Kunst zurückerobert, im Hinblick auf Weiterentwicklung und Befreiung des Lebens. Sie haben sich das Leben zurückerobert, im Hinblick auf das Durchdringen der Kunst mit frischen Lebenssäften.

Ihre physische Präsenz in vielen ihrer Arbeiten – besonders in den frühen oder in den unlängst ent-

MARIO CODOGNATO studiert Kunstgeschichte an der University of East Anglia und schreibt für verschiedene Kunstzeitschriften.

GILBERT & GEORGE EXHIBITIONS:

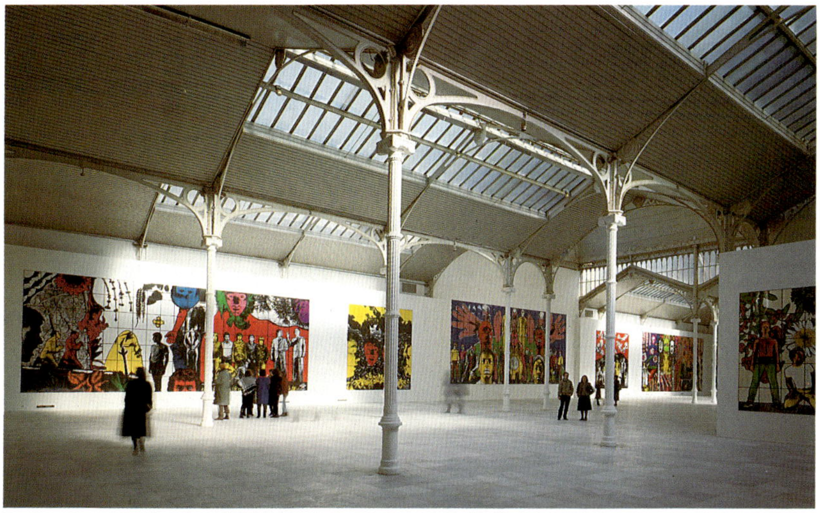

PALACIO DE VELÁSQUEZ, MADRID 1987,
PICTURES / BILDER 1982–1985.

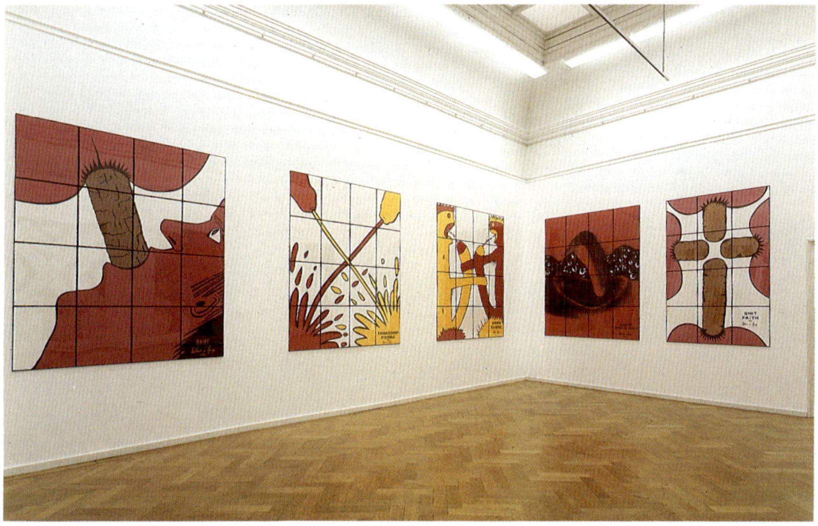

KUNSTHALLE BASEL, 1986,
PICTURES / BILDER 1982–1985.

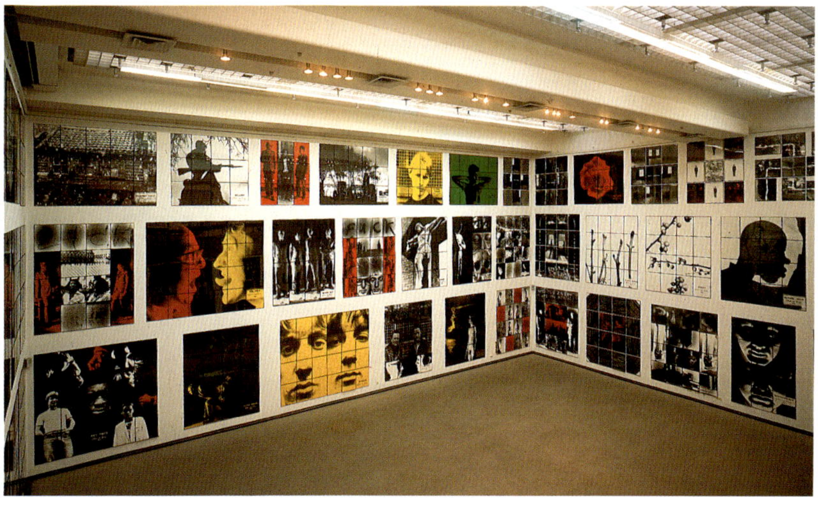

KUNSTHALLE DÜSSELDORF, 1981,
PHOTO-PIECES 1971–1980

GILBERT & GEORGE EXHIBITIONS:

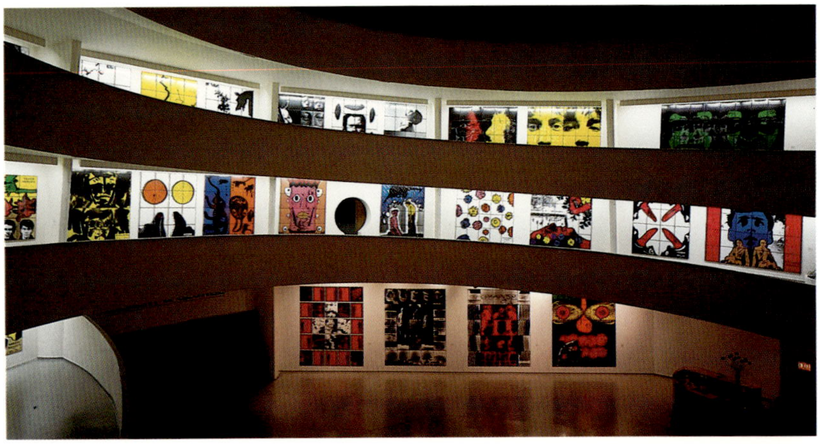

THE GUGGENHEIM MUSEUM NEW YORK, 1985, RETROSPECTIVE.

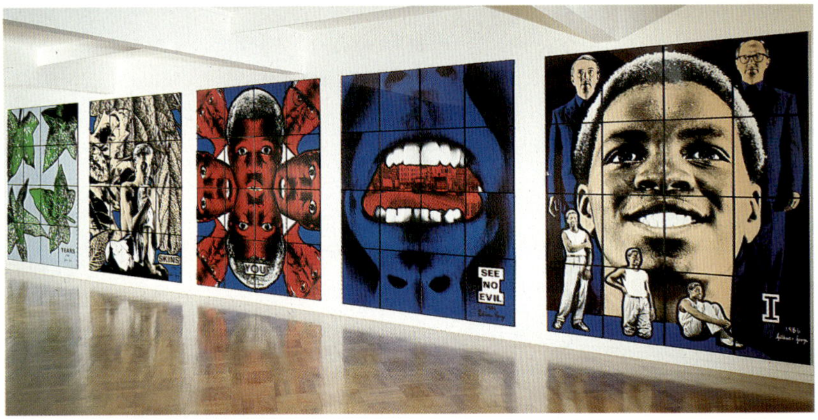

ANTHONY D'OFFEY GALLERY LONDON, 1987.

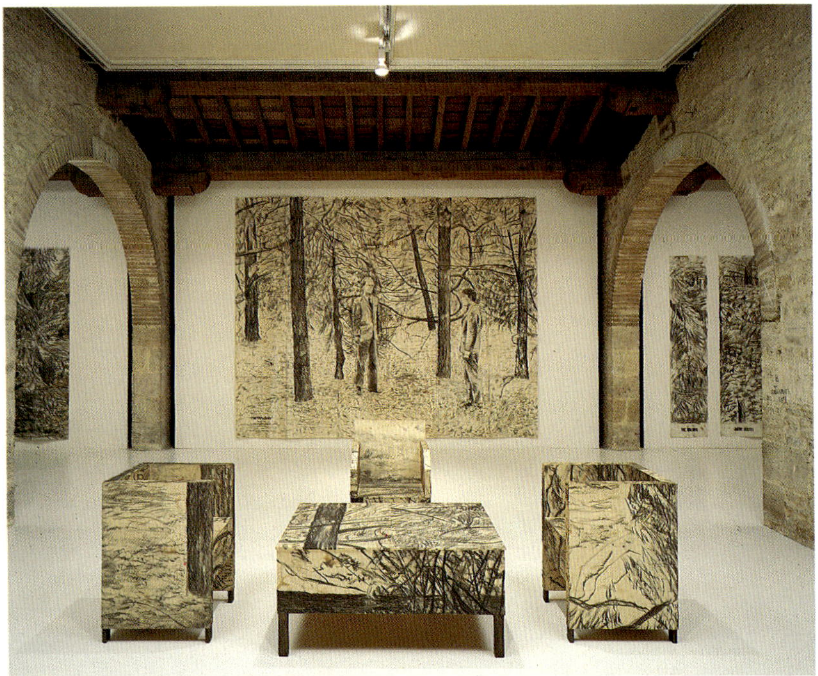

GILBERT & GEORGE, TUILERIES, 1974, A FOUR PANEL, THREE CHAIRS AND TABLE CHARCOAL ON PAPER SCULPTURE / EINE VIER-TABLEAUX-DREI-STÜHLE-UND-TISCH-KOHLE-AUF-PAPIER-SKULPTUR, *INSTALLATION AT CAPC BORDEAUX, 1986.*

standenen – hat Anlass zu zahlreichen Missverständnissen gegeben. Doch ist ganz wichtig zu verstehen, dass ihre Kunst im strengen Sinn nicht autobiographisch ist. Sie stellen sich selbst niemals in Situationen dar, die nicht direkt in Beziehung gebracht werden könnten mit unserem Leben oder dem anderer Einzelpersonen. Ihre Ängste sind Symbole, Metaphern, Darstellungen, Visionen unserer Ängste: ihre Anlässe zu Glück oder Sorge, Liebe oder Hass, Teilnahme oder Isolation stehen für die unseren. Die Essenz der Menschlichkeit ist universell. Es sind die kulturellen und sozialen Umstände, die unsere freiwillige oder unfreiwillige Anteilnahme an unterschiedlichen zufallsbedingten Situationen oder Zuständen erzwingen. Als Künstler zielen Gilbert & George auf das Erschaffen von Bildern, die universelle Werte beinhalten. Als Menschen können sie sich nicht frei machen von einer besonderen kulturellen und sozialen Stellung innerhalb des Systems und der äusseren Lebensbedingungen, in denen sie leben. Unsere Aufgabe als Betrachter ist es, durch ihre Darstellungen, die notwendigerweise persönlich sind, eine universelle Wirklichkeit und Botschaft zu erkennen. Es ist nicht wichtig, uns in den Bildern oder Situationen, die sie erschaffen, selbst direkt zu erkennen; wir müssen sie als eine Art «zeitgenössische Form» der Allegorie der Menschheit akzeptieren, der äusseren Lebensbedingungen, in denen unsere Spezies lebt und die sie fortwährend zu modifizieren neigt. Der Einsatz photographischer Medien in den Arbeiten betont diesen Wunsch, die Botschaft so unzweideutig wie möglich darzustellen, und betont die Funktion ihrer Kunst als ein Spiegel des Einzelmenschen und/oder der kollektiven Tragödie der menschlichen Existenz.

Gilbert & George betrachten sich selbst als Krieger, die «für einen totalen Ausdruck kämpfen», die darauf hinzielen, alle unsere Erfahrungen einzubeziehen, die intellektuellen und die körperlichen, selbst die dramatischsten, die banalsten, die aufgrund sozialer Konventionen am meisten gemiedenen. Ihr tägliches Streben nach künstlerisch kreativer Aktion wird zu einer Metapher der unaufhörlich verzweifelten menschlichen Geschäftigkeit. Wenn Kunst das erhabenste Mittel der Kommunikation ist, so machen Gilbert & George ihre zwingende Notwendigkeit sichtbar, ihre Grösse, aber auch das Ringen, um sie zu erreichen, den Zweifel, die Qual der Aktion.

Die ersten Photoarbeiten, zwischen 1972 und 1974, bringen in dramatischer Weise die Welt des Alkoholismus zur Sprache. Die tragischen Bilder von Gilbert & George als Berauschte vermitteln die Empfindung totaler seelischer Preisgabe, die Vorstellung eines menschlichen Verlangens, der Wirklichkeit zu entfliehen, eine Empfindung ewiger Verdammnis. In ihnen manifestiert sich ein deutliches Gefühl der Selbst-Verunglimpfung, der Suche nach unangenehmen Situationen. Leben wird an den Rand eines Abgrunds geführt. In Gilbert & George vermeint man eine straff gespannte Saite in dem Augenblick zu erkennen, in dem sie reissen wird. In der Serie HUMAN BONDAGE (Menschliches Gefangensein), 1974, *steht Alkoholismus für alle sklavischen Abhängigkeiten unserer Zeit (wie etwa die Abhängigkeit von Heroin, vom Rhythmus des Fliessbands, von der Verbraucherkultur) und für die sklavischen Abhängigkeiten unseres Wesens, unserer Vergänglichkeit, unseres Egoismus, unserer angestammten schlechten Gewohnheiten, unserer sozialen Konventionen. Die Serie DARK SHADOW* (Dunkler Schatten), 1974, *ist eine von einem stummen Schrei begleitete Selbstbeobachtung. Sie vermittelt ein Gefühl von existentieller Langeweile, von Leere, von Flachheit. Es scheint keinen Unterschied zu geben zwischen der Flachheit der Bilder und den Ausdrucksweisen der zwei menschlichen Wesen.*

Die Farbe Rot mit ihrer violent archaischen, endlosen Symbolik dringt in viele der zwischen 1974 und 1978 ausgeführten Arbeiten ein. Die CHERRY BLOSSOMS (Kirschblüten), 1974 *sind die ersten, die vergehen. In Japan verwendet man diesen Begriff für die jungen Soldaten, die die ersten sind, die sich im Falle einer Gefahr für das Vaterland freiwillig melden, die ersten, die sterben. Das verzweifelte Rot von BLOODY LIFE* (Verdammtes Leben), 1975, *ist ein Blutspucken von der Seele. Gilbert & George leben gemäss jenem menschlichen Gefühl der Lebensverweigerung, des Müdeseins oder der Langeweile an dieser Welt, einem Gefühl, das den Lebenswillen des Menschen erschüttert. Auch dieses Gefühl hat, obschon auf verschiedene Arten und Weisen oder Frequenzen, stets das Leben eines jeden Einzelmenschen*

gekreuzt. Die beiden Künstler laden uns ein, es wie einen Bestandteil der menschlichen Natur zu betrachten. Sie zeigen uns das Allumfassende dieses tragischen, aber menschlichen Gefühls. Der Betrachter erkennt seine Verzweiflung in der der anderen Menschen. Die pessimistische Vision vom Leben wird zu einem Gefühl von Verständnis für andere Individuen. Die Serie BAD THOUGHTS (Schlimme Gedanken), 1975, *fungiert als ein flammender Spiegel. Die unergründlichen schlimmen Gedanken von Gilbert & George werfen uns erbarmungslos auf uns selbst zurück. Isolation ist auch das Leitmotiv des verzweifelten Grautons von DUSTY CORNERS* (Staubige Ecken), 1975, *und DEAD BOARDS* (Tote Planken), 1976.

Leben tendiert dahin, sich im Kosmos auszudehnen, es tendiert dahin, sich das Universum anzueignen. Gleichzeitig neigt das Leben dazu, einen Zufluchtsort für seinen Daseinsgrund, eine verlassene Ecke zu suchen, um darin einen Frieden oder eine Verdammung zu finden, die ganz allein ihm gehört. MENTAL (Geistig, intellektuell), 1976, *in der umgangssprachlichen Bedeutung von geistesgestört, ist die Route nach Nirgendwo, die die Künstler beschreiben; isoliert von der natürlichen Welt (den Blumen) und der Welt der Menschen (dem Asphalt der Grossstadt) schreiten sie dahin. Die Entfremdung, das Unglück, die Erniedrigung, die Frevelhaftigkeit, die Einsamkeit des modernen Grossstadtlebens «explodieren» in den Serien RED MORNING* (Roter Morgen) *und DIRTY WORDS* (Unflätige Wörter) *des Jahres 1977. Jedes einzelne Wort trägt einen anderen Titel mit einer ihm angehängten «negativen», «polemischen» oder «sexuellen» Nebenbedeutung. Die unflätigen Wörter der Graffiti werden zur «natürlichen» Bildunterschrift der Untergangsstimmung der Metropolis. Von diesem Augenblick an wird das moderne Grossstadtleben in ihrem Werk das zentrale Thema sein. Ihrer Auffassung nach ist es das typischste Beispiel für das Verhalten der Leute. Es enthält, preist und betont die Beziehungen und Konflikte zwischen den Menschen. Es wird zu einem Spiegel und einer Metapher des menschlichen Verhaltens. In den Arbeiten von 1978 «durchbrechen» die Künstler «die Mauer» ihrer Isolation und richten ihre Aufmerksamkeit auf die sie umgebende Wirklichkeit. Sie scheinen die Zuschauer eines bewegungslosen Tanzes zu sein, in dem Menschen und natürliche Phänomene, Gebäude und Bäume dieselbe tragische plastische, unvermeidliche Gegenwart miteinander teilen.*

Die Arbeiten der 80er Jahre stellen einen radikalen Wendepunkt dar. Die Bilder und Themen umfassen die gesamte Wirklichkeit. Wie eine zeitgenössische Version der mittelalterlichen Fresken schildern und untersuchen sie das Leid und den wirklichen oder vermuteten Beweggrund des Lebens aller Menschen mittels ihrer Existenz – bald mit einem groben Realismus, bald mit einer symbolischen Umsetzung oder einer

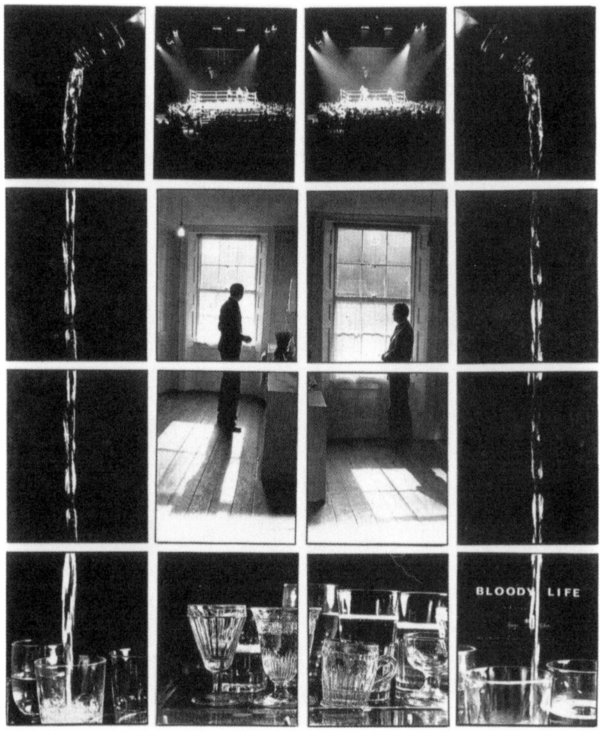

GILBERT & GEORGE, BLOODY LIFE / VERDAMMTES LEBEN, NO. 3, 1975, *97 x 81"* / 247 x 206 cm.

delirierenden Vision. Wie die bildlichen Darstellungen auf den Kirchenglasfenstern einer nordischen Kathedrale neigen sie dazu, moralisch zu mahnen, zu warnen, sie neigen dazu, auf die Seele desjenigen zu wirken, der sie betrachtet. Die Haut der lebendigen Wesen oder die Oberflächen-Strukturen der unbelebten Gegenstände werden auf grausame Weise augenfällig gemacht. Die Schwarzweisstöne versteinern die Körper und die Dinge in einen statuenhaften Zustand scharf

umrissener und unehrerbietiger Schönheit. Die Farben, bald symbolisch, bald gefühlsmässig eingesetzt, werden selbst zu einem reinen und benommen machenden Element der lebenden Wirklichkeit. Die Orte, die Leute im alltäglichen Leben des Londoner East End, in dem Gilbert & George wohnen, werden zur Inspiration einer visuellen Parabel.

Eine künstlerische Praxis, die das Leben der Menschen als ihr Leitmotiv voraussetzt, führt zur Erkennung der Lebenskräfte, die unsere Existenz in der Welt bestimmen. Gilbert & George glauben, dass diese Kräfte Sex und Religion sind. Die Darstellung und das Verstehen der zahllosen Formen, mittels derer diese zwei Kräfte unsere Existenz bestimmen, sind das Motiv ihrer Kunst, weil sie das Motiv ihres und unseres Lebens sind. Trotz ihrer universellen, dominierenden Rolle ist die Sexualität immer noch mit einem Tabu belegt.

Jede Zivilisation, jede Einzelperson gründen ihr sittliches Verhalten auf ihre Einstellung gegenüber Sex und errichten eine Schranke gegen alle die sexuellen Formen, die nicht Teil ihrer Gewohnheit sind. Die Künstler laden uns ein, Betrachtungen darüber anzustellen, dass jeder einzelne Mensch dem Sex gegenüber unterschiedlich denkt und handelt, seine Rolle als treibende Kraft zu akzeptieren, jegliche Heuchelei aufzugeben. Arbeiten wie SHIT (Kot), 1982, *oder SPERM EATER* (Sperma-Esser), 1982, *zeigen bildliche Darstellungen, die in unserer Gesellschaft normalerweise als anstössig gelten, und zwar für beide, den Empfänger und den Macher. Gilbert & George neigen, indem sie sie in den künstlerischen Zusammenhang stellen, dazu, uns zu ent-schocken, jegliches Vorurteil zu eliminieren oder uns dieses zumindest vor Augen zu führen.*

In ihrem Werk gibt es häufig nackte Körper. Diese decken auch unsere Zugehörigkeit zu einer natürlichen und instinktmässigen Welt auf. Es sind stets männliche Körper. Für Gilbert & George ist das eine Notwendigkeit, weil nackte Frauenkörper in unserer Gesellschaft, wegen ihrer als Werkzeug dienenden Verwendung durch die Massenmedien, einen unvermeidlich pornographischen Beigeschmack haben. Die Künstler betrachten Religion als die andere treibende Kraft des Menschen. Sie glauben, dass ein jeder Mensch zu einem gewissen Grad religiös ist. Die Kräfte, die diese universelle religiöse Empfindung bestimmen (was auch immer sie sein mögen), werden für ihre Photoarbeiten zu einer anderen grundlegenden Quelle der Inspiration. Es geht um eine Darstellung der immerwährenden existentiellen Revolution zwischen der geistigen und der körperlichen Welt. In vielen Arbeiten können wir Kreuze finden. Sie übernehmen die Bedeutung von Symbolen einer universellen geistigen Wirklichkeit. Der Glaube an etwas muss als tief in unserer Wirklichkeit verwurzelt betrachtet werden, als Teil unserer Existenz. In SHIT FAITH (Scheiss-Glaube), 1982, *wird der tägliche, natürliche Ablauf der Darmentleerung mit religiöser Symbolik in Verbindung gesetzt. Darmentleerung ist – wie Sex – universell, aber im gesellschaftlichen Leben anstössig. Die Assoziation mit dem Glauben versöhnt beide auf der Ebene der natürlichen menschlichen Welt.*

Die Welt der Pflanzen, der Blumen und Früchte ist ein grundlegender Bestandteil vieler Arbeiten. Pflanzen haben schon immer an den Menschen appelliert. Der Mensch fand in ihnen Analogien zu seiner Existenz, er gab ihnen häufig Namen, die einen deutlichen Bezug zu seinem Leben haben. Jede Pflanze hat ein unterschiedliches Erscheinungsbild, ist aber in ihren elementaren Bestandteilen den anderen Pflanzen gleich, wie auch jeder Mensch unterschiedliche Situationen «lebt», in seinen elementaren Bestandteilen aber den anderen gleich ist. Die flüchtige Schönheit der Blumen ist eine Allegorie der flüchtigen Freuden des Lebens und seiner Kürze. Die augenscheinliche Degeneration eines alten Baumes stellt eine Allegorie des physischen und psychischen Verfalls beim menschlichen Altern dar, und ein trockener Ast ist eine Allegorie unseres leichenhaften Zustands nach unserem Tod. Pflanzen haben auch eine mit blossem Auge wahrnehmbare sexuelle Bedeutung. Ihr einfaches und spontanes Sexualleben ist ein Beispiel für das unsrige. In SLEEPY (Schläfrig), 1985, *werden Schlaf und Gewicht des Körpers (des Lebens?) durch die Torheit des blütentragenden Astes ebenso wie durch die geschlossenen Augen des Knaben sichtbar gemacht.*

(Übersetzung: Udo Breger)

GILBERT & GEORGE, THE DIRTY WORDS /
DIE UNANSTÄNDIGEN WÖRTER
(BOLLOCKS WE'RE ALL ANGRY), 1977, 95 x 79" / 241 x 201 cm.

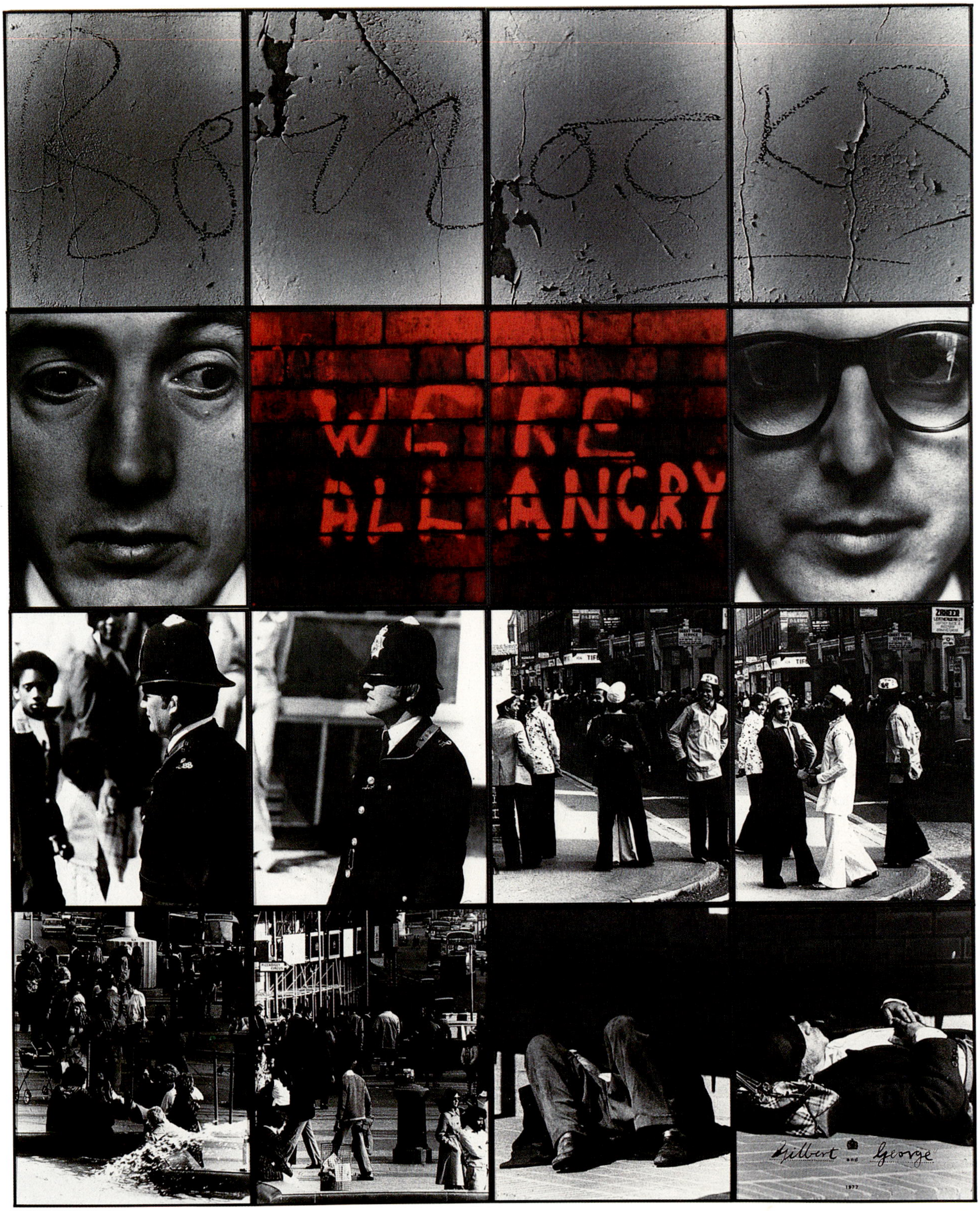
WE RE
ALL ANGRY
Gilbert and George
1977

JEREMY COOPER

GILBERT & GEORGE "AT HOME"

Gilbert & George is singular.
They are he.
Gilbert can still often be Gilbert, George invariably George. But together Gilbert and George are mostly Gilbert & George.
Gilbert & George is, I would say, their greatest creation. A living sculpture of such dominant authority that if Gilbert & George was somehow to fail – to die – it is difficult to imagine how either Gilbert or George could continue to live. It is in order to preserve their singular lives as much as their plural art that Gilbert and George have created an ambience for Gilbert & George in which he and they can feel equally "At Home".

From the summer of 1978, for over a year, Gilbert and George ceased entirely the actual production of works of art and concentrated instead on completing the restoration of their eighteenth century weaver's house in Spitalfields, in the East End of London. They continued, no doubt, to work in their heads and on their walks and down their drinks, but the daily labour was confined to the task of hand-stripping and polishing the original pine which lines the walls throughout all four floors of their house. As students, in the late 1960s, they had rented a floor of the house. Ten years later they owned the whole building, as well as a vast studio in the rear yard, previously a Bangladeshi textile factory. With their limited domestic needs serviced by a narrow, non-public extension up the back of the house, the immaculately empty period interior of the main building was finally ready in autumn 1979 for ... Well, for what, exactly?

For living sculpture, of course. For guests at teatime sculpture (with marmite on toast). For magazine interview sculpture. For collection sculpture. For occupying the odd evening sculpture.

For watching T.V. sculpture?

Yes, for that too, eventually.

But how? And in what style?

For Gilbert and George the essential precondition was that the overall effect had, somehow, to be unique. They, unlike others, were barred the easy solutions. No fashionable decorator for Gilbert & George. No quick trip to multi-purpose Conran. Nor, even, to one-off Zvi Aram. (Too often had they vilified their contemporaries in art and design to turn to them now for help.) They might have decided to build for themselves a revivalist stage-

---

JEREMY COOPER, until turning in 1983 to full time writing, was an antiques dealer in Bloomsbury. He has recently published "Victorian and Edwardian Furniture and Interiors" (Europe: Thames and Hudson; U.S.A.: Abbeville). His novel "Ruth" is shortly to appear in paperback (Hodder and Stoughton).

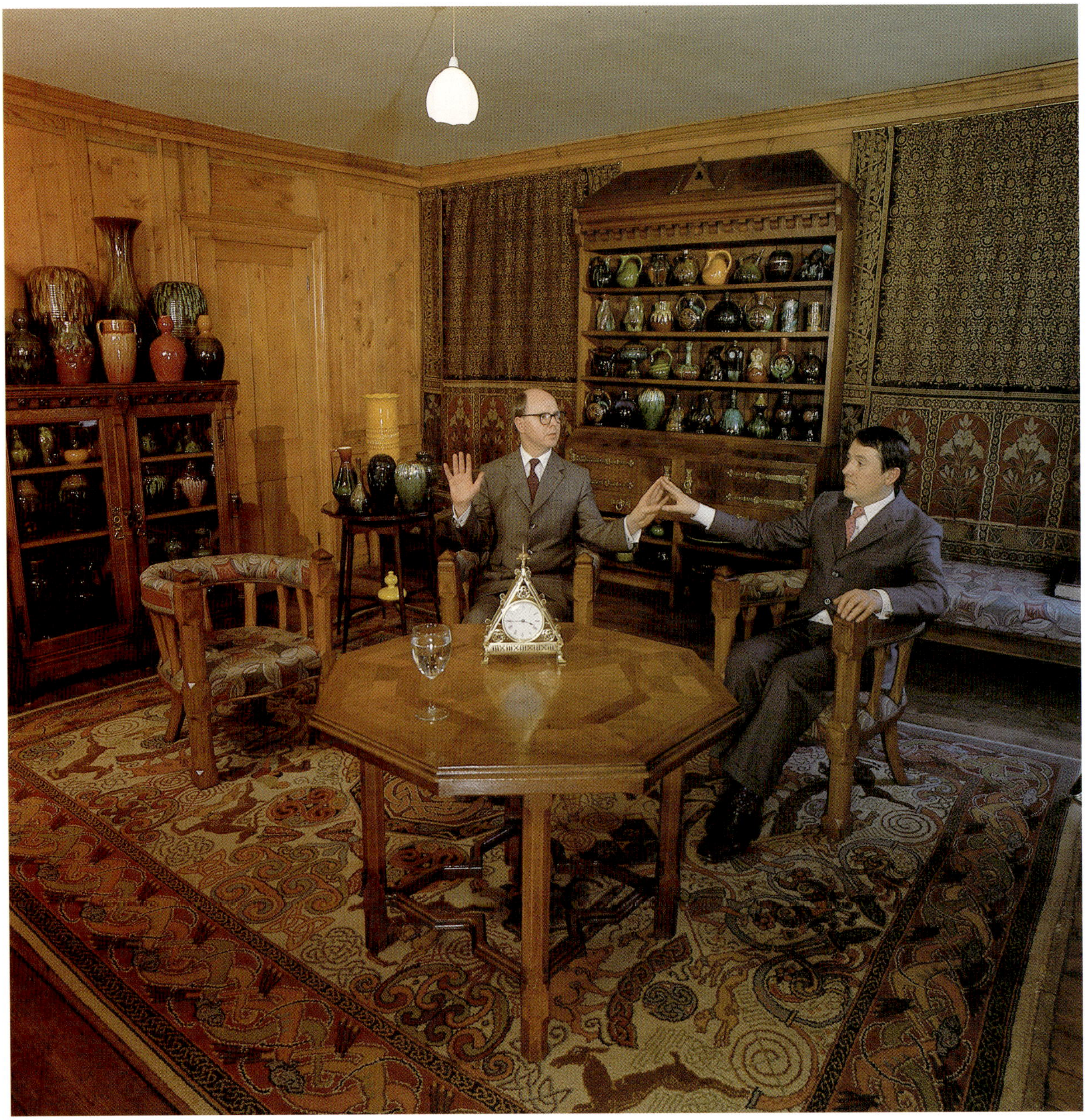

CHRIS GARNHAM, PORTRAIT OF GILBERT & GEORGE FOR THE OBSERVER MAGAZINE, 1984.

set had this not already been done – to Gilbert-&-Georgian excess – by a Spitalfields neighbour. Another solution could have been to design their own furniture and objets d'art, but Gilbert and George seemed to shy away from the idea of living face-to-face twenty-four hours a day with Gilbert & George. As he had also – I believe – become weary of forever confronting his own image, all three of them went off together in search of something new for their old house.

They discovered the ideal furniture, largely by chance, in the work of progressive English architect-designers of the period 1830 to 1890: from the reformed gothic of A.W.N. Pugin, through the geometric gothic of B.J. Talbert and C.L. Eastlake, to the aesthetic sophistication of E.W. Godwin and Dr. Christopher Dresser.

Their first tentative purchase was of two wing chairs, arts-and-craftily relief-carved with fruit. For months afterwards they found nothing else to please them, until a poster in the Underground drew them, in September 1979, to an antiques shop in Bloomsbury specializing exclusively in the period to which (as they then discovered) their chairs belonged. The slow and careful process by which Gilbert and George set out to furnish the house gathered speed after the purchase in March 1980 of three gothic revival armchairs and a pair of matching benches (on one of which they posed for the frontispiece portrait in GILBERT & GEORGE. THE COMPLETE PICTURES 1971–1985). With the stylistic parameters thus established, Gilbert and George began to take a serious historical interest in the period, and eventually, in June 1981, came to make their first major purchase: a Gillow's sideboard designed by B.J. Talbert, similar to his prize-winning piece for the 1872 London International Exhibition, now in the Victoria and Albert Museum. The owners already by then of two pieces of furniture by A.W.N. Pugin (decorator of the Palace of Westminster), Gilbert and George had become collectors.

Meanwhile, they had also been introduced to the work of Dr. Christopher Dresser (1834–1904), a botanist turned commercial designer whose name, until then, they had never heard of. The extreme adventurousness of Dresser's pottery designs appealed instantly to Gilbert and George who from that moment bought every single piece of his Linthorpe (1879–89) and Ault (1887–1923) pottery they could find. At the same time they began buying, in similar quantities, the products of two Devon potteries already known to George, C.H. Brannum's Barumware of the period 1879 to 1913 and Watcombe terracotta produced (some to Dresser's design) in Torquay from 1867 to 1901. They also discovered the wildly underrated studio pottery of Sir Edmund Elton, made at Clivedon in Somerset from 1879 until his death in 1920.

By 1983 their interest in the gothic revival had been extended to include the slightly later aesthetic movement. Christopher Dresser cast-iron furniture began to appear at their house, and in 1984 several ebonised pieces by E.W. Godwin were hauled up to the large attic room. The following year Gilbert and George further enhanced the sense of richness, of colour density, in their rooms by hanging textiles on the walls: bold geometric designs by Talbert and Dresser. At the same time they also discovered the qualities of mid-Victorian chromolithography, and speedily formed an impressive collection of pattern books by Owen Jones, the Audsley brothers, Dresser and others. All their purchases were made through dealers, including the acquisition of three complete private collections: of exceedingly rare Dresser Clutha glass; of some outstanding Elton pottery; and another collection of several hundred pieces of Brannum. They once bid at auction. In January 1986 when, despite Christie's high estimate on Talbert's Pericles sideboard, their even higher bid was unsuccessful. By the summer of 1986 barely an inch of spare space remained in the house, and only certain additions to their extraordinary collection have since been made. Such was their dedication to chosen themes that, in six busy years, Gilbert and George's collection grew to be rivalled by only one other in the world for its size and quality – that formed over the previous twenty years by an England rugby international and born-again property developer (the man, incidentally, who had dared outbid them for the Pericles sideboard).

It would be a mistake, however, to think of Gilbert & George as a mere collector. He, and all he does, is primarily a work of art. In denying the original excitement of discovery, Gilbert & George now claims to derive no pleasure from the collection other than as benevolent curator of a neglected slice of his British heritage. Gilbert & George takes his collection as seriously as he does himself. He, and therefore it, is by self-definition unique.

Originally Gilbert and George had, in fact, acted with many of the same motives as other dedicated explorers in unfashionable fields of collecting. As for others so for Gilbert and George, collecting was, in part, a way of escape – if only from Friday night hangovers: "The worse we feel the more we spend," George used to explain. "Today (the Saturday morning of June 16, 1981 when they spent a lot) we felt very ill. We feel much better now, thanks." They were also openly proud of their collection, always keen to display and discuss new acquisitions. In those years they used to amuse themselves by testing inexpert visitors on the date of some particularly bizarre nineteen-twenties-looking Dresser pot.

"Wrong. It's eighteen-eighty," Gilbert would chortle.

"Amazing, what?" George would add.

Gilbert and George used readily to admit to having made mistakes in the early days – mistakes of omission rather than commission, by failing to appreciate the quality of pieces they would now like to own. As with other collectors, financial restriction also played a part, and it is no coincidence that Gilbert and George's heaviest period of buying coincided with their international success as artists. For a time in the mid-1980s they completely dominated the London market in their fields, buying everything and anything they liked. As with other fanatical collectors, Gilbert and George may also at times feel weighed down by the burden of their valuable possessions.

While Gilbert & George's work expresses no direct visual debt to the collection (Pugin's Big Ben tower is as much a national/phallic symbol as a sign of enthusiasm for the neo-gothic), there are many connecting resonances. The moralising zeal and overt religiosity of Pugin, for example, appeals to Gilbert and George. Like them, Pugin believed an artist has both the power and the duty to improve society. "The present condition of architecture is deplorable," Pugin wrote in 1840. "Truth reduced to the position of an interesting but rare and curious relic." Moving on to Christopher Dresser, not only the sentiment but even the language is positively Gilbert-&-Georgian. KNOWLEDGE IS POWER Dresser inscribed in capital letters above his studio door. "Ornamentation must be powerful in its utterance," he wrote in 1876. "If power is absent from a composition weakness is the result, which cannot be pleasant. Weakness is childish, is infantine; power is manly; power is Godlike." The identification of power and manhood – to the exclusion of womanhood – with Godliness finds many echoes in the words and works of Gilbert & George. Like Queen Victoria, Margaret Thatcher, and Gilbert & George, Christopher Dresser believed steadfastly in the individual's moral obligation to seek self-advancement through hard work. "Think not that there is a royal road to success," Dresser wrote in a series of polemical articles published in Cassell's Technical Educator from 1870 to 1873. The road is through toil ... I am a worker, and a believer in the efficacy of work."

Given the limitation of space, and Gilbert and George's refusal to sell anything from the collection, it is difficult to see how further progress with the collection is possible. Except that for some time they have been trying to buy another house. If they succeed in this then, with typical single-mindedness, they plan to create a mirror image of their house. For themselves, of course, not for guests. (Every year Gilbert and George separate for two weeks to stay with their respective mothers; although Gilbert & George has not once invited the mothers to pay him a return visit.)

Maybe, in years to come, this remarkable COLLECTION SCULPTURE will end up on view in three identical houses, one each for the unavoidably ageing Gilbert and George, and a third for the ever-young Gilbert & George.

JEREMY COOPER

GILBERT & GEORGE «ZU HAUSE»

*Gilbert & George ist singularisch.
Sie sind er.
Gilbert kann immer noch häufiger Gilbert sein, George unveränderlich George, aber zusammen sind Gilbert und George meistens Gilbert & George.
Gilbert & George ist ihre grösste Schöpfung. Eine lebende Skulptur von solch überragender Autorität, dass, sollte Gilbert & George irgendwie verlorengehen – sterben –, man sich nur schwer vorstellen kann, wie entweder Gilbert oder George weiterleben könnte. Um ihre singularischen Leben ebenso aufrechtzuerhalten wie ihre pluralische Kunst, haben Gilbert und George für Gilbert & George ein Ambiente geschaffen, in dem er und sie sich gleichermassen «zu Hause» fühlen können.*

Vom Sommer 1978 an stellten Gilbert und George über ein Jahr lang die eigentliche Produktion von Kunstwerken ein und konzentrierten sich statt dessen darauf, die Restaurierung ihres aus dem achtzehnten Jahrhundert stammenden Weber-Hauses in Spitalfields, im Londoner East End, abzuschliessen. Zweifellos fuhren sie fort, in ihren Köpfen, während ihrer Spaziergänge und über ihren Drinks zu arbeiten, aber die alltägliche Aufgabe beschränkte sich auf die Tätigkeit, das ursprüngliche Kiefernholz, das die Wände auf allen vier Etagen ihres Hauses bedeckte, eigenhändig von Farbe zu befreien und zu polieren. In den ausgehenden sechziger Jahren hatten sie, als Studenten, eine Etage des Hauses gemietet. Zehn Jahre später nannten sie das ganze Gebäude ihr eigen, dazu ein geräumiges Atelier im Hinterhof, eine ehemalige bangladeschische Textilfabrik. Mit ihren bescheidenen häuslichen Bedürfnissen, die in einem schmalen, nicht öffentlichen Anbau hinten am Haus abgewickelt werden, war das vollkommen leerstehende historische Innere des Hauptgebäudes im Herbst 1979 schliesslich bereit für... ja, wofür eigentlich?

Für lebende Skulptur natürlich. Für Gäste-beim-Tee-Skulptur (mit marmite, einer Art Extrakt aus frischer Brauhefe, auf Toast). Für Zeitschriften-Interview-Skulptur. Für Sammlung-Skulptur. Für Den-einsamen-Abend-ausfüllen-Skulptur.

Für Fernsehen-schauen-Skulptur?

Ja, gelegentlich auch dafür.

Aber wie? Und in welchem Stil?

Die wesentliche Vorbedingung für Gilbert und George war, dass das Gesamtergebnis irgendwie einzigartig sein musste. Einfache Lösungen waren ihnen, anders als anderen, versperrt. Keine modischen Dekorateure für Gilbert & George. Kein rascher Besuch

---

JEREMY COOPER, war bevor er sich 1983 dem hauptberuflichen Schreiben zuwandte, Antiquitätenhändler in Bloomsbury. Kürzlich veröffentlichte er «Victorian and Edwardian Furniture and Interiors» (Europe: Thames and Hudson; USA: Abbeville). Sein Roman «Ruth» wird in Kürze als Paperback erscheinen (Hodder and Stoughton).

bei Multizweck-Conran. Nicht einmal bei Einzelstück-Zvi Aram. (Viel zu oft hatten sie ihre Zeitgenossen in Kunst und Design mit Zoten bedacht, um sich jetzt hilfesuchend an sie zu wenden.) Sie hätten beschliessen können, sich ein gotisch-historistisches Bühnenbild zu bauen, hätte dies nicht schon – in Gilbert & Georgeianischem Übermass – ein Spitalfields-Nachbar getan. Eine andere Lösung hätte sein können, eigene Möbel und kleinere Kunstgegenstände zu entwerfen, doch schienen Gilbert und George vor dem Gedanken zurückzuschrecken, vierundzwanzig Stunden am Tag von Angesicht zu Angesicht mit Gilbert & George zu leben. Wie er – meine ich – es auch müde geworden war, immerzu sein eigenes Bild vor Augen zu haben, machten sich alle drei auf die Suche nach etwas Neuem für ihr altes Haus.

Das ideale Mobiliar entdeckten sie, grösstenteils durch Zufall, in der Arbeit fortschrittlicher englischer Architekten/Designer aus der Zeit zwischen 1830 und 1890: von der streng-reformierten Neo-Gotik A. W. N. Pugins über die geometrische Neo-Gotik B. J. Talberts und C. L. Eastlakes bis zur ästhetischen Differenziertheit E. W. Godwins und Dr. Christopher Dressers.

Ihr erster zaghafter Kauf bestand aus zwei Ohrensesseln mit kunstvoll/dekorativ reliefgeschnitzten Früchten. Auf Monate hinaus fanden sie anschliessend nichts weiteres, das ihnen gefallen hätte, bis ein Plakat in der U-Bahn sie im September 1979 zu einem Antiquitätenladen in Bloomsbury hinzog, der sich ausschliesslich auf die Epoche spezialisierte, in die (wie sie sodann herausfanden) ihre Sessel gehörten. Das langsame und sorgfältige Verfahren, mit dem Gilbert und George sich daranmachten, ihr Haus einzurichten, nahm, nach dem Erwerb dreier neugotischer Lehnstühle und zweier dazu passender Bänke (auf einer davon posierten sie für das Titelporträt in GILBERT & GEORGE, THE COMPLETE PICTURES 1971–1985), im März 1980 an Geschwindigkeit zu. Mit solchermassen festgelegten stilistischen Parametern fingen Gilbert und George an, ein ernsthaftes historisches Interesse an dieser Epoche zu entwickeln, und fanden, im Juni 1981, schliesslich die Gelegenheit, ihren ersten grösseren Kauf zu tätigen: Ein von B. J. Talbert entworfenes Gillow-Sideboard, ähnlich seinem preisgekrönten Entwurf für die London International Exhibition 1872, der sich heute im Viktoria-und-Albert-Museum befindet. Bis dahin bereits Besitzer zweier Möbelstücke von A. W. N. Pugin (Dekorateur des Westminster-Palastes), waren Gilbert und George damit zu Sammlern geworden.

Inzwischen hatte man sie auch mit dem Werk von Dr. Christopher Dresser (1834–1904) bekannt gemacht, einem Botaniker, der den Beruf eines kommerziellen Designers eingeschlagen hatte und dessen Namen sie bis dahin niemals gehört hatten. Die aussergewöhnliche Abenteuerlichkeit von Dressers Töpferwaren fand bei Gilbert und George sogleich Anklang, die von dem Augenblick an jedes einzelne Stück von Dressers Linthorpe-(1879–89-) und Ault-(1887–1923-)Keramik kauften, das sie aufspüren konnten. Zur gleichen Zeit fingen sie – in ähnlichen Quantitäten – an, die Erzeugnisse zweier Devontöpfereien zu kaufen, die George bereits kannte – C. H. Branums BARUMWARE (Töpferei) aus der Zeit von 1879 bis 1913 und Watcombe-Terrakotta (einige nach Dressers Entwürfen), produziert zwischen 1867 und 1901 in Torquay. Auch entdeckten sie die stark unterbewertete Studiokeramik von Sir Edmund Elton, hergestellt von 1879 bis zu seinem Tod, 1920, in Clivedon, Somerset.

Spätestens 1983 hatte ihr Interesse an der Neugotik soweit zugenommen, dass sie die zeitlich ein wenig spätere ästhetische Bewegung mit einschlossen. Christopher Dressers Gusseisen-Mobiliar begann in ihrem Haus aufzutauchen, und 1984 wurden mehrere schwarz gebeizte Stücke von E. W. Godwin auf das ausgedehnte Dachgeschoss gehievt. Im darauffolgenden Jahr steigerten Gilbert und George das Gefühl der Pracht, der Farbendichte in ihren Räumlichkeiten, indem sie Textilien an die Wände hängten: gewagte geometrische Entwürfe von Talbert und Dresser. Gleichzeitig entdeckten sie die Qualitäten des – die Mitte der viktorianischen Epoche kennzeichnenden – Mehrfarbensteindrucks und stellten umgehend eine eindrucksvolle Sammlung von Musterbüchern von Owen Jones, den Gebrüdern Audsley, Dresser und anderen zusammen. Alle ihre Käufe wurden über Händler abgewickelt, einschliesslich des Erwerbs dreier vollständiger Privatsammlungen: überaus seltenes Dresser-Clutha-Glas; einige hervorragende Elton-Keramik sowie eine weitere Sammlung von

mehreren hundert Stücken von Brannum-Töpferei. Einmal boten sie bei einer Versteigerung mit; im Januar 1986, als ihr Gebot für Talberts Perikles-Sideboard, das weit über Christie's an sich schon hohem Schätzwert lag, nochmals überboten wurde. Bis zum Sommer 1986 blieb kaum ein Quadratzentimeter freier Raum übrig, und seither wurden ihrer aussergewöhnlichen Sammlung lediglich einige weitere Stücke hinzugefügt. Ihre Hingabe an ausgewählte Gegenstände war so gross, dass Gilbert und Georges' Sammlung innerhalb von sechs geschäftigen Jahren wuchs, um nur von einer anderen in der Welt um ihrer Grösse und Qualität wegen übertroffen zu werden – von jener über zwanzig Jahre zusammengetragenen Sammlung eines englischen Rugby-Internationalen und wiedergeborenen Grundstückserschliessers (zufälligerweise der Mann, der es gewagt hatte, sie bei dem Perikles-Sideboard zu überbieten).

Es wäre allerdings ein Fehler, an Gilbert & George als blossen Sammler zu denken. In erster Linie sind er, und alles, was er tut, ein Kunstwerk. Und indem er den ursprünglichen Reiz der Entdeckung in Abrede stellt, behauptet Gilbert & George heute, keine andere Freude an der Sammlung zu finden als die des wohlwollenden Konservators eines vernachlässigten Teils seines britischen Erbes. Gilbert & George nimmt seine Sammlung ebenso ernst wie sich selbst. Er, und deshalb auch sie, sind per Selbstdefinition einzigartig.

Ursprünglich hatten Gilbert und George tatsächlich aus vielfach denselben Beweggründen heraus agiert wie andere hingebungsvolle Forschungsreisende auf nicht modischen Sammelgebieten. Wie für andere auch war das Sammeln für Gilbert und George teilweise eine Möglichkeit der Flucht – und sei es nur vor dem Freitagabend-Katzenjammer: «Je schlechter wir uns fühlen, desto mehr geben wir aus», pflegte George zu sagen. «Heute (jener Samstagmorgen des 16. Juni 1986, an dem sie sehr viel Geld ausgaben) fühlten wir uns s e h r krank. Jetzt fühlen wir uns v i e l besser, danke.» Auch waren sie unverhohlen stolz auf ihre Sammlung, stets erpicht darauf, neue Errungenschaften zu zeigen und zu diskutieren. In jenen Jahren pflegten sie sich zu amüsieren, indem sie unerfahrene Besucher hinsichtlich der Datierung eines besonders seltsamen Dresser-Gefässes, das wie aus den zwanziger Jahren unseres Jahrhunderts aussah, auf die Probe stellten.

«Falsch. 1880», pflegte Gilbert zu frohlocken.

«E r s t a u n l i c h, was?» pflegte George hinzuzufügen.

Gilbert und George waren es gewohnt, bereitwillig einzugestehen, in frühen Tagen Fehler begangen zu haben, indem sie es versäumten, die Qualität von Stücken, die sie heute gern besitzen würden, richtig einzuschätzen. Wie bei anderen Sammlern spielten auch finanzielle Beschränkungen eine Rolle, und es ist kein Zufall, dass Gilbert und Georges' belebteste Kaufperiode mit ihrem internationalen Erfolg als Künstler zusammenfiel. Mitte der achtziger Jahre beherrschten sie den Londoner Markt – auf ihren Gebieten – eine Zeitlang vollständig und kauften alles und jedes, das ihnen gefiel. Wie andere fanatische Sammler mögen Gilbert und George sich heutzutage gelegentlich auch von der Last ihrer wertvollen Besitztümer niedergedrückt fühlen.

Obwohl Gilbert & Georges' Werk keine direkten visuellen Anleihen bei der Sammlung macht, gibt es viele verbindende Resonanzen (Pugins Big Ben ist ebenso ein nationales/phallisches Symbol wie ein Ausdruck der Begeisterung für das Neugotische). Der moralisierende Eifer und die offene Religiosität Pugins finden zum Beispiel bei Gilbert und George Gefallen. Pugin glaubte, wie sie auch, ein Künstler habe die Macht und die Pflicht, die Gesellschaft zu verbessern. «Der gegenwärtige Zustand der Architektur ist beklagenswert», schrieb Pugin 1840. «Wahrheit wurde herabgesetzt in den Rang eines interessanten, aber seltenen und sonderbaren Überbleibsels.» Geht man weiter zu Christopher Dresser, so ist nicht nur das Empfinden, sondern gar die Sprache ausdrücklich Gilbert & Georgeianisch. WISSEN IST MACHT, schrieb Dresser in Grossbuchstaben über seine Ateliertür. «Ornamentierung muss in ihrem Ausdruck m a c h t v o l l sein», führte er 1876 aus. «Wenn einer künstlerischen Anordnung Macht fehlt, ist Schwäche das Resultat, welches nicht angenehm sein kann. Schwäche ist kindisch, ist infantil; Macht ist mannhaft; Macht ist gottgleich.» Die Gleichsetzung von Macht und Mannhaftigkeit – unter Ausschluss von Weiblichkeit – mit Rechtschaffenheit findet in den Worten und Werken von Gilbert & George viele Echos.

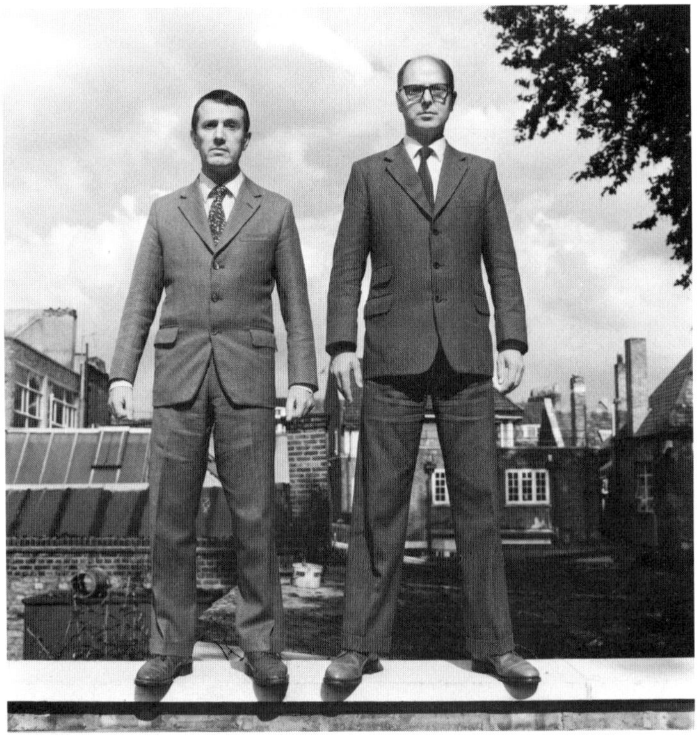

LIAM WOON, PORTRAIT OF GILBERT & GEORGE, 1987.

Wie Königin Viktoria, Margaret Thatcher und Gilbert & George glaubte Christopher Dresser unerschütterlich an die moralische Verpflichtung eines jeden Menschen, durch harte Arbeit die eigenen Fortschritte zu stärken. «Glaubt nicht, dass es einen mühelosen Weg zum Erfolg gibt», schrieb Dresser in einer Reihe in Cassell's Technical Educator von 1870 bis 1873 veröffentlichter polemischer Artikel. «Der Weg führt durch Plackerei ... Ich bin ein Arbeiter und ein an die Wirksamkeit von Arbeit Glaubender.»

Geht man von den räumlichen Beschränkungen aus und von Gilberts und Georges Weigerung, irgend etwas aus der Sammlung zu verkaufen, ist es nur schwer vorstellbar, wie ein weiterer Fortschritt hinsichtlich der Sammlung möglich ist. Ausser, dass sie seit einiger Zeit versucht haben, das Haus nebenan zu erwerben. Wenn sie damit erfolgreich sind, dann planen sie, mit typischer Zielstrebigkeit, ein Spiegelbild ihres Hauses zu schaffen. Natürlich für sich selbst, nicht für Gäste. (Jedes Jahr trennen Gilbert und George sich für zwei Wochen, um ihre jeweiligen Mütter zu besuchen; obwohl Gilbert & George die Mütter nicht ein einziges Mal eingeladen hat, ihm einen Gegenbesuch abzustatten.)

Möglicherweise wird diese bemerkenswerte SAMMLUNG-SKULPTUR eines Tages in drei identischen Häusern zur Besichtigung freigegeben werden – je eine für die unvermeidlich alternden Gilbert und George, und eine dritte für den ewig jungen Gilbert & George.

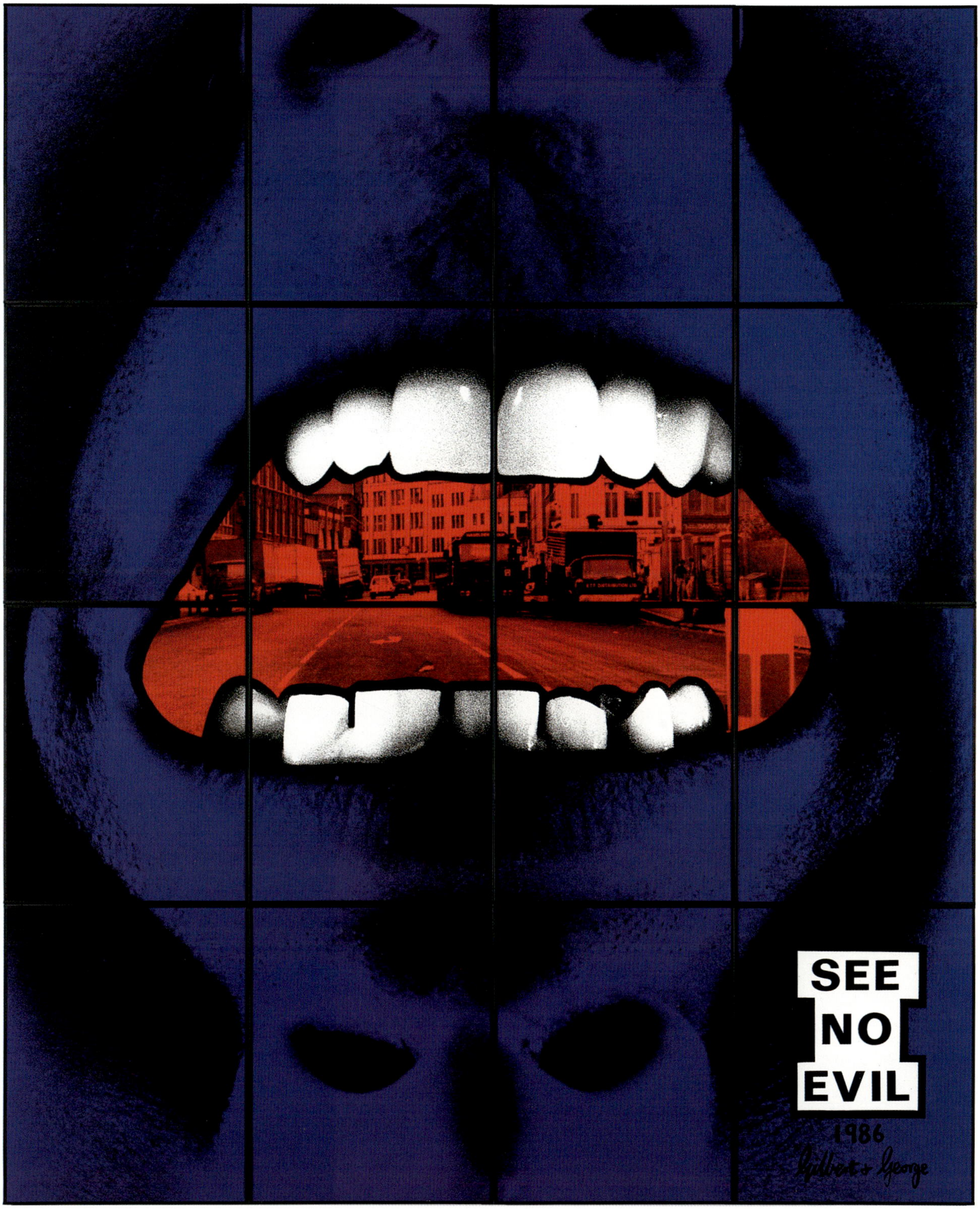

GILBERT & GEORGE, SEE NO EVIL / SIEH NICHTS BÖSES, 1986, *95 x 79½" / 242 x 202 cm.*

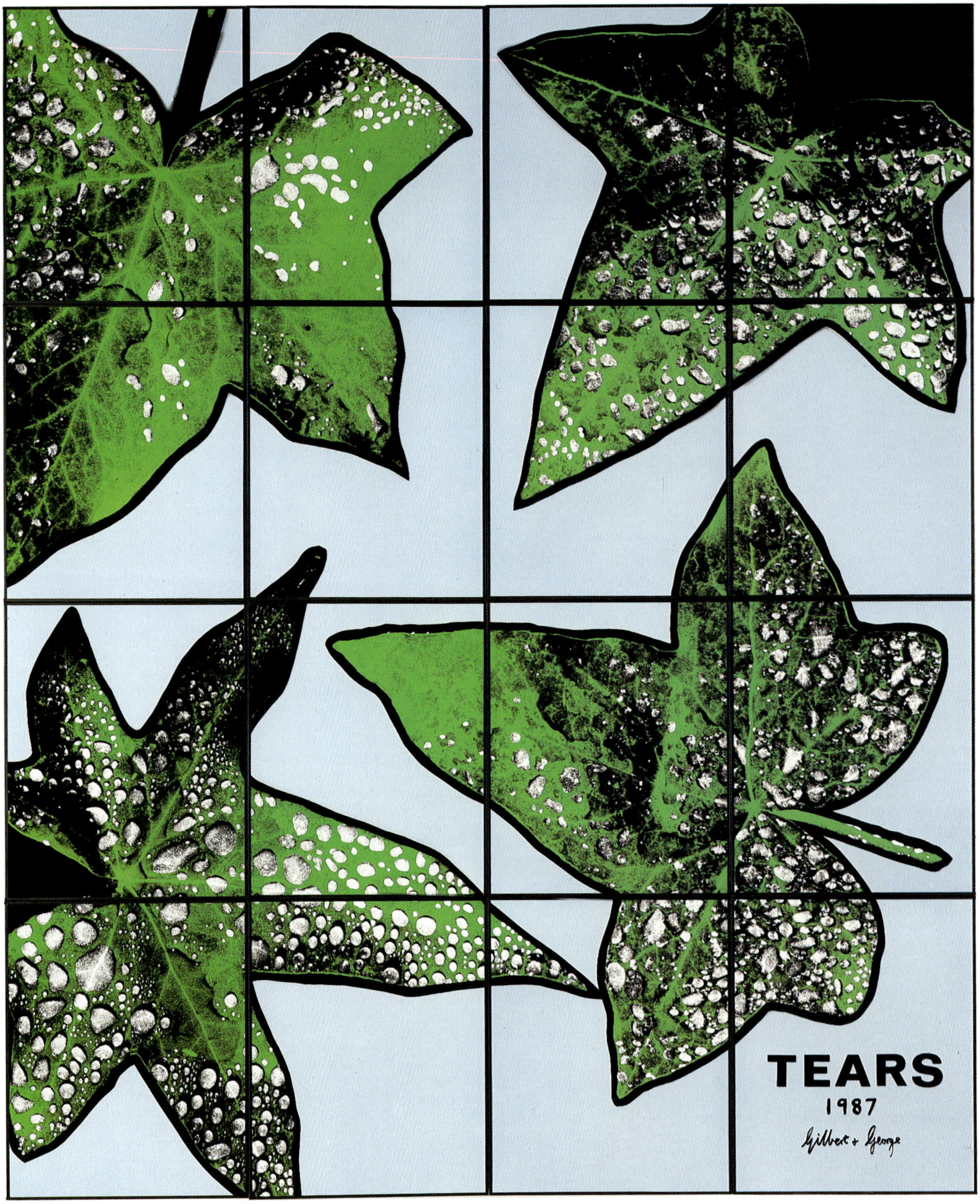

GILBERT & GEORGE, TEARS / TRÄNEN, 1987, *95 x 79½"* / 242 x 202 cm.

DER GESANG DER CIRCE

DEMOSTHENES DAVVETAS

Erfahrung wird aus Erinnerung geboren; oder, um es anders auszudrücken: mehrere Erinnerungen gleicher Bedeutsamkeit erlangen den Status von erworbener Erfahrung. Im Gegensatz zu Unerfahrenheit, welche Zufälligkeit erzeugt, vermag aus dieser erworbenen Erfahrung Kunst zu entstehen.

Ich denke, dass diese – im ersten Band von Aristoteles' «Metaphysik» entwickelte – Betrachtung sehr gut zu Gilbert und George passt. Die von ihnen geschaffenen Bilder sind nicht Produkte bloss zufälliger Handbewegungen, sondern von Wissen und Logik; sie drükken das Verlangen ihrer Schöpfer aus, das Irrationale zu beherrschen und es neben dem Rationalen koexistieren zu lassen.

Dieser Wunsch ist Ausdruck des Anspruches, den diese beiden Künstler an die Kunst stellen – ein Mittel zur Kommunikation, ein Instrument des Zwiegesprächs zu sein, das den Austausch von Ideen ermöglicht. Wer Kunst aus dieser Wahrnehmung heraus versteht, wird sich folgerichtig bemühen, auch ihre stoffliche Erscheinung von diesem starken Wunsch nach Dialog her zu begreifen. Was gäbe es für einen besseren Weg, um dies zu erreichen, als jene Materialien und jene Ikonographie zu verwenden, die jedermann – ungeachtet seines Ranges und Standes – zugänglich sind? Aus dieser Logik muss der Einsatz der menschlichen Gestalt im Werk von Gilbert und George verstanden werden.

In der Bildsprache der beiden Künstler erscheint die menschliche Gestalt wie der Gesang der Circe: gesungen, um Interesse und Aufmerksamkeit eines anderen Menschen zu provozieren und ihn so weit zu reizen, dass er dem Gesang und der Musik bewusst zu lauschen beginnt (also das Bild der Künstler anschaut). In diesem Moment gibt der Gesang seine flüchtig zarte Form auf und wird zu einem Kerker, zu einer unaufhörlichen Berauschung, die ihren Zuhörer gefangenhält. Die menschliche Gestalt ist im Werk von Gilbert und George eine Methode des Sprechens; oft von Wörtern oder Sätzen begleitet, wird sie für den Betrachter zu einer Art Spiegel. Dieser Spiegel besitzt magische Eigenschaften: Er «hört zu» und er «spricht».

Das «Zuhören» drückt sich durch den Inhalt aus (dem, was bildlich erschaffen wurde) – in der menschlichen Gestalt. Wir können sagen, dass der Betrachter beim Anschauen der Bildnisse in den Werken dieser Künstler sich selbst erkennt, aus der Verbindung zwischen Wörtern und Gestalt oder aus inneren, unsichtbaren Aspekten seiner selbst heraus, über die er vielleicht nachsinnt und über die er auch gern sprechen würde. Aber irgend etwas bereitet ihm Angst und veranlasst ihn, es nicht zu tun. In der Konfrontation mit Gilbert und Georges Bildern indes verspürt er das Bedürfnis, zu sprechen und sich, teilweise oder ganz, mit einigen der Gestalten zu identifizieren, aus denen die

DEMOSTHENES DAVVETAS ist Schriftsteller und lebt in Paris. Er schreibt regelmässig für Libération und ist Autor des Romans «Oreste», erschienen 1986 bei Flammarion.

Bilder zusammengefügt sind. Dieser Zug zu einer Art Beichte seitens des Betrachters ist ein Beweis der Macht des «Zuhörens» im Werk dieser beiden Künstler, welches sogleich moralische Dimensionen annimmt und zwingend zum «Sprechen» führt.

Wie prähistorische und heidnische Priester, und wie gewisse Priester (natürlich aus der Kirchenhierarchie) des christlichen Zeitalters, oder sogar wie manche umherschweifende, um die Geheimnisse der Seele wissende Visionäre, entlassen Gilbert und George den, der ihnen gebeichtet hat, nicht, ohne ihn zärtlich zu liebkosen. Ihre Berührung ist gleichzeitig sanft und brutal und häufig voller Melancholie und Ironie, mit einem Hang zu Disziplin und Spiel, sie ist vielschichtig und einfach zugleich, wie Kinder oder alte Männer. Zuweilen ist ihre Berührung wie der Schrei eines Menschen, der seine tiefe Verzweiflung zu verbergen weiss, zuweilen wie die vertrauten Worte des Weisen: dass die ihn umgebende Wirklichkeit, was wir als die existierende Welt bezeichnen, nichts anderes ist als ein führerloses Schiff auf stürmischer See. Ihre Berührung (das stoffliche Vorhandensein des «Sprechens») findet in der Verbindung der menschlichen Gestalt mit den sie begleitenden Wörtern oder Sätzen ihren Ausdruck.

Welches Medium die Künstler auch benutzen (sei es Malerei, Photographie, Zeichnung etc.): Die menschliche Gestalt ist Sprache, und die begleitenden Wörter sind musikalische Noten, schlichte Buchstabenpersönlichkeiten. Zwischen dem Bild und dem Wort existiert die Beziehung des Unsichtbaren und des Sichtbaren: Was die beiden Elemente dem Auge darbieten, ist insofern nur ein Teil der Gesamtbedeutung, als es auch einen Teil gibt, der hinter dem sichtbaren Inhalt im Werk der beiden Künstler verborgen bleibt.

Die Gestalt ist gleichzeitig Gestalt – und ist es auch nicht. Was dargestellt wird (zum Beispiel die Gestalt Christi, ein nackter Knabe und sogar Gilbert und Georges Selbstdarstellung), ist, was wir zu sehen meinen, aber es ist auch etwas anderes, jenseits davon. Es ist eine Metapher, ein Symbol, etwas Zeitloses, von Zeit sich Entfernendes, beweglich und statisch, es sind die aus der Tiefe kommenden ewigen Werte, die menschliche Beziehungen leiten.

Die Gestalt ist verwandelt worden: sie ist die Sprache selbst, mit den Möglichkeiten, ein Bild zu werden. Wenn wir tiefer in das Werk der Künstler eindringen wollten und versuchten, einige Wurzeln zu finden, würden wir gewiss darauf stossen, dass die Entstehung der Gestalt parallel und identisch mit der des Schreibens verlaufen ist. So wie die Linie im Alphabet zum Schriftzeichen wird, zum Buchstaben, so formen die Buchstaben, wenn sie sich vereinen, Wörter oder Sätze. Andere Male wird eine Linie gleicherweise zu einer Zeichnung werden, einem Bild, welches jedoch nicht einfach als die Vollendung einer Linie in Gilbert und Georges Werk zum Vorschein kommt. Dieses eher unsichtbare Bild kommt statt dessen in der Bestimmtheit des Denkens und Wollens zum Ausdruck, die sich auf Erneuerung von Materialien richten, als ein Bild, dem der Raum eines Stücks Papier oder einer Photographie Hintergrund ist.

Kurz, in diesem Fall will Sprache nicht auf ihrer ursprünglichen, formalen Stufe verharren, sondern will, bereits bearbeitet und untersucht, als Produkt streng kontrollierter Arbeit erscheinen. Und dies, weil sie nicht eine Sprache ist, die sich innerhalb der Struktur und der Möglichkeit ihres eigenen Baus genügen und erschöpfen will. Sie ist kein Mechanismus, der nur Fragen stellt. Sie ist im Gegenteil ein Werkzeug, das dem Denken des Künstlers und jener Überzeugung gehorcht, dass es in der Kunst eine Absicht, ein Ziel geben muss. Wer sein Ziel erkennt, wird erfolgreich sein. Folglich ist Kunstgeschichte nicht etwas – und darf es nicht sein –, das nach und nach (infolge von Bewegungen) und im Kollektiv voranschreitet, sondern das vorrückt und zurückgeht, etwas, das von dem Augenblick an, da es seinen Anfang nahm, mit dem Bewusstsein vom Ende konfrontiert war. Deshalb hat sie mit einem Kreis zu tun, und sie handelt von der Beziehung zwischen Künstler und Publikum: eine Beziehung, die auf Wechselseitigkeit beruht, die das Ergebnis von «Zwiegespräch» ist.

Es ist genau dieser Sinn von «Zwiegespräch», der die Arbeit von Gilbert und George bestimmt. Sie rühren an alles, was verboten ist, an alles, was versteckt ist, auf das man moralisch und gesellschaftlich mit Missfallen blickt, und sie bringen es zum Leben zurück, indem sie ihm eine andere Verwendung und damit eine andere Dimension geben. Auch rühren sie an alles, was moralisch und gesellschaftlich bereits akzeptiert ist, und stellen es in ihrem Werk verändert dar. Es ist, als sei ihre Berührung (der Akt der Kunst) von einer beharrlichen, subversiven und konservativen Haltung gegenüber der existierenden Welt gelenkt. Es ist, als spielten sie mit Moral. Es ist, als vernähmen sie in quälendem Gesang die Worte des Dichters Manolis Anagnostakis: «Es gibt immer zwei Kategorien: Handelnde und Betrachter.»

(Übersetzung: Udo Breger)

THE SONG OF CIRCE

DEMOSTHENES DAVVETAS

Experience is born of memory, or to put it differently, a number of memories with the same function obtain the status of acquired experience, which, contrary to inexperience – itself producing accidentalism – gives birth to Art.

This viewpoint expounded in the first volume of Aristotle's "Metaphysics" seems, I think, to suit Gilbert and George's case very well. The pictures they create are not the product of a mere chance movement of the hand. They are a product of knowledge and logic – the desire of the creator to attempt to dominate the irrational and make it co-exist with the rational.

This desire is born of these two artists' conception of art as a medium of communication, an instrument for dialogue which allows for the transfusion of ideas between people. Someone who perceives art from this viewpoint is consequently interested in working toward its material presentation and is directed by the spirit of the need for "dialogue". What better way than by using materials and iconography within everyone's reach? It is against this background that we must understand the use of the human figure in the work of Gilbert and George.

The human figure in the pictorial language of these two artists is like the song of Circe: sung to provoke the interest and attention of the listener and to incite him even further so that once he has consciously begun to listen to this music (to look at the image made by the artists), the song immediately ceases to have a simple form and becomes prison-like, a continuous intoxication holding its listener captive. The human figure in the work of Gilbert and George is a way of speaking; often joined by words or phrases, it becomes a type of mirror for the spectator. This mirror possesses magical qualities: it "listens" and "speaks".

"Listening" is expressed from within the contents (that which is created) – the representation of the human figure. We can say that the spectator, on looking at the images of the artists' work recognizes himself from within the connection between words and figure, or recognizes interior, invisible aspects of himself which he perhaps contemplates and wants to speak about, but something frightens him, causing him not to. However, confronted with Gilbert and George's pictures he feels the need to speak and to identify partly or wholly with some of the figures which make up the pictures. This tendency towards a kind of confession from the spectator is proof of the power of "listening" in these two artists' work which consequently takes on moral dimensions, and inevitably leads on to "speaking".

Like prehistoric and pagan priests and like certain priests (from, of course, the ecclesiastical hierarchy) of the Christian age, or even like some kind of wandering visionary, wise in the secrets of the soul, Gilbert and George cannot abandon the confessor without first affectionately touching him. Their touch is both gentle and savage, full of melancholy and irony, with a tendency for discipline and sport, full of extremity and simplicity, like children or old men. It is

DEMOSTHENES DAVVETAS is a writer who lives in Paris. He writes regularly for "Libération" and is the author of the novel "Oreste" published by Flammarion in 1986.

sometimes like the cry of someone who knows how to conceal his profound desperation, or at other times it is like the familiar words of the wise man: that reality around him, i.e. what we call the existing world, is nothing but a ship without a navigator in a tempestuous sea. Their touch (the material existence of "speaking") is expressed in the connection of the human figure with the words or phrases which accompany it.

Whatever medium they use (be it painting, photography, drawing, etc.), the human figure is language and the accompanying words are musical notes, plain letter characters. The relationship between picture and word rests on the interplay between the invisible and the visible: what the two elements present to the eye is merely part of the overall meaning since there is also a part that remains invisible behind the visible content of the two artists' work.

The figure is, and at the same time is not, a figure. What is represented (e.g. the figure of Christ, a naked boy and even Gilbert and George's self-presentation) is what we think we see but it is also something else, beyond that. It is a metaphor, a symbol, something timeless, wandering away from time, moving and static; it is the deep eternal values that govern human relationships.

The figure has been transformed: it is language itself with the possibilities of becoming a picture. If we wanted to delve further into the artists' work and try to find some roots, we would be sure to find the birth of the figure parallel and identical to that of writing. Therefore, as the line of the alphabet ends and acquires the character of a letter, here too, a line sometimes becomes a letter and collectively the letters form words or phrases. Similarly, at other times, a line becomes a drawing, a picture, which does not, however, simply emerge as the completion of a line in Gilbert and George's work. It is rather from the guidance of thought and the desire for the renewal of materials that the work emerges, as a picture with the space of the paper (drawing) or a photograph as a background.

Briefly, in this case, language does not want to remain in its primary, formal stage, but wants to appear already worked-upon and inspected, the product of strictly controlled labour. This is due to the fact that it is not language which feels adequate and wants to exhaust itself within the framework and possibilities of its own structure. It is not a mechanism which only begs questions. On the contrary, it's a tool which obeys the artists' thought – that in Art there must be a target, an aim. He who succeeds is he who realizes his aim. Consequently, art history is not and must not be something that progresses successively (in movements) and collectively, but that proceeds and recurs, something that from the moment it began is faced with the consciousness of the end. Therefore, it is concerned with a cycle, and it is about the relationship between the artist and the public; a relationship based on reciprocity, a relationship which is the product of "dialogue."

It is precisely this sense of "dialogue" that dictates the work of Gilbert and George. They touch upon everything that is forbidden, everything that is tucked away, morally and socially frowned upon, and they bring it back to life by giving it another use, another dimension. They also touch upon what is already morally and socially accepted and present it altered in their work. It is as if their touch (the act of the art) is directed by a persistent subversive and conservative attitude towards the existing world. It is as if they were playing with morals. It is as if they themselves hear, in a haunting song, the words of the poet Manolis Anagnostakis: "There are always two categories: the actors and the spectators."

(Translation from the Greek: Vivian Constantinopoulos)

WOLF JAHN

SINNSTIFTER UND ZEUGEN VON WELT

Kunst ist immer Produktion von Sinn. Ob sie ihn schafft, kritisiert, negiert, vortäuscht oder heraufbeschwört, spielt dabei eine untergeordnete Rolle. Ihr Metier ist der Sinn, egal auf welche Art dies geschieht. Sie ist sogar in zweifacher Weise mit Sinn beschäftigt, da sie es dank ihres bildnerischen Ausdrucks stets mit SINN-lichem zu tun hat. Die Sinne anzusprechen und den Sinn oder dessen Widerpart zu visualisieren ist ihr eigentliches Terrain. Dieses muss sie behaupten, schaffen, umackern und tagtäglich neu bestellen.

Auf Gilbert & George trifft die Sinnforderung von Kunst in ganz besonderem Maße zu. Schon von Anfang an formulierten sie ihr Anliegen, das zweifellos nach mehr Sinn und Inhalt verlangte: «To be with art is all we ask.» Sie wollten Kunst mit transportablen Inhalten schaffen, Kunst, die für alle da ist, das heisst deren Sinn allen zugänglich ist, und eine Kunst, die auch den Sinn von Sinn neu zu formulieren vermag. Gerade dieser formalen Seite des Sinns haben sie ihren Stempel aufgedrückt, indem sie diese mit «Skulptur» umschrieben oder wie erst vor kurzem mit einer «frozen representation» verglichen. Sinn ist demnach nichts Globales, Allumfassendes oder Ewig-Währendes, sondern schlichtweg Figur, die ihren spezifischen Inhalt sinnlich veräussert. Sinn gleicht hier dem Phänomen Sprache und ihren Tausenden von Einzelbausteinen. Wie jedes Wort einen spezifischen Sinn, eine ihm eigene Bedeutung aufweist, so gibt auch jedes Bild einen entsprechenden Inhalt wieder. Sinn und Bedeutung erweisen sich im Werk von Gilbert & George als eine Angelegenheit der Differenzierung, nicht der Verabsolutierung.

Als Beispiele für eine derartige Form von Sinngebung – Autonomie und differenziert-spezifischer Inhalt – seien mehrere Bilder von Gilbert &

WOLF JAHN lebt als freischaffender Kunstjournalist in Hamburg. Er verfasste eine Monographie über Gilbert & George, die demnächst publiziert wird.

George vorgestellt. HERE und THERE, beide 1987, entstammen der jüngsten Produktion von Gilbert & George. Wie schon frühere ihrer Arbeiten stehen auch sie innerhalb eines antithetischen Aufbaus. Zugute kommt diese Gegensätzlichkeit dem einzelnen Bild. Dadurch gewinnt es an Prägnanz und Aussage. Bei den hier genannten drehen sie sich um den menschlichen Raum, dessen «Hier» und dessen «Dort». Der Mensch erfährt die örtliche Bestimmung seines Daseins, seiner Existenz.

Um diesen inhaltlichen Kontext zu erstellen, verwenden Gilbert & George für beide Bilder betont unterschiedliche Hintergründe. Bei «Here» besteht er aus einem Blick in eine Strasse, auf der jede Menge Kisten und Abfall von geschäftigem Treiben zeugen, während er sich bei «There» aus Bäumen, Gebüsch und Zweigen zusammensetzt. Diesen kontrastierenden Bildgründen entsprechen auf analoge Weise die Vordergründe; in beiden Fällen mit jeweils zwei Menschen angegeben. «Here» präsentiert Gilbert & George nebeneinander im Stand und mit ihren Händen zum Boden weisend. Damit nehmen sie den Bildtitel auf, indem sie auf jenes «Hier», die Strasse zeigen. «There» hingegen präsentiert zwei Jungen, die auf Kisten sitzen. Der rechte von ihnen stützt mit den Händen sein etwas trauriges Gesicht, während der linke mit einer Latte in den Händen leicht staunend aus dem Bild blickt.

Gemeinsamkeiten (zwei Menschen – Kisten) und Unterschiede (Stehen/Sitzen – Stadt/Natur – Oben/Unten der Bildtitel) definieren hier den Raum des Menschen, seine Heimat und seine Fremde. HERE lokalisiert das Zuhause des Menschen ganz offensichtlich innerhalb der Stadt, und zwar dort, wo sie kommerziell, laut, treibend, fliessend, aber auch mit Wohnung und Privatraum anzutreffen ist. Die Menschen «hier» – und dies demonstrieren Gilbert & George mit ihrem Stand – erkennen sie als ihre Heimat, ihren Existenzraum an. «Hier» lebt, arbeitet, erholt sich, isst und stirbt der Mensch.

THERE hingegen hält danach Ausschau, ob es im Gegensatz zum «Hier» der Stadt noch einen anderen Platz auf dieser Welt gibt. Und es gibt ihn tatsächlich, nämlich die Natur, jener traurige Ort, in der sich kein Mensch befindet, sich weder Geschäftigkeit noch menschliches Leben vollziehen. Selbst die Kisten, bei THERE wie bei HERE Indizien des menschlichen Tuns, finden keinen Einlass in die Natur. Ausserhalb ihres Territoriums müssen sie verweilen. Kein Wunder, dass die beiden Jungen vor diesem menschenleeren und unkultivierten Raum etwas traurig dreinblicken. Sie wirken wie abgeschoben, entfernt vom eigentlichen Leben der Stadt, dem «Hier» ihrer Existenz.

Auf letzteren Umstand – das Abschieben in die Fremde, in den menschenleeren Raum – deutet noch ein drittes Bild hin. PARKED, 1987, schliesst dabei zwei Wortbedeutungen von «Park» bzw. «Parken» zu einer einzigen zusammen. Denn ähnlich zwei hintereinander parkenden Autos sitzen auch Gilbert & George hier in einem Park in räumlicher Staffelung. Sie haben wortwörtlich «geparkt» (d.h. sie sind abgestellt), und dies in einem Park, dem Raum der Natur. Wenngleich dieser menschlich erbaut ist, gibt er sich dennoch menschenleer, da sich das Leben ausserhalb seiner Grenzen abspielt. Traurig, wer sich in ihm befindet, dort sinnbildlich gesehen «parkt». Er muss zusehen, wie das Leben ohne ihn stattfindet.

«Here» sowie «There» und «Parked» verdeutlichen auf eine sehr bildliche und einfache Weise, dass es den so oft zitierten «anderen» Ort des «eigentlichen» menschlichen Lebens gar nicht gibt. Jenen imaginären und utopischen Ort des Noch-Nicht, der immer zweierlei voraussetzt: erstens die Unwirtlichkeit unserer Städte und zweitens ihre angebliche Entfremdung von einer ehemaligen Leibhaftigkeit. Aus diesem fast feindlich zu nennenden Denken gegenüber der Zivilisation ist stets die Flucht aus ihr entstanden, hin zu einem imaginären Ort, der die wahre Heimat des Menschen symbolisierte. Bislang hat ihn allerdings noch kein Mensch gefunden. Trotzdem hat sich das Bild der angeblich menschenfeindlichen Zivilisation erhalten.

Indem Gilbert & George für diese Welt und für den Menschen im wesentlichen nur zwei Orte benennen, nämlich «Hier» und «Dort», verdeut-

GILBERT & GEORGE, HERE / HIER, 1987, *119 x 139"* / 303 x 354 cm.

GILBERT & GEORGE, THERE / DORT, 1987, *119 x 99½"* / 303 x 253 cm.

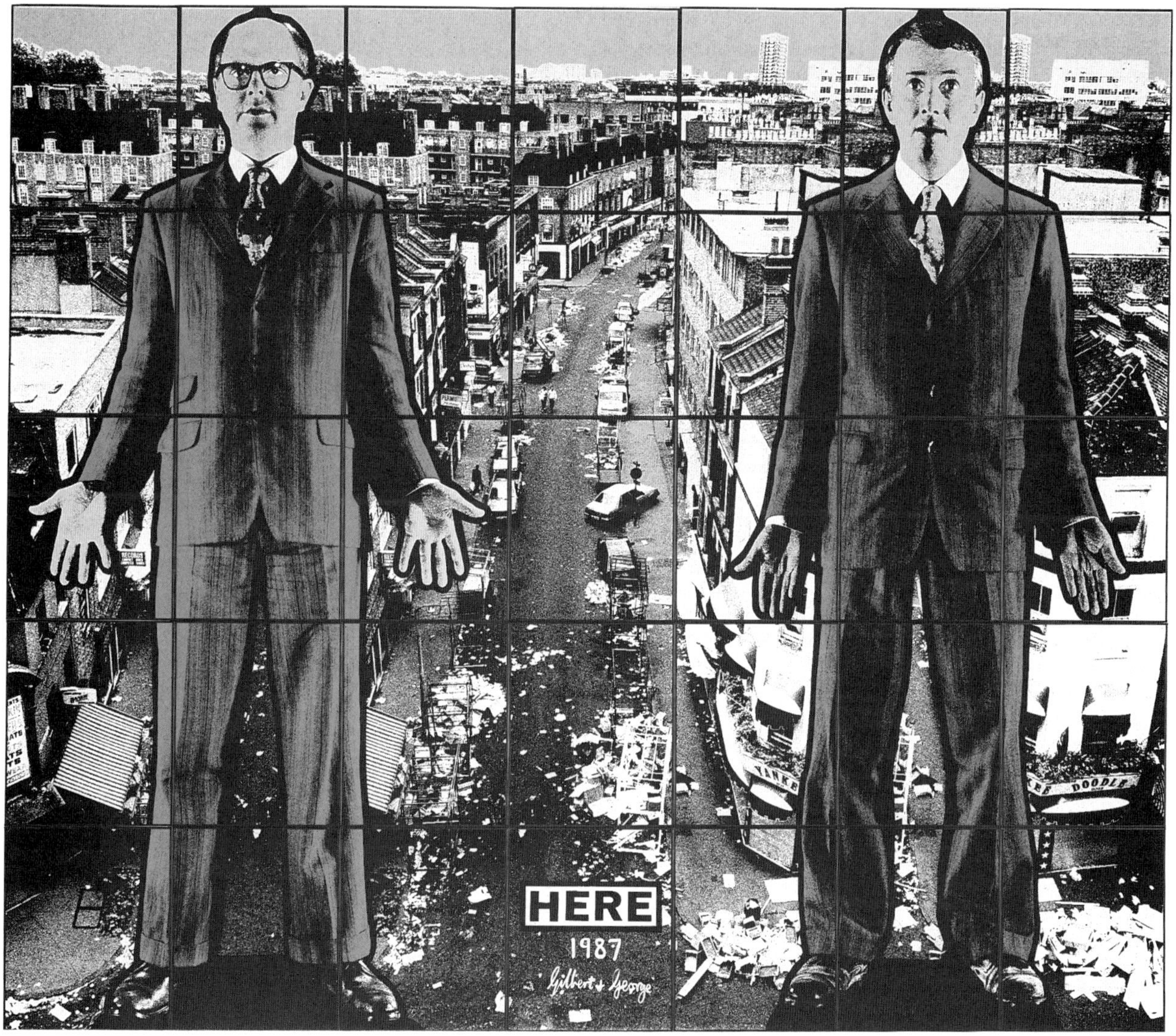

lichen sie, dass die Utopie (wörtlich: der Nicht-Ort) von jener angeblich wahren Heimat eine Illusion darstellt. Es gibt nur das «Hier» der Stadt, die Heimat des Menschen, und jenes «Dort», die unkultivierte und menschenleere Natur. Mehr nicht. Das mag zwar traurig für die abendländische Seele klingen, befreit aber dennoch von einer schmerzlichen Sehnsucht nach dem fiktiven Ort jenseits der Zivilisation.

In der Kunst von Gilbert & George geht es um Inhalte, und zwar um solche, die dem Menschen sein Leben gestalten, indem sie dessen Welt und Um-Welt bildlich formulieren. Kurzum, es geht um BILDung ganz im ersten Sinne des Wortes.

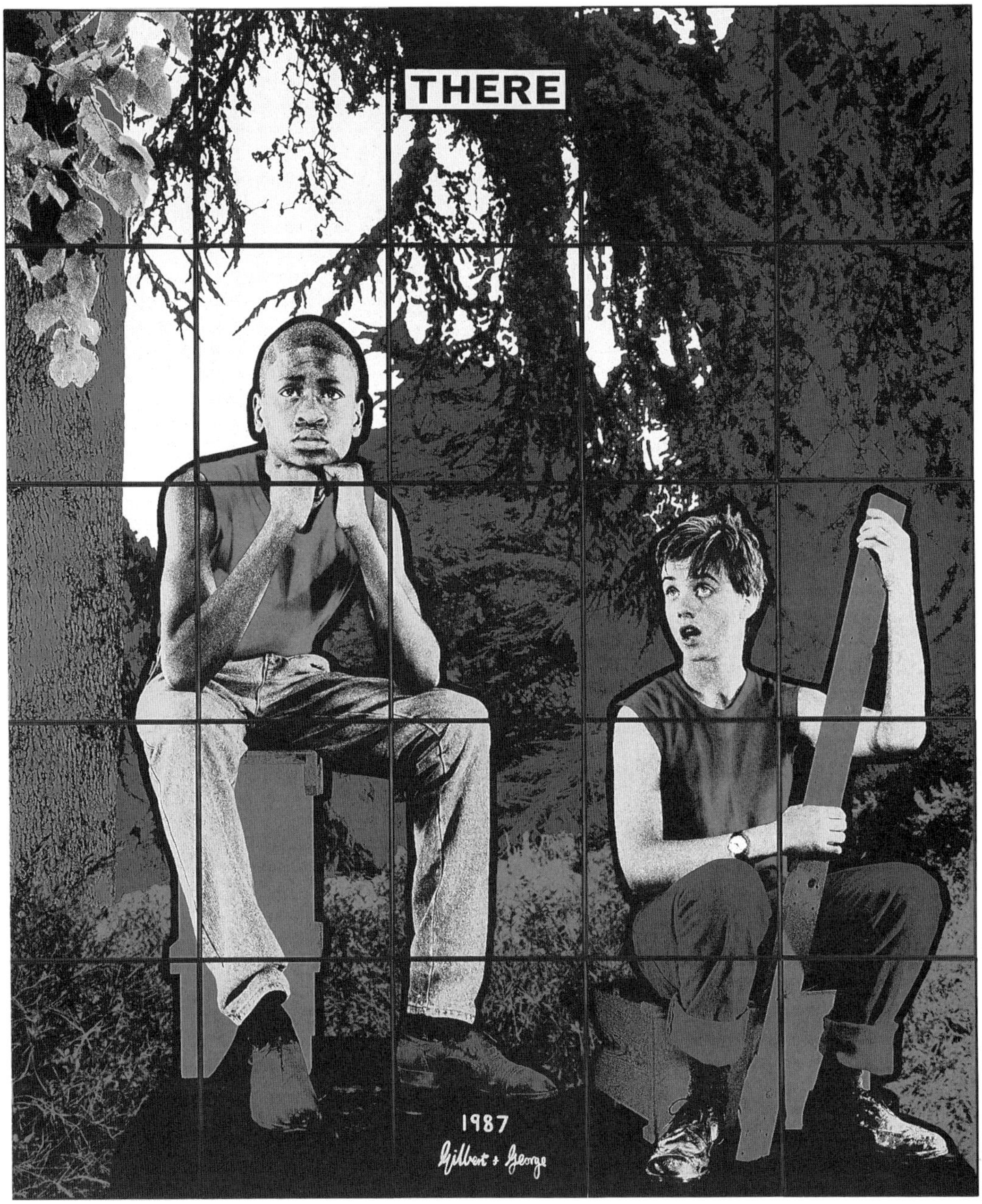

HERE und THERE leisten eine solche dort, wo sich die Frage nach den Orten dieser Welt stellt. Die Bilder versuchen eine sprachliche wiewohl bildliche Selbstverständlichkeit für das zu geben, was wir meinen, wenn die Rede von «hier» beziehungsweise «da» ist. Sie wollen uns mit der Welt und ihren Räumen vertraut machen.

HERE und THERE behandeln augenscheinlich nur einen Teil von Welt. In der Kunst von Gilbert & George aber geht es um mehr als nur einen ihrer Teile, es geht um ihre Komplexität und Differenziertheit. Um diese Vielfältigkeit hier zu demonstrieren, sei ein zweiter inhaltlicher Komplex vorgestellt, der jedoch eine ganz andere Thematik als

HERE und THERE zum Gegenstand hat. Statt Raum herrscht hier Zeit vor. Zeit, die ihr Ende findet. DEATH AFTER LIFE (Tod nach dem Leben) spricht von einer Vision des Endes, und zwar dem Ende als Er-Füllung und Zeitlichung des Lebens.

Auf dem über elf Meter langen und knapp fünf Meter hohen Bild DEATH AFTER LIFE, 1987, deutet in der Mitte ein junger Mann auf den Titel, bzw. dessen Personifizierung hin. Seine Arme auf den Boden gestützt, den Blick frontal nach vorne gerichtet, präsentiert er seinen Oberkörper als Bild einer zunächst befremdenden Szenerie. Sie zeigt einen weissen Vollmond hinter kahlen Bäumen und oberhalb eines modernen Hochhaustraktes. Doch zusammen ergeben der junge Mann sowie sein «Oberkörper» das Bild jenes «Todes nach dem Leben». Bildlich formuliert er sich als vollständiges Auswachsen, als voll-endete und damit auch ge-endete Form. Darauf spielen vor allem Mond, Bäume und Haus an, alle drei zusammen Inbegriffe des Voll-Endeten, des Vollbrachten: Der Mond hat seinen Weg vollbracht, er ist voll geworden. Zudem zeichnet ihn Weiss aus, die Vermengung aller Farben und somit auch deren vitale Auflösung. Die Bäume haben ihr Wachstum vollbracht und nun, im Zustand ihrer Kahlheit, liegt der Weg des Lebens, der Blüte und der Frucht hinter ihnen. Schliesslich ist auch das Haus, die Architektur schlechthin, Hinweis auf die Vollendung. Nur in der Silhouette als monolithischer Block zu sehen deutet es auf Fertig-Stellung hin. Es ist errichtet. Um diesen Weg der Voll-Endung im Sinne seiner zeitlichen Er-Füllung und damit auch seines Gefüllt-Seins zu betonen, umschliesst der junge Mann die genannten Bilder mit seinen Armen. Umschliessen und Voll-Endung sind hier die Bilder, die den Tod nach dem Leben auszeichnen.

Veranschaulicht die zentrale Figur das Thema mit allgemeinen Motiven, erfährt es seine weitere Gestaltung an den Bildseiten mit menschlichen Motiven. Auffallend stechen vor allem vier grosse Köpfe sowie menschliche Glieder hervor. Jeweils zwei dieser Köpfe errichten sich rechts und links der Zentralfigur zu «Stämmen», während sich die Glieder, Hände, Füsse und Finger, unmittelbar oberhalb von ihnen befinden. Dabei ragen jeweils eine Hand sowie ein Finger aus den Kopffigurationen heraus, während sich die übrigen zusammen mit den Porträts von Gilbert & George in einer Horizontalen ausbreiten.

Die Betonung der menschlichen Glieder sowie der zu den Bäumen analoge Bildaufbau der Köpfe samt Händen und Fingern wiederholt das zentrale Bildmotiv. Denn wie dort Mond und Bäume vollendet sind, hat sich auch hier der menschliche Körper samt seinen «Enden» – nämlich Kopf, Fuss, Hand und Finger – regelrecht ausgebreitet und seinem Endpunkt genähert. Baumästen gleich ragen Hände und Finger in den Raum, während die vier massiven Köpfe ihre Träger bilden. Der menschliche Körper hat sein Ende gefunden. Er hat sich aus-gegliedert und ist in fast absoluter Kongruenz seiner Er-Füllung nahe.

Zu seiten der beiden Motive, der Zentralfigur sowie ihrer körperlichen Umschreibung durch Köpfe und Glieder, befinden sich schliesslich eine Anzahl weiterer Personen. Unmittelbar oberhalb der Zentralfigur stehen Gilbert & George, während sich ihr links und rechts zugeordnet jeweils fünf Jungen befinden. Zeichnen sich schon die beiden grossen Motive durch symmetrischen Aufbau, fast vollständige Form- und Farbkongruenz aus, geschieht dasselbe mit den übrigen Personen. Sowohl die Künstler entsprechen sich durch Deckungsgleichheit in Haltung und Farbe als auch die zehn Jungen. Jeder hat sein Pendant auf der gegenüberliegenden Bildseite. Auch dies erneut eine Anspielung auf Mond und Bäume der Zentralfigur. Denn auch sie weisen dank ihrer Voll-Endung eine mehr oder weniger perfekt körperliche Symmetrie auf. Die Farbkongruenz beider Bildseiten zielt dabei noch einmal auf das Weiss des Vollmondes ab. Die Farben decken sich, haben ihre Vitalität zugunsten eines nahtlosen In-Eins-Seins aufgegeben.

Für sich genommen stellt DEATH AFTER LIFE erneut ein antithetisches Bild dar. Antithetisch insofern, als der Titel hier den Tod in bezug auf das Leben abhandelt. Voll-Endung des Lebens und zugleich sein Tod stellen hier die perfekte Symmetrie und Kongruenz der Leiber dar, ihre endliche Aus-

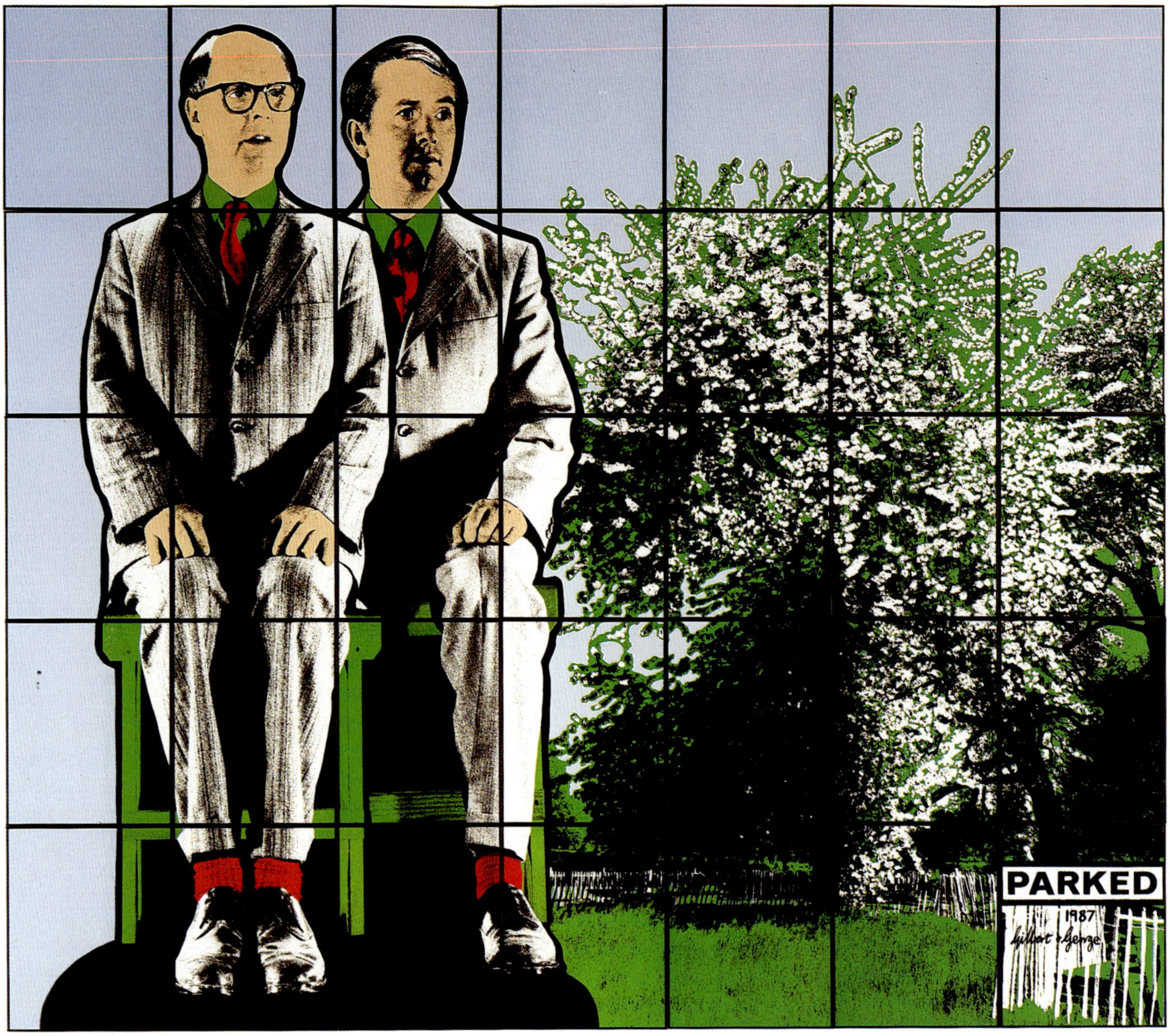

GILBERT & GEORGE, PARKED / GEPARKT, 1987,
119 x 139" / 303 x 354 cm.

gliederung und eben darin ihre Er-Füllung. Der Tod steht somit unmittelbar in Zusammenhang mit dem Leben, indem er sich durch die Beendigung der vitalen Kräfte in Form von Kongruenz und der Erlösung des Lebens durch Er-Füllung auszeichnet. DEATH AFTER LIFE fragt nicht, was nach dem Leben kommt, sondern danach, was das Leben an seinem Ende und seinen Enden auszeichnet, es bildlich manifestiert.

Gaben HERE und THERE den Orten dieser Welt ihren Sinn, verleiht DEATH AFTER LIFE dem Tod seinen Sinn. Auch hierbei allerdings ein Eingeständnis. Ein Leben nach dem Tod ist uns nicht geschenkt, ein Gott, der uns aufnimmt, auch nicht, dafür aber ein Bild, das das Ende des Lebens human gestaltet. Sind es nicht Menschen, die hier den Tod visualisieren und ihn damit um so menschlicher, oder besser: nur menschlich, bilden?

WOLF JAHN

SENSING AND WITNESSING WORLD

Art is always the production of sense. Whether it creates, criticizes, negates, fakes or invokes sense is of secondary importance. Its job is sense, regardless how the job is done. In fact, its involvement with sense is two-fold since its pictorial expression goes hand in hand with its SENS-ual aspect. To appeal to the sense and to visualize sense or its opposite is the terrain that art must claim, create, plow and re-plant day after day.

This requirement of art applies most aptly to Gilbert & George. They made their objective perfectly clear from the start, namely, more sense and more content: "To be with art is all we ask." They wanted to create art with transportable contents, art for everyone, in other words, art whose sense is easily accessible, and finally, art that is able to reformulate the meaning of meaning. They impressed their stamp on this formal aspect of meaning very early, by calling it "sculpture" or, more recently, comparing it with "frozen representation." Accordingly, sense is not something global or comprehensive or eternal, but a figure, plain and simple, which gives physical shape to its particular contents. This notion of sense is similar to the phenomenon of language and its many thousands of building blocks. Just as every word transmits a specific meaning, a sense of its own, every picture conveys its own contents. Sense and meaning in Gilbert & George's work is obviously a matter of differentiation rather than a question of absolutes.

WOLF JAHN lives and works as an art journalist in Hamburg. He has written a monograph about Gilbert & George which is to be published soon.

Several works shall serve to illustrate this form of meaning-investment, of autonomy and differentiated, specific content in Gilbert & George's pieces. HERE and THERE, both 1987, are among their most recent works. Like earlier pieces, they are also based on an antithetical structure. This opposition is to the advantage of the individual picture. It enhances the impact and the message. The pictures deal with the human environment, its "here" and its "there." Man experiences the concrete location of his being, his existence.

To provide the context for their subject matter, Gilbert & George intentionally use very different backgrounds. In HERE, it consists of a view of a street on which piles of boxes and garbage indicate bustling activity; in THERE, it is composed of trees, bushes and branches. These contrasting backgrounds correspond by analogy to the respective foregrounds, showing two people in both cases. HERE presents Gilbert & George standing next to each other, their hands indicating the ground. They visualize the title by physically referring to "Here," to the street. THERE shows two boys sitting on boxes. The one on the right is sadly resting his head in his hands; the one on the left, holding a board, has a slightly astonished expression on his face.

Common ground (two people – boxes) and differences (standing/sitting – city/nature – top/bottom of the titles) define the environment of man, his home territory and his foreign territory. HERE obviously locates man's home within the city, commercial, noisy, bustling, flowing, but also with room for apartments and private spaces. As demonstrated by their stance,

Gilbert & George recognize the people "here" as their homeland, as their space of existence. "Here," man lives, works, relaxes, eats and dies.

THERE, on the other hand, wants to know if there is any other place on earth in contrast to the "here" of the city. And there is: namely nature, that sad place without a single person, with no bustling activity, no human life. Even the boxes, indications of human activity in both HERE and THERE, are not admitted to nature. They have to linger outside of their territory. No wonder the two boys look a bit sad in front of this deserted, uncultivated space. They look like outcasts, evicted from the life of the city, from the "here" of their existence.

This sense of banishment to deserted spaces devoid of people is the subject of another picture as well. PARKED, 1987, unites the two meanings of the word "park." Gilbert & George are sitting in a park and recede into the picture behind each other like two parked cars. They have literally "parked" themselves in a park, in nature's space. Although erected by humans, it is still deserted since life takes place beyond its boundaries. Sad, those who are emblematically "parked" inside it. Forced to watch life pass by without them.

HERE, THERE and PARKED simply and graphically illustrate that the often cited "other" place of "actual" human life does not exist – that imaginary, utopian place of Not-Yet that automatically implies two assumptions: first, the inhospitality of our cities and second, their supposed estrangement from a former incarnation. This hostile attitude towards civilization has generated the notion of escape to an imaginary place symbolizing man's real home. But although nobody seems to have found it yet, the image of a civilization hostile to humans still prevails.

By reducing the locus of the world and of people to basically two places, "here" and "there," Gilbert & George demonstrate that the utopia (literally, the no-place) of a supposedly real home for man is an illusion. All we have is the "here" of the city, the home of man, and the "there" of the country, uncultivated, deserted nature. That's it. This may sound sad to the soul of western man but, at least, it releases him from the painful quest for an imaginary place beyond civilization.

In their art, Gilbert & George talk about the subject matters that design man's life for him by formulating images of his world and his environment. The effect is ultimately one of education, which is what HERE and THERE do in reference to the places of this world. The pictures try to provide a self-evident, linguistic and iconographic context for what we mean when we talk about "here" or "there." They want to acquaint us with the world and its spaces.

HERE and THERE would seem to deal with only part of the world. But Gilbert & George's work speaks of more than just one of its parts, it speaks of its complexity and its subtlety. This diversity is illustrated by a second thematic complex in their pictures, which is quite different from the subject matter of HERE and THERE. Instead of space, it is now time that predominates, time that comes to an end. DEATH AFTER LIFE shows a vision of the end, the end as full-fillment and the mortality of life.

DEATH AFTER LIFE, 1987, is 36 feet long and 16 feet high. The figure of a young man in the middle alludes to or rather personifies the title. His hands are propped on the ground and he is looking straight out of the picture. He presents his body as the vehicle of a curiously enigmatic scene. It shows a white full moon behind leafless trees and above a modern high-rise complex. In combination, the young man and his "body" yield the image of "death after life." Pictorially, the configuration is the formulation of complete maturity, of perfected and therefore terminal form. Moon, trees and houses all epitomize fulfillment, finalization. The moon has come to the end of its path; it is full. And it is white, the sum of all colors and their vital dissolution. The trees have finished growing and are now barren; the path of life, blossoms and fruit lies behind them. Finally, the building, the quintessence of architecture, also refers to fulfillment. This monolithic block, visible only in silhouette, indicates completion. It has been erected. To underscore this path of full-fillment in the sense of passing through time and becoming full, the young man encloses the images in his arms. Enclosure and full-fillment are the imagery used in this picture to depict death after life.

The figure in the center illustrates the theme in terms of general motifs; the theme is specified by human motifs on either side, in particular by the conspicuous presence of four large heads as well as human extremities. A pair of heads each to the right and left of the cen-

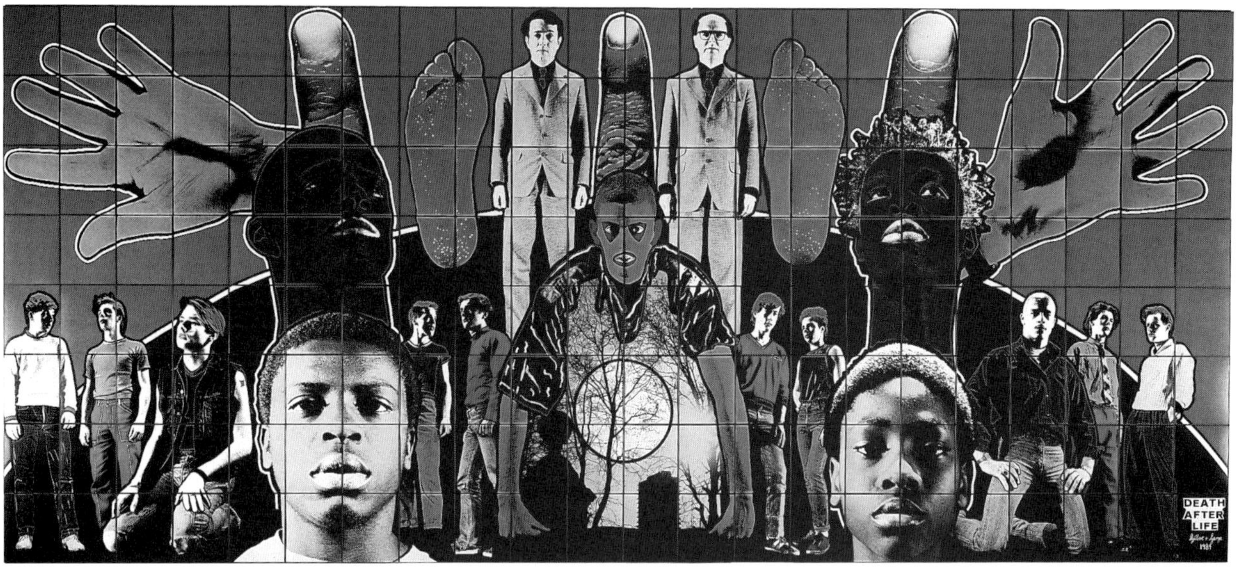

GILBERT & GEORGE, DEATH AFTER LIFE/ TOD NACH DEM LEBEN, 1984, *190 x 435"*/ 482 x 1103 cm.

tral figure form two trunks, with limbs – hands, feet and fingers – placed directly above them. A hand and a finger issuing out of the heads, two feet, one finger, and the portraits of Gilbert & George are spread out over the length of the picture.

The emphasis upon human extremities as well as the composition of the hands and fingers on top of the heads, in analogy to the trees, reiterates the central motif. Just as moon and trees in the center have reached the end of their paths, we see the human body, its "ends" – head, foot, hand and finger – literally spread out on either side, also nearing its end point. Hands and fingers, supported by the four massive heads, reach up into space like the branches of a tree. The human body has come to an end. It has out-limbed itself and is close to fulfillment in almost absolute congruence.

Adjacent to both motifs, the central figure as well as the body's resolution into head and limbs, there are several other people. Gilbert & George are standing directly above the central figure, with five youths each to the left and right below. The symmetrical composition of the two main motifs and their virtually total congruence of form and color applies to the other figures as well. Both the artists and the ten youths correspond in posture and color. They each have a counterpart on the other side of the picture – once again an allusion to the moon and trees of the figure in the middle, because they have also reached full-fillment through a near perfect physical symmetry. The congruence of the colors on both sides of the picture converges on the white of the full moon. The colors cover each other; they have surrendered their vitality in favor of a seamless oneness-of-being.

Taken in isolation, DEATH AFTER LIFE *again represents an antithetical image, inasmuch as the title takes up the issue of death in terms of life. Full-fillment of life and its death at the same time stand for the perfect symmetry and congruence of bodies, their finite delimbitation and their consequent fullness. Death is thus associated with life; it is depicted as the termination of the vital forces in the form of congruence and the release of life through fullness.* DEATH AFTER LIFE *does not ask what follows life but rather what characterizes the end and the ends of life, what does it manifest pictorially.*

While HERE *and* THERE *inform the places of this world with meaning,* DEATH AFTER LIFE *informs death with meaning. But not without making a concession. We have not been given life after death, nor have we been given a God who will shelter us, but we have been given a picture that presents a humane end to life. Is it not people who are here visualizing death, thus making it more humane or rather, just human?*

(Translation: Catherine Schelbert)

FOLGENDE SEITE / *NEXT PAGE*

EDITION FÜR PARKETT / *EDITION FOR PARKETT*

1987, GILBERT & GEORGE

PHOTOGRAPHIE AUF KARTON AUFGEZOGEN, IN DER MITTE FALTBAR, 25,5 x 42 cm, AUFLAGE: 200, NUMERIERT, SIGNIERT.

PHOTOGRAPH MOUNTED ON CARDBOARD AND FOLDED IN THE MIDDLE, 10 x 16 1/2", EDITION OF 200, SIGNED AND NUMBERED.

Jede Nummer der Zeitschrift entsteht in Collaboration mit einem Künstler, der eigens für die Leser von Parkett einen Originalbeitrag gestaltet. Dieses Werk ist in der gesamten Auflage abgebildet und zusätzlich in einer limitierten und signierten Vorzugsausgabe erhältlich.

Each issue of the magazine is created in collaboration with an artist, who contributes an original work specially made for the readers of Parkett. The work is reproduced in the regular edition. It is also available in a signed and limited Deluxe-Edition.

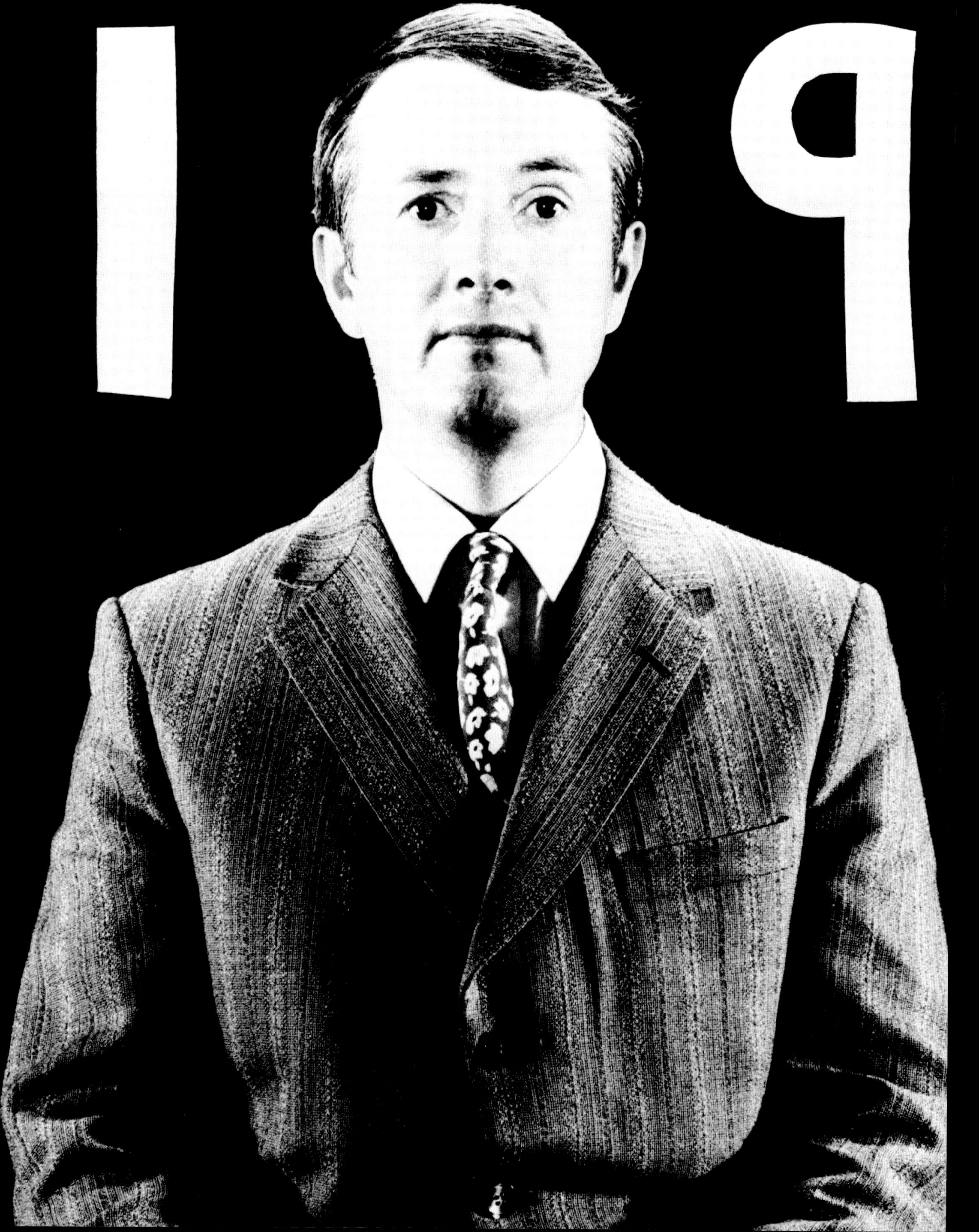
I
P

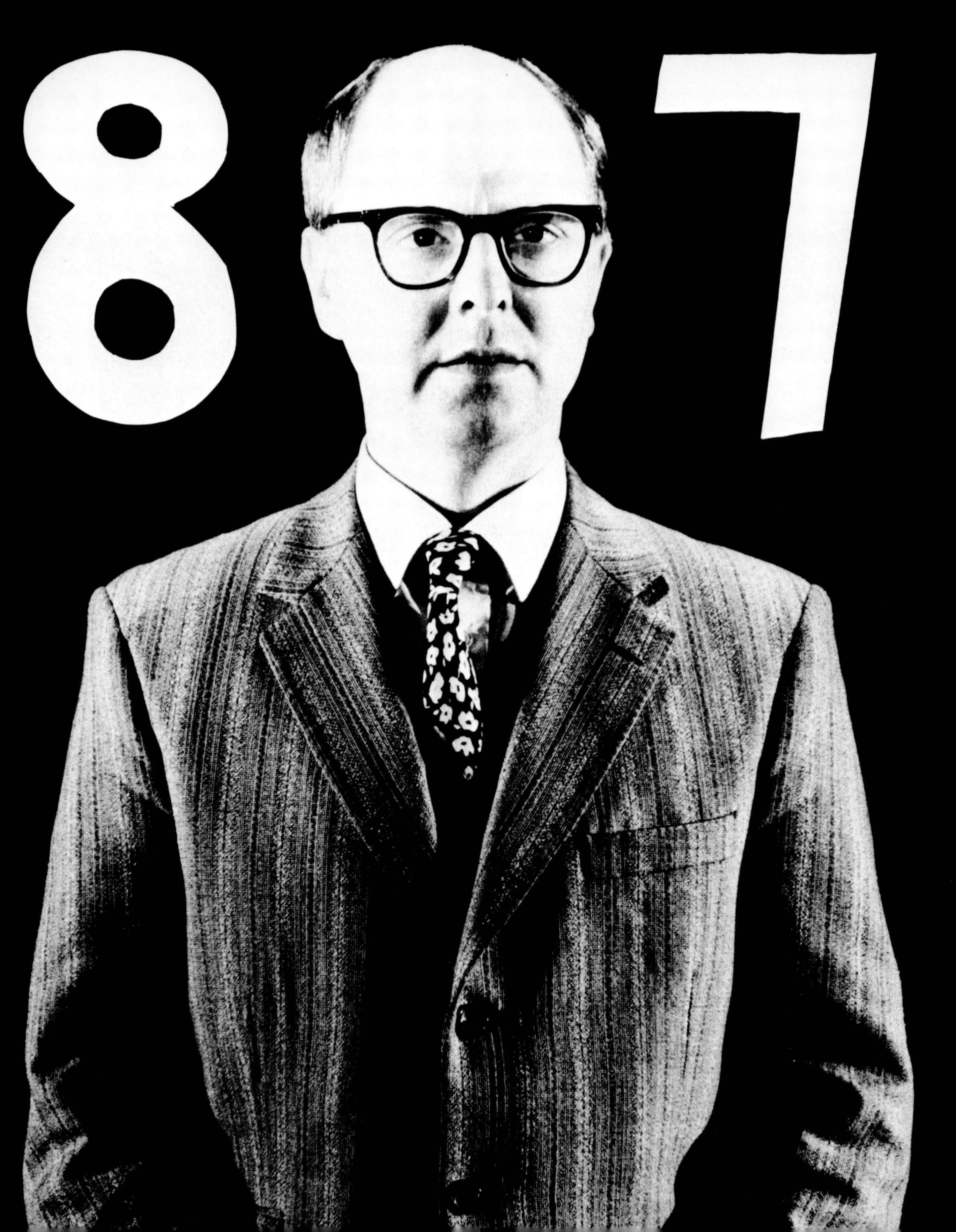
8
7

Gilbert & George & Everyman

PAUL TAYLOR

After twenty years, history may be catching up to Gilbert & George. As their particular blend of British conceptualism begins to thicken around the hips, Gilbert & George are merging imperceptibly into the cultural environment. Formerly gray-suited radicals in the midst of innumerable hippies ("playing flutes," George adds), they are now being out-dressed by the rank and file of young, upwardly-mobile Britons and their tailors. Their early posture of "hyper-conformism," a willingness to conform too much to a standard of appearances, paradoxically set them aside as a kind of Everyman. It is from the archetypal stance of Everyman that Gilbert & George now presume to speak to the modern world.

That Gilbert & George's art is made by an artists' team – that it is the result of a twin authorship – no longer shocks. Artist-teams have multiplied since their initial appearances – think of the Boyle Family in Britain, Marina Abramovic/Ulay and Fortyn/O'Brien in the Netherlands, Fischli/Weiss in Switzerland, General Idea in Canada, Tsk Tsk Tsk in Australia, Castelli/Salomé and Dokoupil/Dahn in Germany, Clegg and Guttmann, Wallace and Donohue, and McDermott and McGough in the States. But Gilbert & George are lodged in the popular imagination as a single artistic unit. Moreover, no artist-team since Gilbert & George has so cleverly perpetuated the idea of collaboration.

Dispensing with the complicated rhetorics of art ("post-object" sculpture, fluxus, live art, etc.) that acted as a kind of accompanying text to Gilbert & George's emergence in London's St. Martin's School of Art in 1967, the artists now insist on utter simplicity. In numerous interviews since the early '80s, Gilbert & George stress the

As a teenager, *PAUL TAYLOR* saw Gilbert & George do "Underneath the Arches" in Melbourne, Australia in 1973.

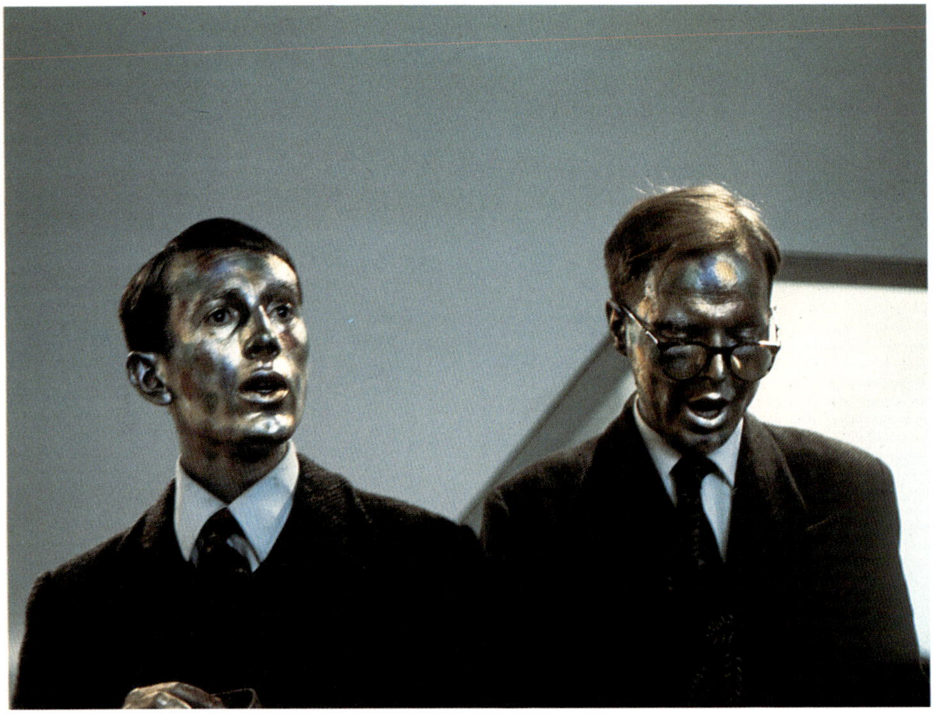

GILBERT & GEORGE, THE SINGING SCULPTURE,
KUNSTHALLE DÜSSELDORF, 1970.

directness of their message. In INTERVIEW magazine, for example, they insisted, "Art is completely abstract, intellectual, and you cannot learn it... Who wants to know the history of art?... We don't need to know the history of art to do art... our main interest is to speak very clearly to the viewer... We hate obscurity in art. We like direct contact." And to ART & TEXT they proposed that "every single person should get something from our art, that's what we like, a normal person, not just specialists."

Pure simplicity comes from pure complexity. But naturally enough, the change in Gilbert & George's attitude has been accompanied by a change in their art. Their self-simplification is worth recounting. When George (b. 1942) met Gilbert (b. 1943) in 1965, and the two began immediately (they say) to make art together, their first task was the elimination of their biographies in favor of a unified p e r s o n a. Immediately, in their first cosigned works, they became mirrors of each other and therefore two versions of the same thing.

Gilbert & George's first public appearances were in the guise of living sculptures, metallic, robotized, and identically attired. Of course, ever since antiquity, statuary has embodied the essence/appearance dichotomy. Multiplied by two, Gilbert & George extended this fundamental dichotomy to infinity. In the beginning, they paraded themselves around pop music events and public youth-culture happenings. Such "self"-display not only exhibited Gilbert & George's difference-in-sameness, but also cut right to the heart of their enterprise. From the start they proclaimed that they saw themselves as spectacle – spectacle in the context of spectacular 1960s pop culture. As bronze statues, they not only appeared as casts in an edition of sculptures but as multiples of high culture cast among the popular masses.

Then, in 1969, came UNDERNEATH THE ARCHES, Gilbert & George's marathon living sculpture that they toured, like a vaudeville act, to museums and what were then called "avant-garde commercial galleries" around the world. UNDERNEATH THE ARCHES was a series of doubles, an exercise in multiplication: an artwork of two men miming to Hardy and Hudson's rendition of Flanagan and Allen's old-time popular song. In the history of the theater, the mime is the first figure to represent an exact double. In these days of mechanical reproducibility, as is especially evident in drag shows, the mime usually mimics the gestures, dress, and hence the "image," of celebrated individuals like Shirley Bassey and Diana Ross. Gilbert & George, accompanied by a portable cassette player, instead mouthed lyrics that were written about that most anonymous class, those populous individuals most visible in their loss of social identity – the homeless, the tramps who sleep underneath the arches.

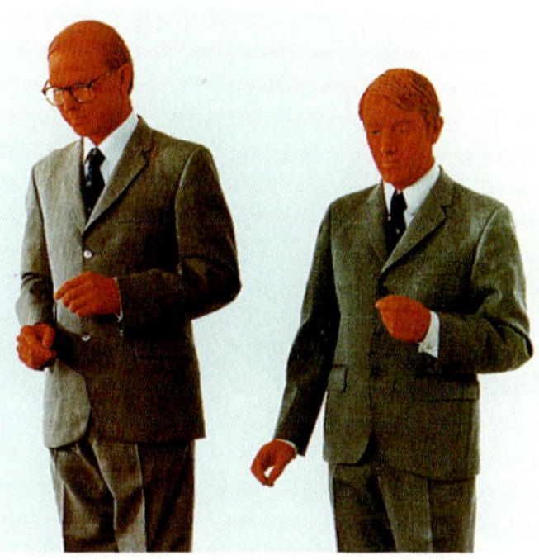

COMING

In the tramp figure, Gilbert & George found their medium. Devoid of personal identity, like Everyman, they streamlined their lives into a mixture of the outsider roles of clochard and dandy. Their essence and appearance became the same thing. Simultaneously the subject and object of their art, they fused their identities, made portraits of each other in a gesture of personality transference, and went about the business of art in the manner of a totally deadpan expressionism. Propounding the aesthetics of boredom – the underbelly of the society of spectacle – Gilbert & George announced that their life was art. They therefore took a further existential step in the direction of the tramps in that they did nothing in particular and yet their special non-employment became their entire profession.

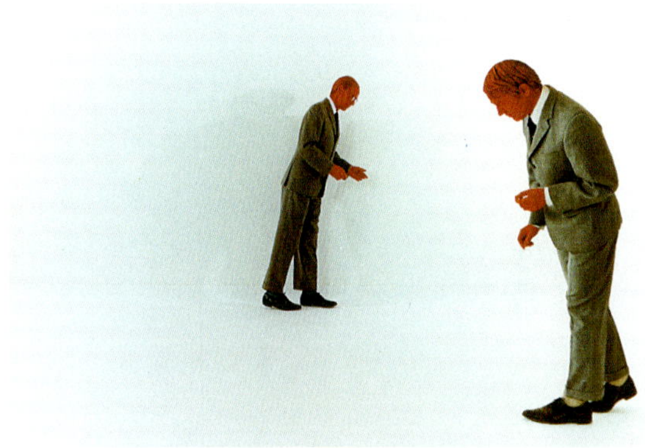

CHERRY BLOSSOM

Their inverviews perpetuate this myth. "On leaving college and being without a penny, we had no studio," George said to A.E.I.U.O. magazine. "So we were just there. That was mainly physical. It was just the two physical presences... But that changed with time." "We became more and more two objects," added Gilbert. "There is no divison between ourselves and our production," concluded George. "Us and our work is completely together – we don't even know the difference."

GILBERT & GEORGE,

DETAILS FROM THE RED SCULPTURE, 1975.

In the mid-1970s, Gilbert & George made their moodiest and most poignant works. Their black and white photographic pieces, like BLOODY LIFE, DUSTY CORNERS (1975) and DEAD BOARDS (1976), were a fictitious docu-drama of intellectual melancholy. But in their subsequent photo-works they underwent a change. Gilbert & George no longer presented an image of themselves as pitiable young artists. Instead, they became born-again tramps in the trappings of monks. After all, the asceticism of their life together, their seemingly womanless world, their clothes and pseudo-spiritual devotion to art-as-life is nothing if not a parody of a religious vocation.

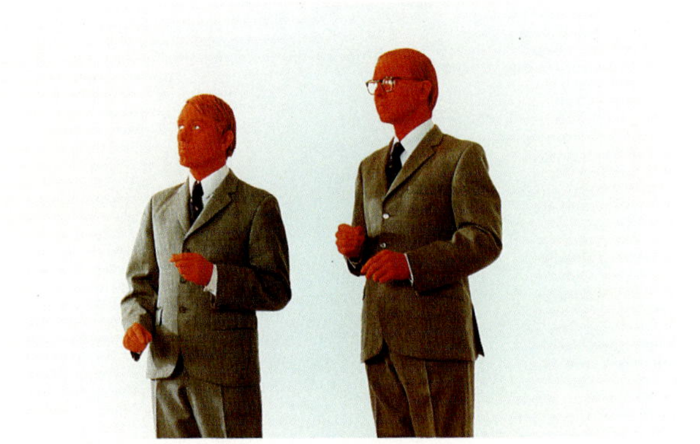

READY

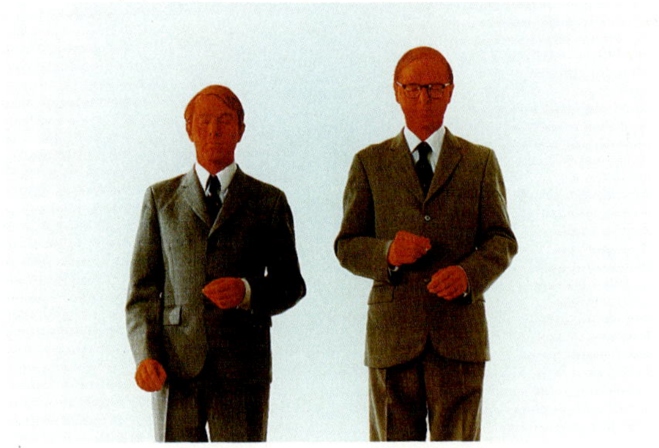

GONE

When Gilbert & George appeared and seamlessly incorporated art into their lives, art as we knew it seemed to dissolve in favor of the aestheticization of life. Ironically, their own art "events" signalled the end of the eventfulness of art. Like monks, Gilbert & George transcended self-expression and stripped themselves of many of the characteristics that make one man different from another. That was twenty years ago. Now they are sending directives to the masses from the other side of conformity.

Like missionaries, Gilbert & George took their new morality outdoors, and substitutes of themselves as tramps abounded in portrayals of young men (many of them unemployed) and such social outcasts as the old, the insane and the "queer." In a sense, all of Gilbert & George's life as doubles of art and each other suddenly ceased to be meaningful, and a message became necessary. Their self-images (still in regulation suits) became more and more the stuff of manipulation, and their photo pictures took on the didactic look of stained-glass windows, formerly the commonest kind of instruction. Similarly, their art's titles and the poses of its figures assumed a religious air.

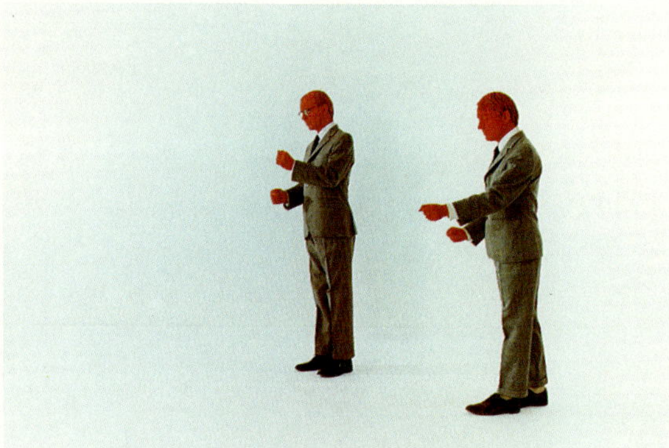

WOODEN AIR

GILBERT & GEORGE,
DETAILS FROM THE RED SCULPTURE, 1975.

Gilbert & George & Jedermann

PAUL TAYLOR

Heute, nach zwanzig Jahren, werden Gilbert & George möglicherweise von der Geschichte eingeholt. Während ihre spezifische Variante britischer Konzeptkunst etwas Hüftspeck anzusetzen beginnt, scheinen Gilbert & George unmerklich mit ihrem kulturellen Umfeld zu verschmelzen. Die einstmals in grauen Strassenanzügen unter zahllosen («flötenspielenden», würde George hinzufügen) Hippies wandelnden Radikalen werden nunmehr vom Tross der jungen, aufwärtsstrebenden Briten und deren Couturiers übertrumpft. Die früh eingenommene Pose des «Hyperkonformismus», jene Bereitschaft, sich allzusehr den gängigen Erscheinungsformen anzupassen, liess sie paradoxerweise als eine Art Jedermann aus dem Rahmen treten. Und von dieser archetypischen Warte des Jedermann wollen Gilbert & George die Moderne ansprechen.

Nicht länger schockiert es, dass die Kunst von Gilbert & George diejenige eines Künstlerteams, das Resultat einer Zwillingsurheberschaft ist. Das Künstler-als-Team-Prinzip ist mittlerweile in Mode gekommen – man denke nur an die Boyle Family in Grossbritannien, an Marina Abramovic/Ulay und Fortyn/O'Brien in Holland, Fischli/Weiss in der Schweiz, General Idea in Kanada, Tsk Tsk Tsk in Australien, Castelli/Salomé und Dokoupil/Dahn in der BRD sowie Clegg und Guttmann, Wallace und Donohue und McDermott und McGough in den USA. Doch bei Gilbert & George handelt es sich nach allgemeiner Auffassung um eine untrennbare künstlerische Einheit. Und kein Künstlerteam hat seither den Kollaborationsgedanken auf so raffinierte Weise umgesetzt und vertreten.

Nachdem sich die Künstler einmal von den umständlichen Kunstbegriffen wie «Post-Objekt»-Skulptur, Fluxus, Aktionskunst, Performance usw., welche 1967 noch den Begleittext zu ihrem erstmaligen Auftritt in der St. Martin's School of Art lieferten, befreit hatten, begannen sie Wert auf äusserste Einfachheit zu legen. Seit den frühen 80er Jahren haben Gilbert & George in ihren Interviews konstant auf die

---

Als Teenager hat PAUL TAYLOR Gilbert & George in Underneath the Arches gesehen, in Melbourne, Australien, 1973.

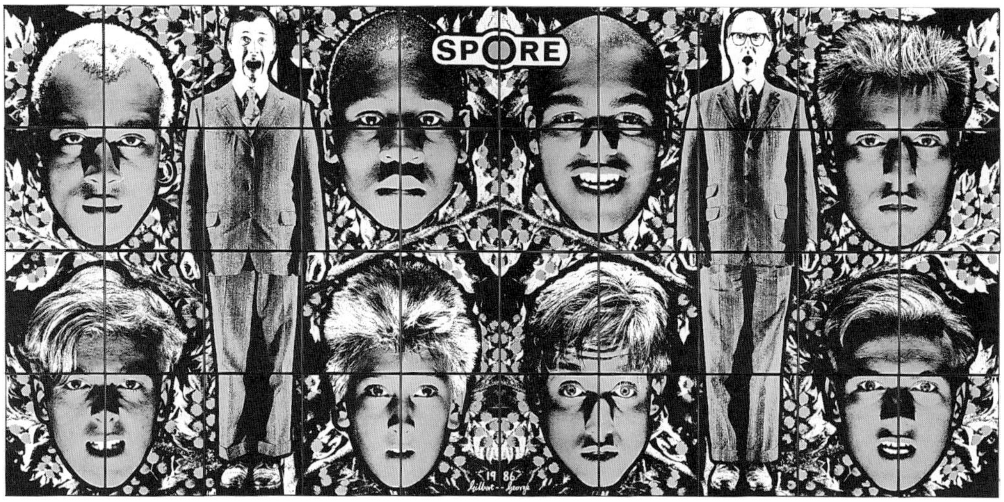

Direktheit ihrer Botschaft verwiesen. In einem in der Zeitschrift «Interview» veröffentlichten Gespräch zum Beispiel betonten sie: «Kunst ist etwas völlig Abstraktes, Intellektuelles, man kann sie nicht erlernen... Wen interessiert denn schon die Kunstgeschichte?... Wir brauchen die Kunstgeschichte nicht zu kennen, um Kunst zu machen... Unser einziges Interesse ist, den Betrachter klar und deutlich anzusprechen... Wir hassen alles Obskure in der Kunst, wir wollen den direkten Kontakt.» Und in einem «Art & Text»-Interview äusserten sie den Wunsch, dass «jeder einzelne Mensch etwas von unserer Kunst bezieht, denn das mögen wir, ganz normale Leute, nicht nur Spezialisten».

Äusserste Einfachheit kommt von reiner Komplexität. Mit der veränderten Einstellung von Gilbert & George veränderte sich selbstverständlich auch ihre Kunst. Es lohnt in diesem Zusammenhang, die Stationen ihrer «Selbst-Vereinfachung» nochmals in Erinnerung zu rufen. Als George (Jahrgang 1942) Gilbert (Jahrgang 1943) kennenlernte, begannen sie nach eigener Aussage sogleich, zusammen Kunst zu machen, wobei ihre erste Aufgabe darin bestand, ihre Biographien zugunsten eines einzigen, vereinheitlichten Erscheinungsbilds auszulöschen. So wurden sie bereits in ihren allerersten, gemeinsam signierten Werken zum Spiegelbild des andern und damit zu zwei Versionen ein und derselben Sache.

Gilbert & Georges erste Auftritte in der Öffentlichkeit erfolgten als lebende Skulpturen in metallischer, roboterhafter, identischer Aufmachung. Natürlich verkörperte das Standbild seit jeher, seit der Antike, die Dichotomie von Wesen und Erscheinung. Mit zwei multipliziert, steigerten Gilbert & George diese fundamentale Zweiteilung ins Unendliche. Zu Beginn marschierten sie als lebende Skulpturen an Popkonzerten und anderen Jugendveranstaltungen auf. Diese «Selbst»-Ausstellung war nicht bloss Illustration ihres Andersseins-in-der-Gleichheit, sondern zielte geradewegs ins Zentrum ihres Unternehmens. Denn von Anfang an verkündeten sie, dass sie sich als Spektakel verstanden – ein Spektakel innerhalb der spektakulären Popkultur der 60er Jahre. In ihren leibhaftigen Auftritten als Bronzestatuen erschienen sie nicht nur als Abguss in einer Skulpturen-Serie, sondern ebenso als ein aus der Massenkultur geformtes multiples Objekt.

1969 kam dann der Marathonlauf als lebende Skulptur in UNDERNEATH THE ARCHES (Unter den Bögen), und Gilbert & George gingen damit wie mit einer Varieténummer in Museen und Kunstgalerien («avant-garde commercial galleries» war damals der englische Ausdruck) auf Welttournee. UNDERNEATH THE ARCHES war eine Verdoppelungsserie, ein Multiplikationsakt: das Kunstwerk zweier Männer, die zu Hardys und Hudsons Interpretation eines alten Volkslieds von Flanagan und Allen mimen.

Im klassischen Theater stellt der Mime oder Possenspieler exakt die Figur eines Doubles dar. Im Zeitalter der mechanischen Reproduzierbarkeit imitiert der Mime – wie man es vor allem bei Transvestitenshows beobachten kann – gewöhnlich Gesten und Kleidung und somit das «Image» berühmter Stars wie etwa Shirley Bassey oder Diana Ross. Gilbert & George jedoch, begleitet von Kassettenmusik, vollführten Mundbewegungen zu Liedstrophen, die von der anonymsten Klasse der Menschheit handelten, von den zahllosen Individuen, die gerade wegen ihres gesellschaftlichen Identitätsverlustes am sichtbarsten sind, nämlich die Obdachlosen, die Clochards, die unter den Bögen, «underneath the arches», schlafen.

In der Figur des Tramps haben Gilbert & George ihr Medium gefunden. Sie formten sich ein Leben, wie Jedermann aller Identität entblösst, aus den zwei Aussenseiterrollen des Clochard und des Dandy. Wesen und Erscheinung wurden eins. Gleichzeitig Subjekt und Objekt ihrer Kunst, fusionierten sie ihre beiden Persönlichkeiten, porträtierten sich gegenseitig in einem Akt der Persönlichkeitsübertragung und gingen gleichsam ohne eine Miene zu verziehen dem Kunstgeschäft im Stil eines völlig ausdruckslosen Expressionismus nach. Indem sie eine Ästhetik der Langeweile, die unterschwellig in der Welt des Schauspiels vorhanden ist, propagierten, verkündeten Gilbert & George, dass ihr Leben Kunst ist. Damit gingen sie einen weiteren wichtigen Schritt in Richtung Tramp, denn sie unternahmen nichts Besonderes, wenngleich ihre spezifische Unbeschäftigtheit zum ausschliesslichen Beruf wurde.

Ihre Interview-Aussagen bestärken diesen Mythos. «Nach Verlassen des College waren wir ohne einen Penny, wir hatten kein Atelier», sagte George einmal im «A.E.I.U.O.»-Magazin. «So waren wir einfach da. Das war vor allem physisch. Einfach diese zwei physischen Präsenzen ... Doch das änderte sich mit der Zeit.» «Mehr und mehr wurden wir zwei Objekte», fügte Gilbert hinzu. «Es gibt keine Trennung zwischen uns und unserem Schaffen», fasste George zusammen. «Wir und unser Werk gehören vollständig zusammen – nicht einmal wir kennen den Unterschied.»

Mitte der 70er Jahre entstanden Gilbert & Georges schwermütigste, berührendste Arbeiten. Ihre schwarzweissen Foto-Pieces wie BLOODY LIFE, DUSTY CORNERS (1975) und DEAD BOARDS (1976) stellten ein imaginäres Dokudrama voll abstrakter Melancholie dar. Doch die darauf folgenden Foto-Arbeiten signalisierten einen Wandel. Gilbert & George projizierten nicht länger das Bild von bemitleidenswerten jungen Künstlern. Der Tramp feierte seine Wiederauferstehung im Gewand des Mönchs. Denn genau besehen ist ihr asketisches Zusammenleben in einer scheinbar frauenlosen Welt, ihre Kleidung und ihre pseudo-spirituelle Hingabe zur Kunst-als-Leben nichts anderes als eine Parodie der religiösen Berufung.

Wie Missionare trugen Gilbert & George ihre neue Moralität hinaus, und ihre Porträts von jungen Männern (viele von ihnen arbeitslos) und gesellschaftlichen Aussenseitern wie Alte, Geisteskranke und Schwule (queers) waren voll von Stellvertreter-Parts für die Figur des Tramp. In gewisser Weise verlor plötzlich das gesamte Leben von Gilbert & George als Verdoppelung der Kunst und ihrer selbst an Bedeutung, und eine Botschaft wurde notwendig. Ihr Selbst-Bildnis (immer noch in konventionellen Anzügen) nahm zusehends manipulativen Charakter an, und ihre Photo-Bilder erinnerten in ihrer Didaktik an gewisse Glasmalereien, die einmal die verbreitetste Form von Kunstgewerbe gewesen waren. Ebenso erhielten die Titel ihrer Kunstwerke und Posen ihrer Figuren einen religiösen Anstrich.

Als Gilbert & George in Erscheinung traten und die Kunst nahtlos in ihr Leben integrierten, schien sich unsere Vorstellung von Kunst aufzulösen, und an ihre Stelle trat eine Ästhetisierung des Lebens. Die Ironie will es, dass ihre eigenen Kunst-«Ereignisse» das Ende der Kunst als Ereignis ankündigten. Geradezu mönchisch wuchsen Gilbert & George über die Selbst-Darstellung hinaus und entledigten sich so mancher Wesenszüge, die einen Menschen vom anderen unterscheiden. Und nun senden sie den Massen, auf der anderen Seite der Konformität stehend, ihre Signale.

(Übersetzung: Corinne Schelbert)

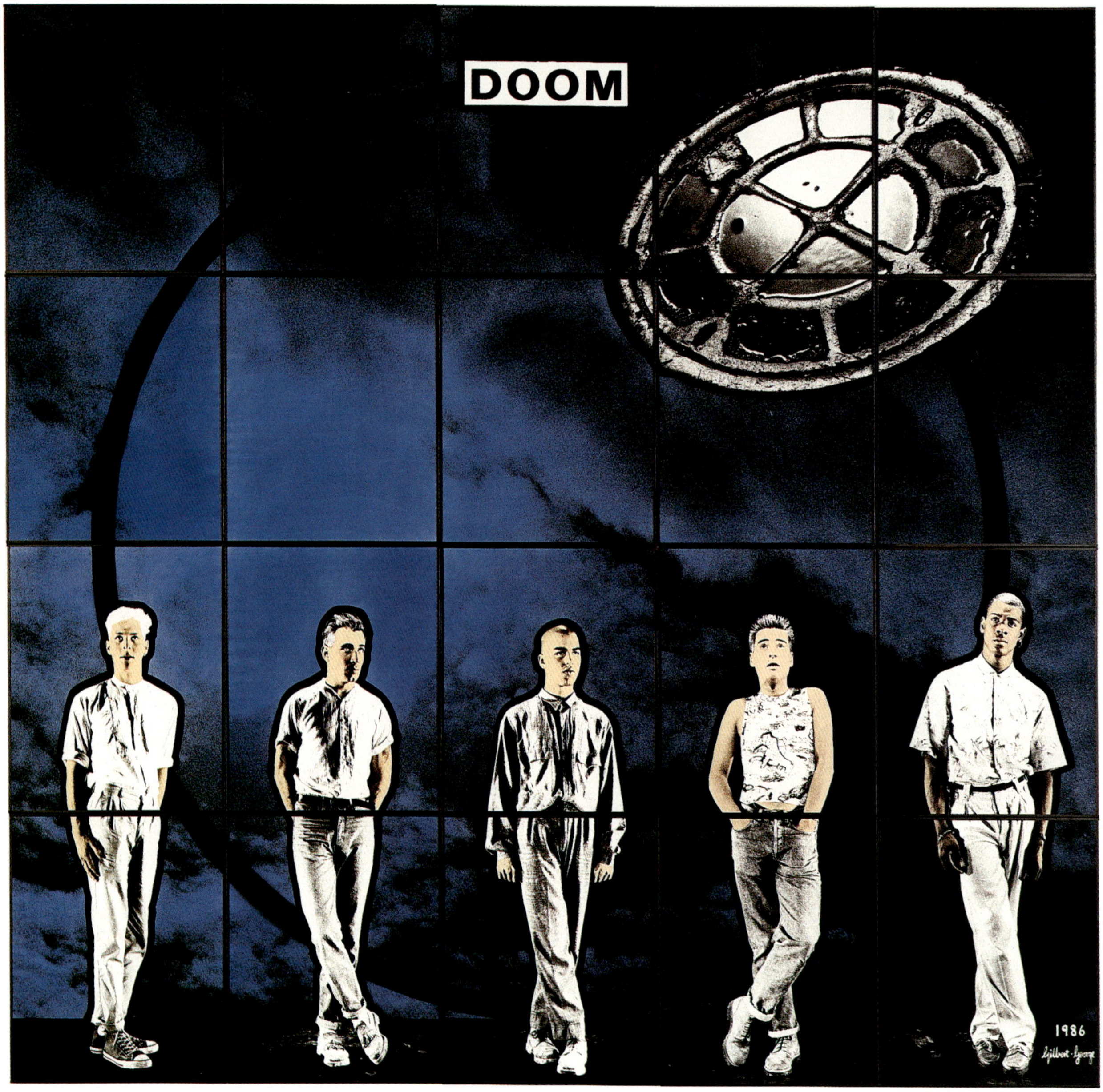

GILBERT & GEORGE, DOOM / SCHICKSAL, 1986,

95 x 99½" / 242 x 253 cm.

PRECEDING PAGE: / VORANGEHENDE SEITE:

GILBERT & GEORGE, SPORE / KEIMKORN, 1986, *95 x 199" / 242 x 505 cm.*

Ian Hamilton Finlay oder EIN SPIELVERDERBER IN DER DIALEKTISCHEN SPEKULATION

BERNARD MARCADÉ

«JEDER GROSSE GEIST IST BEIDHÄNDIG, ER ARGUMENTIERT NACH ZWEI SEITEN HIN»
BALTASAR GRACIAN

1. UT PICTURA, POESIS. Das proteushafte Werk Ian Hamilton Finlays, das gänzlich auf die Sprache angewiesen scheint und dennoch zweifellos als visuell aufgefasst werden muss, zwingt uns dazu, die vielzitierte Debatte über Horaz' UT PICTURA, POESIS mit neuen Augen zu betrachten: Die Dichtkunst gleicht den Gemälden: gewisse werden dich mehr ansprechen, wenn du nah davor stehst, andere von weiter weg. Dieses liebt den Schatten, jenes will bei vollem Licht gesehen werden und scheut des Kenners durchdringenden Scharfblick nicht; dieses gefiel einmal nur, ein anderes wird auch zehnmal noch gefallen. (Horaz, ARS POETICA, 361–365.)
Da Finlays Werk beide Dimensionen zugleich in sich vereinigt – und dies weder kompromisshaft noch ausschliesslich –, widersetzt es sich damit vehement den traditionellen wie auch den modernistischen Lehren, die jede auf ihre Art versuchen, das Spezifische einer «Kunst der sich zeitlich abfolgenden Worte» und einer «Kunst der im Raum nebeneinanderstehenden Formen» (Lessing) hervorzuheben.
Indem Finlay auf der sprachlichen und der visuellen Ebene zugleich wirkt – eine nicht ungefährliche Position –, übertritt er mutig die (formalistische) Fatalität, dass eine Partei der anderen ihre Überlegenheit weismachen will. Der eigentliche Kampf – und bleibt er auch meist hinter stilistischen Fragen verborgen (besser: getarnt) – findet für Finlay eindeutig woanders statt.

2. ÄSTHETIK UND MORAL. Ian Hamilton Finlay benützt die Sprache weder zu logischen noch zu ontologischen Zwecken. Ebenso benützt er das Bild nicht illustrativ (es bildet nicht ab, sondern z e i g t). Damit entzieht sich seine Kunst den erforschten Grundlagen von Wahrheit und Einbildung; sie ist weder ein Denken in Bildern noch ein (Ge)Bild(e) des Denkens. Finlays Werk sollte zum einen als ein visuelles Denken, aber vielmehr noch als eine v i s u e l l e M o r a l aufgefasst werden, in der Tradition der I m p r e s e und manieristischen Devisen. Von die-

BERNARD MARCADÉ ist Schriftsteller und Kunstkritiker in Paris. 1986 erschien von ihm «L'éloge du mauvais esprit» in der Edition de la différence, Paris.

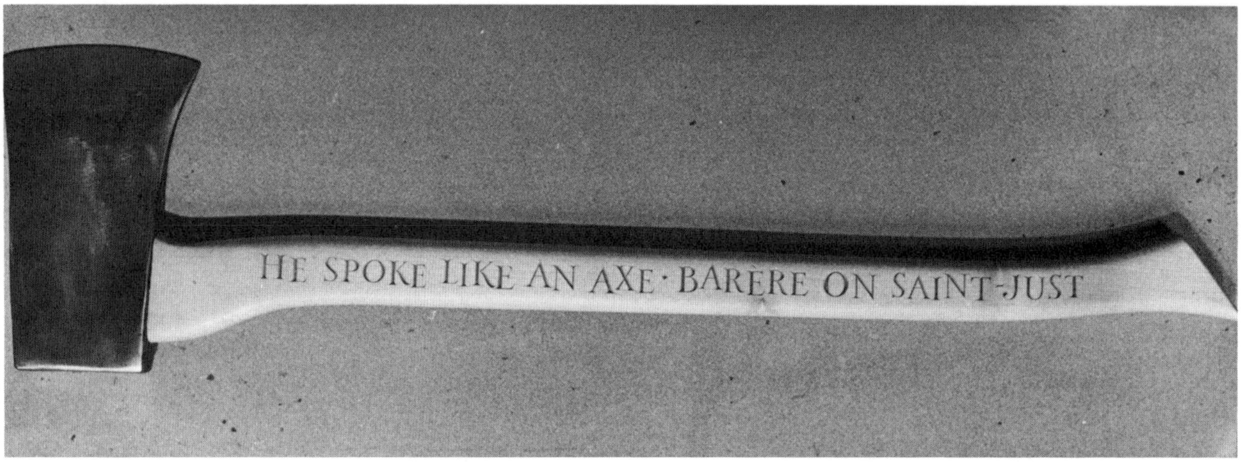

IAN HAMILTON FINLAY WITH KEITH BROOKWELL AND JOHN ANDREW,
(«ER SPRACH WIE EINE AXT. BARÈRE ÜBER SAINT-JUST.»), 1985,
OBJECT IN THE GARDEN TEMPLE, LITTLE SPARTA.

ser Moral (die von der moralisierenden Moral unterschieden werden muss) besitzt dieses Werk nämlich die Grösse, die Distanz, die Schärfe und die Ironie...

3. TOTALITÄT, FRAGMENT. Das visuelle Universum Ian Hamilton Finlays – aus Splittern, Fetzen, Strichen, Zitaten bestehend – ist unleugbar fragmentarisch. Finlays Zerstückelung darf aber nicht als nostalgisches Manifest einer verlorenen Einheit und Wahrheit verstanden werden, sondern vor allen Dingen als die Verteidigung und Veranschaulichung des Fragments gegenüber einer bestehenden spekulativen und totalitären Auffassung des Universums. Damit bekennt sich Ian Hamilton Finlay zu einer Tradition, die, obgleich sie stark am «Totalitätssinn» haften bleibt, sich stets gegen die einheitliche und eindeutige Weltauffassung aufgelehnt hat, dies seit den Vorsokratikern bis zu den ersten deutschen Romantikern und bis zu Nietzsche. Obwohl eindeutig fragmentarisch, bleibt Finlays Werk dennoch von der Frage des Stils durchsetzt. Denn ist nicht das Fragment – das durch Klären und Destillieren wirkt, das einschneidet, zuspitzt, veredelt – mit Stil gleichzusetzen? Ist das Fragment nicht die Ablehnung schlechthin der Idee von Totalität und als solches auch deren verzweifeltste Erscheinung?

4. EINE ANTI-DIALEKTIK. Ian Hamilton Finlays Kunst versucht nicht, diese Widersprüche aufzuheben, denn sie selbst geht aus von der Zweideutigkeit, die Baltasar Gracian mit «einem zweischneidigen Wort, einer doppellichtigen Bedeutung» vergleicht. Seine Art, etwas zu sagen und zu zeigen und im gleichen Moment das Gegenteil dieses Gesagten und Gezeigten zu beweisen – Schatten und Licht, Terror und Tugend, Natur und Kultur, Grösse und Kleinheit –, steht in krassem Gegensatz zu einem dialektischen Vorgehen. Finlays Kunst besteht gerade darin, niemals etwas mittelfristig anzugehen, sondern die Widersprüche in ihrer Unlösbarkeit und Vieldeutigkeit zu belassen und zum Wirken zu bringen. So hebt sich auf dem Hintergrund des unheilvollen SS-Zeichens die elegante Figur Apollos und Daphnes ab. So erscheint an

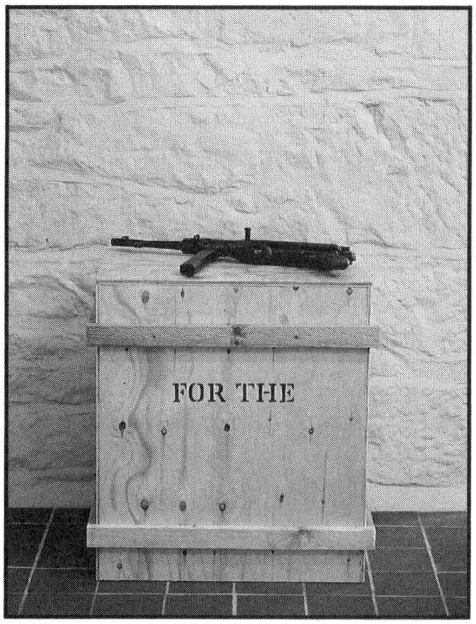

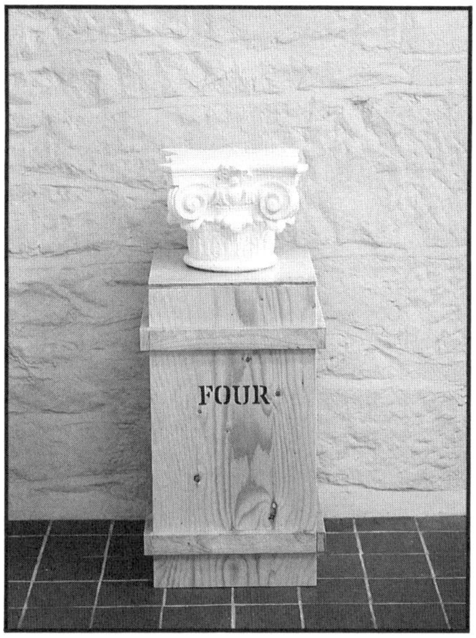

IAN HAMILTON FINLAY, REPUBLIC FOR THE FOUR KINGS / REPUBLIK FÜR DIE VIER KÖNIGE, 1987.
FONDATION CARTIER, JOUY-EN-JOSAS. *(Photo: Antonia Reeve)*

Stelle der rätselhaften Grabstätte von Poussins HIRTEN VON ARKADIEN ein gespenstischer Panzer, bedrohend und lächerlich zugleich... Stets will Finlay eine konflikthafte Dualität, einen innerhalb der Dinge und Werte ausgetragenen Zweikampf in Szene setzen, ohne jemals eine vermittelnde (und daher normative) Lösung in Aussicht zu stellen. Seine Kunst: im Gleichartigen die Andersartigkeit zu finden und alle Disparitäten, Irrtümer und Versagen einer Welt, die ihre Integrität, Einheitlichkeit und Transparenz ängstlich zu wahren versucht, zum Vorschein treten zu lassen. Diese Kunst versteht es, bestehende Werte und Hierarchien zu stören und aus dem Gleichgewicht zu stürzen. Auf beissende, oft anmassende, ja grausame Art will sie die Dinge (und vor allem die Werte) von ihrem Platz verstossen und eben das zeigen (sichtbar machen), was diese Dinge verfolgt, beeinflusst und sie bedroht.

5. DIE VERBÜNDETE KEHRSEITE. Ian Hamilton Finlay lässt nichts durch. Die geringste Lücke, der kleinste Riss in unserem Kultur- und Zivilisationssystem wird für ihn zur Zielscheibe eines erbarmungslosen genealogischen Sperrfeuers. Was nämlich die genealogische Betrachtungsweise von dialektischer Spekulation unterscheidet, ist gerade das Voranstellen und nicht etwa das Entschärfen oder gar das Aufheben (die berühmte Hegelsche Aufhebung!) der Konflikte. Die «erhabenen, grosszügigen Ideale» – Natur, Kultur, Freiheit, Brüderlichkeit ... –, auf denen unsere politischen, moralischen und ästhetischen Werturteile beruhen, werden von Finlay unablässig aufgespürt und auf ihre Schwächen hin untersucht. Jedem der Werturteile weist er nach, dass sie mit ihrem absoluten Gegenteil im Bunde stehen, dass sie sich – oft unwissentlich – zu einer Welt bekennen, die sie ja gerade ablehnen: Terror, Knechtschaft, Krieg ... und dass umgekehrt auch diese negativen Werte Spuren einer verlorenen, oder zumindest entstellten Idealität tragen ... Jede Münze hat ihre Kehrseite, doch ist es nicht immer jene, die man glaubt: Ein Tempel verbirgt oft die Guillotine, Natur ist eine Idee, ein Wert unserer Kultur und umgekehrt. Friede ist bekanntlich die Fortsetzung – mit anderen Mitteln – des Krieges.

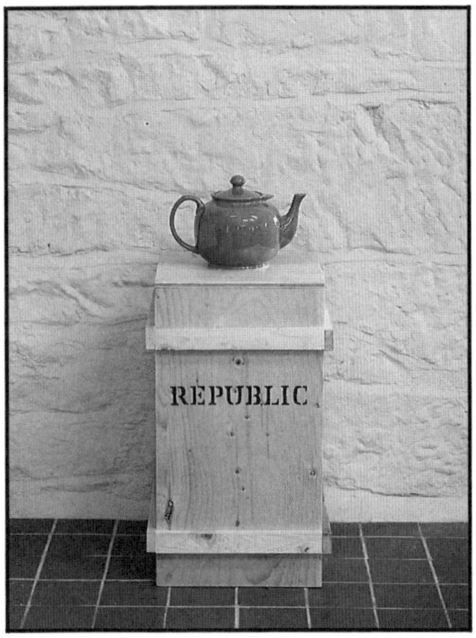

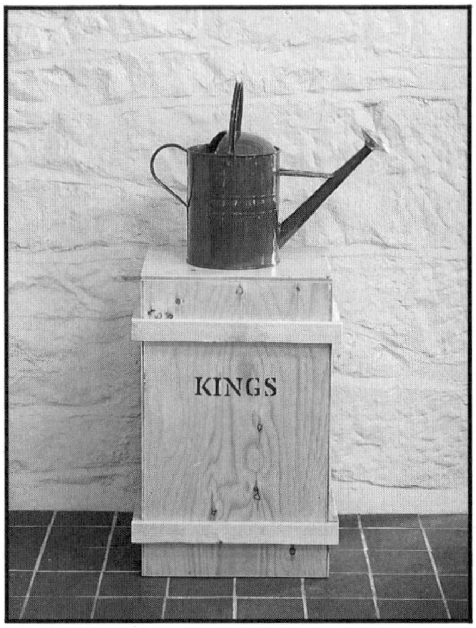

IAN HAMILTON FINLAY, REPUBLIC FOR THE FOUR KINGS / REPUBLIK FÜR DIE VIER KÖNIGE, 1987.
FONDATION CARTIER, JOUY-EN-JOSAS. *(Photo: Antonia Reeve)*

6. ET IN ARCADIA EGO. Als König George III. vor dem Bild Joshua Reynolds stand, auf dem ein sitzendes Paar vor einem Grabstein «von beglückender Erregung beseelt» dessen Inschrift liest, übersetzte er sogleich das Epigraph *ET IN ARCADIA EGO* mit: «DEN TOD GIBT ES SOGAR IN ARKADIEN.» Erwin Panofsky hat hervorragend bewiesen, wie richtig diese Interpretation war und in welcher Hinsicht sie mit der akademischen Übersetzung «AUCH ICH HABE IN ARKADIEN GELEBT» im Widerspruch steht.

Arkadien ist einer der Namen Utopias: der ideale Ort des Glücks und des Schönen, das Land des ewigen Frühlings, das goldene Zeitalter des ursprünglichen Lebens, des Überflusses und der Unschuld. Aber diese Devise, von der sich die Geschichte der klassizistischen (Guercino, Poussin, Cipriani...) und romantischen Kunst (Kolbe, Reynolds) genährt hat, liest sich nun, mit Panofsky, wie ein klaffender Riss (wie ein Zeichen des Todes) im bis dahin unbefleckten Muster der menschlichen, politischen und sozialen Transparenz des Westens. Utopia wäre also vom Tod gestreift worden, vom Negativen, von der Zerstörung... Krieg und Konflikte wären somit in unserer Auffassung der Natur, in unseren ästhetischen und moralischen Werturteilen zum vornherein enthalten.

Gegen diese Fatalität kämpft der von Finlay eingerichtete Garten *LITTLE SPARTA* in Stonypath (es handelt sich um einen philosophischen Garten, Pan gewidmet), aber zugleich nährt er sich von dieser Fatalität (*LITTLE SPARTA* ist für die Natur ein Monument, für das englische Establishment aber ein befestigtes Lager).

7. NEOKLASSIZISMUS UND TARNUNG. *LITTLE SPARTA* ist die utopische Verkörperung einer unmöglichen Utopie (also der Ort eines Ortlosen), eine Stätte der Fiktion und somit der Ernüchterung; die Versöhnung zwischen Natur und Kultur wird sich nie anders als mittels Tarnung abspielen. «In der Kunst ist jeder Stil eine Tarnung, durch welche hindurch wir die wahre Natur sehen können, indem wir sie selbst wiederherstellen...», gesteht Finlay.

Wenn Finlay so hartnäckig die Formen des Neoklassizismus aufgreift, so deshalb, weil sein Ideal, seine Moral und seine Ästhetik darin aufbewahrt

(getarnt!) sind. In der Tat ist der Neoklassizismus ein Ort der Ambivalenz, der Spannung zwischen Leidenschaften und gestellten Forderungen, zwischen Gefühl und Strenge, Zitat und Neuerung ...; und in diesem Sinn verkörpert er das Tarnen als Stil schlechthin. «Das Tarnen eines Tanks», meint Finlay, «heisst, wie Shenstone sagt, dem Unerbittlichen das Freundliche, dem Erhabenen das Schöne, den Trommeln die Flöten beifügen.»

8. SMALL IS QUITE BEAUTIFUL. Das traditionelle (historische und formale) Schema, das den Neoklassizismus in zwei Phasen aufteilt, nämlich in eine aufsteigende, triumphale (das 18. Jahrhundert) und eine absteigende und dekadente (die 30er und 40er Jahre), wirft Ian Hamilton Finlay über den Haufen, indem er diesen beiden Phasen Mittäterschaft und Kompromisshaltung nachweist. Beide Formen des Neoklassizismus werden nämlich von einer Utopie getragen: die eine ist fortschrittlich und leuchtend (die Französische Revolution), die andere zerstörerisch und dunkel (die totalitären Staatsformen im Europa der 30er Jahre), und diese Unvereinbarkeit verwirrt Finlay endlos.

Ist die Französische Revolution, dieses ausgehende 18. Jahrhundert, nicht der Schauplatz grausamer und unerbittlicher Konfrontation von Schatten und Licht? Weist nicht die sinnbildliche Figur Saint-Just darauf hin, dass Terror und Elegie und Revolution und Eleganz in gewisser Hinsicht vereinbar sind? «Die Französische Revolution», sagt Finlay, «hat zwei Aspekte: den epischen und den häuslichen, die Guillotine und die Teekanne ...» Der «geheime Garten» des Spandauer Gefängnisses, sagt er weiter, sei für den berühmten Hitler-Architekten Albert Speer der geeignete Ort, um seine Architektur-Utopien zu verwirklichen. «Grösse», sei sie nun auf der Seite des Erhabenen oder auf jener des Terrors, beinhaltet stets ihre Kleinheiten, Schwächen, ja Niedlichkeiten ... *«Small is quite beautiful»*, so lautet die spöttische Devise, mit der Finlay die Fassade der Reichskanzlei in seinem «3rd Reich Revisited» schmückt.

9. VERRÄTER UND HELD. Ian Hamilton Finlays «neoklassizistische Aufrüstung» ist eine Strategie, die ihm erlaubt, keinem der Widersprüche, die unsere intellektuellen Werturteile bestimmen – darunter vor allem der (traditionelle!) Gegensatz von Modernität und Tradition –, Recht zu geben, sondern sie alle in ihrer Unvereinbarkeit zu belassen. In der Tat ist ja der Neoklassizismus als Stil eine Herausforderung an den Begriff Stil überhaupt, da er die verschiedenartigsten Dimensionen in sich vereinigt und nebeneinander existieren lässt: antikisierende Nostalgie, romantische Gefühlswelt und modernistische Utopie ...

In dieser Hinsicht greift Ian Hamilton Finlays Schaffen besonders heftig in die heutige Debatte um Modernismus/Postmodernismus ein, und zwar deshalb, weil es von einer visuellen Moral ausgeht und daher jenseits der formalistischen und historischen Auffassungen von Kunst und Kultur steht. Sein Werk weist die zyklische – und daher notgedrungen spekulative – Bewegung der Dinge energisch zurück (was indessen nicht einer dogmatischen Ausschliessung gleichkommt!) und widersetzt sich einer Welt, in der sich Avantgarde mit «Rückkehr zur Ordnung» periodisch ablöst (ja, Avantgardismus ist, klassisch gesehen, auch ein Militarismus!).

Ian Hamilton Finlay wirft auf brennende und eigentümliche Art die (zugleich aktuelle und inaktuelle!) Frage von Ordnung und Unordnung auf (siehe dazu den Satz von Saint-Just: die gegenwärtige Ordnung ist die Unordnung der Zukunft, in dem jedes Glied auswechselbar ist). In einer Welt, in der die Spielregeln von Anfang an gefälscht sind, weigert Finlay sich, eine Wahl zu treffen, und lässt sein Werk in einem labilen und gewagten Gleichgewicht wirken. Denn Ian Hamilton Finlay ist zu klarsichtig, zu romantisch, zu distanziert, zu leidenschaftlich, zu absolut, zu relativ, um nach dem Beispiel J.L. Borges' nicht zu erkennen, welch kleine Distanz den Verräter vom Helden trennt.

(Übersetzung: Mariette Müller)

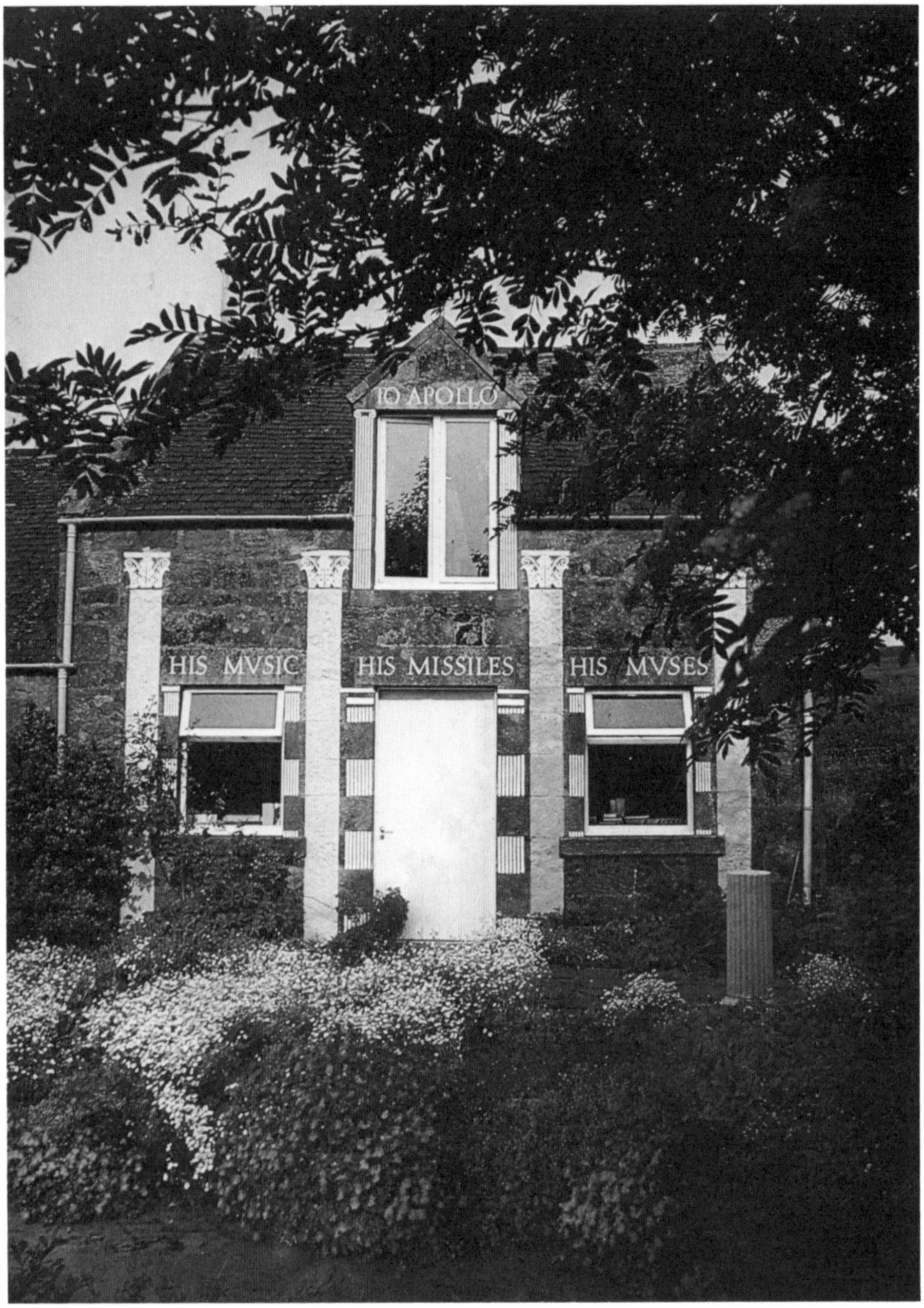

IAN HAMILTON FINLAY, THE GARDEN TEMPLE, LITTLE SPARTA.

Ian Hamilton Finlay or A SPOILSPORT IN DIALECTICAL SPECULATION

BERNARD MARCADÉ

EVERY GREAT SPIRIT IS AMBIDEXTROUS, HE ARGUES ON BOTH SIDES.
BALTASAR GRACIAN

1. UT PICTURA, POESIS. At once totally dependent on language and nevertheless deliberately visual, Ian Hamilton Finlay's metamorphic work obliges us to reconsider from another viewpoint the famous debate generated by Horace's UT PICTURA, POESIS: "Poetry is like painting; some works more pleasing when looked at closely, others when seen from a distance; one likes darkness, the other wants to be viewed in the light and does not fear the connoisseur's penetrative judgement; this one pleases but once, that one will please ten times over." Horace, ARS POETICA, 361–365. Because it relates to both of these dimensions, without compromise or exclusive commitment, this work sternly refutes the renaissance and modernist doctrines which, each in their own way, attempt to bring out the specific of an art based on "words succeeding each other in time," on "forms which coexist in space" (Lessing).
Playing on two boards at once – as far from dangerfree intellectual stance –, Finlay's work bravely transgresses that (formalistic) inevitability which aims at stressing the preeminence of one camp over another. Even if, more often than not, it conceals – camouflages itself by stylistic means, to Finlay, war definitely lies elsewhere.

2. AESTHETICS AND MORALS. Ian Hamilton Finlay uses language to ends which are neither logical, nor ontological. Similarly, he uses the visual image to ends which are not illustrative (not to illustrate, but to show). In so doing, his art betrays two causes simultaneously, that of truth and that of the imagination: it is neither a picture of thought, nor thought pictured.
Rather than being like a visual thought, Finlay's work, which thus rejoins the tradition of the impresa and of mannerist emblems, is to a greater extent meant to be perceived and understood as a visual moral. Of such a moral – which must in this perspective be distinguished from moralizing morals –, this work indeed does possess the aloofness, the distance, the edge and irony...

3. TOTALITY, FRAGMENT. Made up of fragments, bits and pieces, lines and quotations, the visual world of Ian Hamilton Finlay is resolutely fragmentary. This parcelled-out vision should

BERNARD MARCADÉ is a writer and an art critic in Paris. His book "L'éloge du mauvais esprit" was published in 1986 by Edition de la différence, Paris.

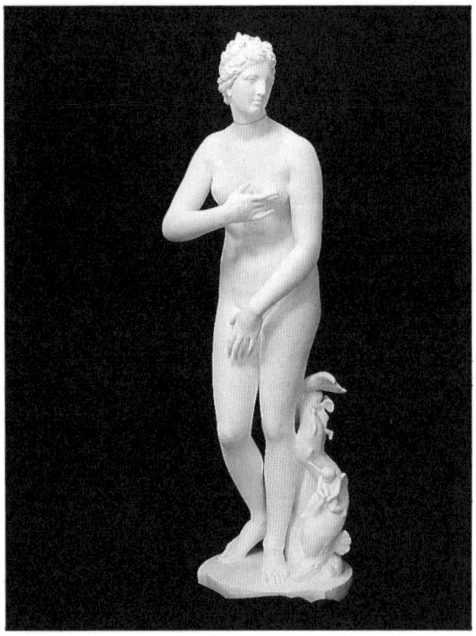

IAN HAMILTON FINLAY, APHRODITE, 1987,
PLASTER / GIPS, *78¾ x 35½" /* 200 x 90 cm.
(Photo: Antonia Reeve)

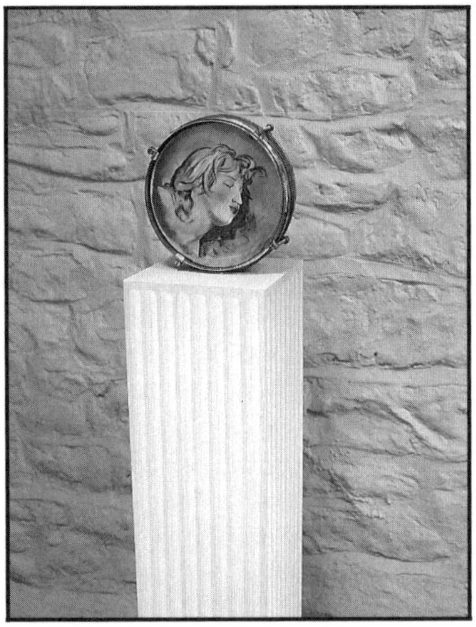

IAN HAMILTON FINLAY WITH GARY HINCKS, PAINTED DRUM /
BEMALTE TROMMEL, */ PORTRAIT OF THE DEAD YOUNG BARA /*
PORTRAIT DES JUNGEN TOTEN BARA VON */ BY J.-L. DAVID, 1987.*

not be read as a nostalgic rendering of some lost unity or truth, but above all as a defence and illustration of the fragment as against (and faced with) a speculative and totalitarian conception of the universe. Hence, Ian Hamilton Finlay sides with a tradition which, while being strongly anchored in a "sentiment of totality," has from the Pre-Socratics to the German Romantics, through to Nietzsche, never ceased to protest against unitary, univocal conceptions of the world. Resolutely fragmentary, Finlay's work nevertheless remains concerned with matters of style. Isn't the fragment which operates via a process of mulled-over distillation, carving and gouging with draughtsmanly refinement, a stylistic effect "par excellence"? Is it not the very denigration of the idea of totality and, as such, its most desperate epiphany?

4. AN ANTI-DIALECTIC. Leaving the contradictions open, rather than attempting to solve them, Ian Hamilton Finlay's art is rooted in that ambivalence which Baltasar Gracian describes "a two-edged word, a meaning seen in two lights." This way of expressing and showing at the same time a certain thing and its contrary: shade and light, terror and virtue, nature and culture, grandeur and puniness, is opposite to any kind of dialectical reconciliation. The art of Finlay consists in never envisaging the mediating term, in letting contradictions stand with all their irresolution and ambiguity. Thus, the elegant outline of Apollo and Daphne shimmers through the grim SS emblem. Instead of the enigmatic tombstone of POUSSIN'S ARCADIAN SHEPHERDS arises a ghost-like Panzer, at once menacing and pretty...
Quite frequently, the art of Finlay consists in a mise-en-scène of conflictual duality, of an inner duel contained within words or values, without it ever being possible to envisage a conciliatory (and therefore, normalizing) solution. This art of uncovering similarity in dissimilarity, of bringing to the surface the disparity, the errors and faults, underlying a world which is so mindful of, so anxious over, its integrity, homogeneity, and "transparency," has the gift of disturbing and disrupting established values and hierarchies. It's a corrosive, sometimes insolent and scathing, means of not letting things (and particularly values) stay in place, a way of demonstrating, of exposing the things that shamefully influence or haunt them.

5. THE CONNIVING REVERSE. In fact, Ian Hamilton Finlay doesn't let anything

go by. The least hiatus, the least crack in the workings of our culture and civilisation is, as far as he is concerned, a target for ruthless genealogical curtain fire.

What indeed differentiates the genealogical attitude from speculative dialectics, is precisely the highlighting of conflicts as opposed to their neutralization, not to say their being swept away completely (the famous Hegelian Aufhebung).

Untiringly, Finlay tracks down the setbacks and shortcomings of the "Great, Generous Ideals": Nature, Culture, Liberty, Fraternity... upon which are built evaluations: political, moral and aesthetic. For each of these, he produces a demonstration according to which, often unknown to themselves, they become the vehicles of a world which upholds those exact notions which they reprove: terror, enslavement, war... According to which, conversely, these same negative values themselves bear the traces – the vestiges – of an ideality, which, if it is not entirely lost, is often misrepresented – a travesty of itself. The other side of a coin is not always what one expects it to be: the temple often conceals a guillotine. Nature is an idea – a value – linked with our culture, and vice versa. Peace, as we well know, is a continuation of war waged by other means!

6. Et in Arcadia Ego.

On seeing a canvas by Joshua Reynolds, which represented, sitting before a tombstone, a couple "moved by the inscription," King George III instantly translated the epigraph ET IN ARCADIA EGO by: DEATH EXISTS EVEN IN ARCADIA. Erwin Panofsky has most convincingly demonstrated the aptness of this translation, and showed how it contradicts the academic translation: I TOO, HAVE LIVED IN ARCADIA.

Arcadia is one of the names given to Utopia: the ideal realm of bliss and beauty, the home and country of eternal spring, the golden age of primitive existence replete with abundance and innocence. This symbol which reappears throughout the history of classical painting (Guercino, Poussin, Cipriani...) and Romantic painting (Kolbe, Reynolds...) should therefore be read as a fantastic breach (a death sign) inscribed within the so far immaculate model of Western, human, political and social transparency. So, Utopia might likewise be impaired by death, negativeness, destruction. War and conflict might emanate from our conceptions of nature, as well as from aesthetic and moral assessments...

This is the inevitability against which Ian Hamilton Finlay's garden LITTLE SPARTA in Stonypath struggles (this is a philosophical garden, a tribute to the God, Pan); but this is also the very inevitability which it feeds on (LITTLE SPARTA is a monument facing nature, as well as an entrenched camp facing the British Establishment).

7. Neo-Classicism and Camouflage.

LITTLE SPARTA is the Utopian incarnation of an impossible Utopia (the site of a non-site), a place for fiction, hence the site of a certain disenchantment: nature and culture can never meet again other than by means of camouflage. In art, admits Finlay, each style is a comouflage through which, by our own reconstructions, we think we see "real nature."

If the latter is so keen to enter into Neo-Classical form, this is perhaps because he finds registered there (camouflaged) his ideal, his moral, as well as his aesthetics. Neo-classicism is indeed the meeting point of a certain ambivalence, of an acute tension between passion and demand, feeling and restraint, quoting and renewing...; in this sense it is the very style of camouflage. "To camouflage a tank," observes Finlay, "is to add what Shenstone calls amiable to severe, the beautiful to the sublime, flutes to drums."

8. Small Is Quite Beautiful.

By rendering them mutually complementary, by making them implicate themselves, Ian Hamilton Finlay does not distinguish the – historical and formal – traditional precept which separates Neo-Classicism in two categories: first, the ascendent, triumphant phase (the XVIIIth century); second, a declining, decadent phase (the 30's and 40's). Both these forms of Neo-Classicism are indeed fostered by a Utopia: one is progressive and luminous (the French Revolution); the other is destructive and dark (the totalitarian regimes in Europe during the 30's). Finlay complicates matters no end, enchancing this antinomy. Wasn't the French Revolution, at the turn of the XVIII th century, a bold and ruthless conflict between light and shade? Couldn't the emblem-like figure of

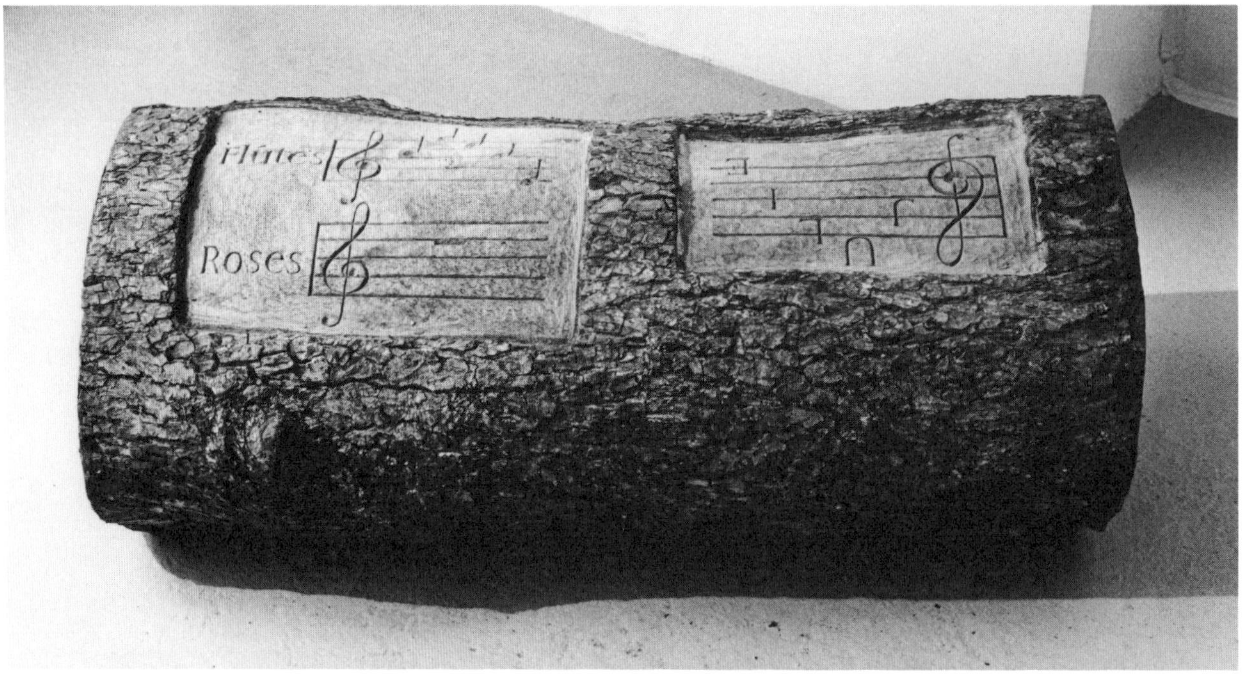

IAN HAMILTON FINLAY, JULIE INSCRIPTION, 1987.

Saint-Just imply a certain compatibility between terror and elegy, revolution and elegance? "There are," notes Finlay, "two aspects of the French Revolution: the epic and the domestic, the guillotine and the tea pot..." It is through "this secret garden" at Spandau prison, where he was held prisoner for so long, that Albert Speer, Hitler's famous architect, was best able to give shape to his Utopian architecture. Be it on the side of the sublime or on the side of terror, "grandeur" always possesses that characteristic pettiness, weakness, even self-indulgence.

... Small is quite beautiful, such is the ironic motto with which Finlay embellishes the lintel of the Reich chancellery, in his "Third Reich Revisited"!

9. TRAITOR AND HERO. Ian Hamilton Finlay's "Neo-Classical re-armament" is a strategy which allows him to pit against each other (and not resolve) the contradictions which direct our own intellectual assessments, mainly the – traditional! – opposition between modernity and tradition. Neo-Classicism is indeed the style which challenges the very notion of style since it allows for the co-existence within itself of the most dichotomous of antiquarian romantic sensibilities and Utopian Modernism. In this light, the work of Ian Hamilton Finlay forcefully finds a place in the contemporary debate surrounding modernism/postmodernism for the simple reason that it is a visual moral which places itself beyond formalist and historicist conceptions of art and culture.

It gently refutes the cyclical and necessarily speculative concept according to which avant-garde movements alternate with "returns to order" (avant-gardism is also, classically, a military concept!).

In a sharp and original way, Ian Hamilton Finlay raises the (both current and outdated) question of order and disorder. (Cf. Saint-Just's saying: "The present order is the disorder of the future," whose fragments can all be permutated.) In a world in which the dice are loaded Ian Hamilton Finlay refuses to choose, dangerously leaving his work to unravel itself in a precarious equilibrium. Ian Hamilton Finlay is indeed too lucid, too romantic, too distant, too impassioned, too much of an absolutist, too much of relativist, not to know like J.L. Borges how narrow the distance is between traitors and heroes. *(Translation: Laurent Sauerwein)*

Vom Werden zum Vergehen

JÖRG ZUTTER

«Die Urgeschichte der Bilder» von Thomas Huber

Die Kunst von Thomas Huber vermittelt keine kurzen Momentaufnahmen des Schöpfungsaktes. Sie spiegelt weder intime Gefühlsmomente noch bringt sie geniale Einfälle zur Darstellung. Der Ausgangspunkt ergibt sich vielmehr aus Hubers Erkenntnis, dass gemalte Bilder nur eine äussere Form, eine Hülle eines vielschichtigen Kernes sind, der sich nie präzis festlegen, sondern nur ungenau andeuten oder umschreiben lässt. Kunst hat deshalb für ihn weniger mit Gestalten und mehr mit Sich-Herantasten an einen universellen Inhalt zu tun.

Jedes Bild trägt unverkennbar die Spuren seines langen, vielschichtigen Entstehungsprozesses in sich und enthält gleichzeitig Elemente seines Werdens und Wirkens. Es kann mit den einzelnen Gliedern einer unendlichen Kette verglichen werden, die vom ersten Ursprung bis in die ferne Zukunft reicht.

JÖRG ZUTTER ist Konservator am Museum für Gegenwartskunst in Basel.

Dieser breite Anspruch, den Huber an seine Kunst stellt, tritt in der im Sommer 1987 entstandenen Arbeit DIE URGESCHICHTE DER BILDER beispielhaft in Erscheinung. Das thematische Umfeld bzw. der Hintergrund der sich aus vier bemalten Holzaquarien zusammensetzenden Installation bildet hier ein querformatiges Bild des Meeres, über dem fünf riesige, sich gegen hinten stark verjüngende Regenwolken gemalt sind. Dieses Seestück bezieht sich ganz konkret auf die verschiedenen Aggregatszustände, welche die Bilder im Laufe ihres Entstehens und Vergehens annehmen können. Der Künstler geht von der festen Überzeugung aus, dass Bilder, bevor sie auf der Leinwand oder auf dem Papier Gestalt angenommen haben, in der Natur bereits ein Vorleben geführt haben. Der ewige Kreislauf des Wassers, das sich in Dampf auflöst, Wolken bildet und anschliessend als Regen wieder auf die Erde fällt, symbolisiert auch den Weg, welchen jedes Bild vor seiner endgültigen Fixierung zurücklegen muss.

Der hier angestellte Vergleich der Entstehung der Bilder mit einem Naturvorgang muss nicht als künstlerisches Dogma, sondern als verdeutlichende Illustration für die Selbstverständlichkeit dieses Prozesses angesehen werden, wie ebenfalls aus dem folgenden Denkbild von Huber abgeleitet werden kann: «Wenn das Bild wie Wasser wäre, eine verbindliche Vorstellung, worunter sich alle Bilder vereinen. Wer hätte nicht Gedanken zum Wasser, Bilder davon in sich gesammelt, die zum gemeinsamen Urbild geschöpft werden können. Die Wasserfläche als gleichnishafter Ort, wo eine Bedingung beginnt und eine andere aufhört zu sein. Grenze zwischen Wasser und Luft. Berührungsebene zweier Reiche. Dort sehe ich die Bilder. Denn sie sind ein Dazwischen. An ihnen berühren sich zwei Medien. So wie es geschieht zwischen Luft und Wasser in den Seen und Meeren, gross und weit, wie die lange Zeit, die verging, seit Geschöpfe aus dem Wasser heraus, diese Grenze durchbrechend, an Land gingen. Die Wasserfläche ist das grosse Bild jenes Ortes uralter Verwandlung.»[1]

Somit kann die tiefgrüne Wassermasse dieser Landschaft als Reservoir unzähliger Bilder angesehen werden. Die Wassergrenze der Aquarien liegt auch auf gleicher Höhe wie der Meeresspiegel. Die Aquarien sind nicht nur Wasserbehälter, sondern auch Beweisstücke für die Vielseitigkeit der im Meer lebenden Tiere und Pflanzen. Die Arbeit symbolisiert somit anhand von vier Beispielen ein gewaltiges Potential an Bildern; die museale Präsentation verleiht dieser Tatsache noch zusätzliches Gewicht, indem hier gewissermassen ein unerschöpfliches Bilderdepot ein Gegengewicht zur chronologischen Vorführung nach Epochen und Schulen schafft.

Obwohl der Titel der Arbeit von der «Urgeschichte der Bilder» spricht, sind Wasserlebewesen dargestellt, und zwar Protozoa (Urtierchen in der Form von Einzellern als Vorstufe anderer Lebewesen), Schwämme (eine Zwischenform von Pflanze und Tier), Goldfische (als Symbol eines domestizierten und somit künstlichen Fisches) und schliesslich die Latimeria chalumne (als eine der ältesten noch lebenden Fischarten; sie stammt vom Quastenflosser ab und gilt als Vorfahre der vierfüssigen Landwirbeltiere).

Thomas Huber hat die symbolische Bedeutung dieser Tierarten am Beispiel der Latimeria kürzlich folgendermassen umschrieben: «Die Latimeria verkörpert den Übergang vom Wasser- zum Landlebewesen, den Wechsel von einem Medium zum anderen. Von Geschichte ist also die Rede, von der Geschichte der Lebewesen, allgemein der Evolution. Verallgemeinernd lässt sich sagen, diese vollziehe sich in Wandlungen oder präziser im Überschreiten der Mediumsgrenzen (Wasser–Luft). Ist es uns heute ein Selbstverständnis, am Lande lebende Wesen zu sein, im Verein mit vielen anderen, werden ähnlich selbstverständlich einmal im Medium Bild Lebewesen diese neuen Welten bevölkern? Die Bilder werden die neuen Lebensräume des Menschen sein. Wir sind eine Vorstufe dieser Spezies, wie die Latimeria eine der unseren. Wir sind halb Körper und halb Geist, vorhanden („vor-händen“) und auch sichtbar, wenn wir uns ganz zeigen, wenn wir uns offenbaren, sichtbar werden, werden wir ganz Bild sein. Die Sichtbarkeit, das Sich-Zeigen wird zur Voraussetzung zu dieser Verwandlung. Bilder sind solche Zeugnisse des Wandels. Die Bilder werden zum evolutionären Schritt in der Geschichte der Lebewesen. Die Evolution als umfassendstes alchemistisches Opus, um die Vorstellung der Verwandlung in einen anderen Zusammenhang zu bringen.»[2]

Somit ruft Huber die Bedeutung der tiefen Ursprünglichkeit des Bildes in Erinnerung und entwirft gleichzeitig dessen zukünftige Entwicklung. Er nimmt hier eine Tradition auf, die letztlich im Schaffen von Paul Klee wurzelt. In seinem Jenenser Vortrag von 1924 umschreibt Klee diese Einstellung, die er als Wechsel vom «Vorbildlichen zum Urbildlichen» bezeichnete, folgendermassen: «Berufen aber sind die Künstler, die heute bis in einige Nähe jenes geheimen Grundes dringen, wo das Urgesetz die Entwicklungen speist».[3] Huber bekennt sich nicht zu einer positivistischen Evolutionstheorie. Mit der Präsentation der bemalten Holzkisten auf brusthohen Sockeln stellt er einen Bezug her zu den Süss- und Meerwasseraquarien

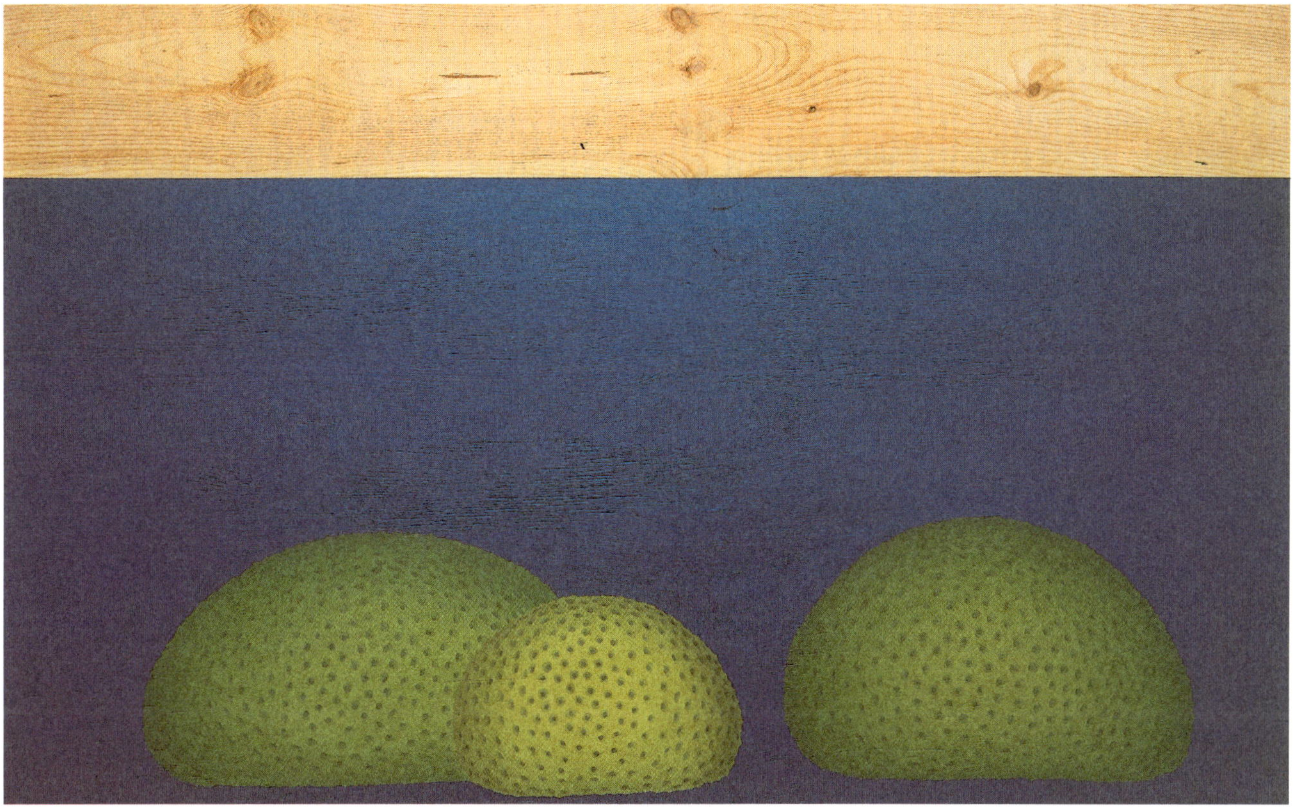

THOMAS HUBER, EUSPONGIA OFFICINALIS, BADESCHWAMM / *SPONGE, 1987,*
SEITE EINES BEMALTEN HOLZAQUARIUMS / *ONE SIDE OF A WOODEN AQUARIUM,* ÖL AUF KIEFERNHOLZ / *OIL ON PINE-WOOD,*
110 x 180 x 70 cm / 43⅓ x 70⅘ x 27½".

eines Zoos oder weckt Assoziationen mit den Schaukästen Naturhistorischer Museen.

Die Propagierung einer neuen, den tiefsten Ursprung der Bilder berücksichtigenden Genese muss als Aufforderung, ja Chance aufgefasst werden, jedes Bild auf seine eigene Urgeschichte hin zu ergründen; d.h. seinen Ursprung nicht in einem logisch-positivistischen Prozess nach dem Motto von Ursache und Wirkung aufzufassen, sondern als geheimnisvollen Organismus, dessen Sinn jenseits des Forschungsbereiches der modernen Wissenschaften liegt.

Der Blick in die Vergangenheit bedeutet jedoch keine Abwendung vom Heute, und die Wiederherstellung des gestörten ökologischen Gleichgewichtes ist für den Künstler nicht nostalgischer Wunsch, sondern zentrales Anliegen. Dieser Blick schliesst die Gegenwart ein und erweitert sie!

Im Vordergrund steht nicht die Wiedergabe einer domestizierten Natur, wie sie das 19. Jahrhundert liebte, keine irdischen Paradiese in der Form künstlicher Felsen- und Grottenlandschaften, riesiger Aquarien, exotischer Gärten samt Seen, sondern einzig und allein die Befreiung des Bildes aus seinem historischen Kontext und die Einordnung in einen breiteren Rahmen im Bereich der allesumfassenden Natur.[4]

ANMERKUNGEN:

1) Thomas Huber, Rede in der Schule, Köln (Vista Point Verlag GmbH) 1986, S. 27. Vgl. auch: Kat. Thomas Huber: Die Urgeschichte der Bilder, Museum für Gegenwartskunst Basel (und weitere Stationen), Basel 1987.

2) Thomas Huber in einem Brief vom 2. Oktober 1987 an den Autor.

3) Paul Klee, Vortrag, gehalten aus Anlass einer Bilderausstellung im Kunstverein zu Jena am 26. Januar 1924 in: Das bildnerische Denken: Schriften zur Form- und Gestaltungslehre, hrsg. von Jürg Spiller, Basel/Stuttgart 1964, S. 93.

4) Werner Hofmann, Das irdische Paradies: Motive und Ideen des 19. Jahrhunderts, München 1974, S. 98.

From Evolution to Devolution

JÖRG ZUTTER

Thomas Huber's "Prehistory of Images"

Thomas Huber's art does not record brief, spontaneous acts of creation. It neither mirrors intimate emotions nor shows ingenious inventions. Instead, the artist's point of departure is based on the realization that painted images are only an external form, a skin around a multi-layered interior that cannot be penetrated or pinned down but only hinted at and circumscribed. Huber is thus less concerned with composition and more with exploring universal contents.

Every image bears unmistakable traces of its lengthy, multi-layered process of growth and contains elements of its evolution. One is reminded of individual links in an endless chain that stretches from the earliest origins to a distant future.

This ambitious target of Huber's work is excellently illustrated by a piece done this past summer, THE PREHISTORY OF IMAGES («Die Urgeschichte der Bilder»). *The environment, i.e. the background for an installation of four painted wooden aquariums, consists of a long, rectangular painting of the ocean with five huge, sharply tapered rainclouds above it. This seascape refers quite literally to the various aggregate states which images can assume in the process of evolution and devolution. Thomas Huber is of the firm conviction that images lead preliminary lives in nature before they take shape on canvas or paper. The eternal cycle of water that turns into vapor, forms clouds and returns to the earth again as rain symbolizes the path that every image has to follow before it reaches a final version.*

The comparison between the growth of these images and a process in nature is not to be taken as artistic dogma but rather as a means of demonstrating how self-evident this process is – a thesis underscored by the following mental image of Huber's, "If the picture were like water, (it would be) a binding idea in which all pictures are united. Who hasn't thought about water, accumulated images of it that could be condensed into a common primal image? The surface of the water, simile of a place where one condition begins and another ends. Borderline between water and air. Point of contact between two realms. That's where I see the

JÖRG ZUTTER is the director of the Museum of Contemporary Art in Basel.

images. Because they are an inbetween. Where two media touch each other. The way it happens between air and water in lakes and seas, great and vast, like the long time that has passed since creatures left the water and broke the barrier to go on land. The surface of the water is the great metaphor of the topos of primeval metamorphosis."[1)] *oldest extant species of fish belonging to the order of Crossopterygii and believed to be ancient ancestors of 4-footed terrestrial vertebrates).*

Thomas Huber himself recently described the symbolic significance of these animals: "The Latimeria embody the transition between aquatic and terrestrial life, the transition from one medium to another. That's

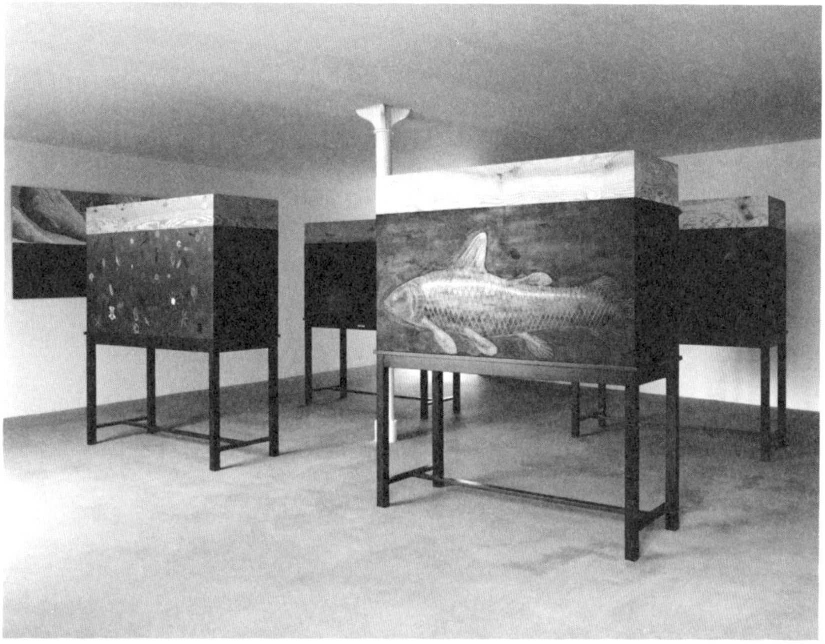

THOMAS HUBER, DIE URGESCHICHTE DER BILDER / *PREHISTORY OF IMAGES, 1987,* INSTALLATION MUSEUM FÜR GEGENWARTSKUNST BASEL. *(Photo: Martin Bühler)*

The green depths of the waters in this landscape can be considered a reservoir of countless images. The water level in the aquariums is the same as the level of the sea. They are not merely containers that hold water: they also bear witness to the diversity of marine animals and plants. The metaphor of the four aquariums thus symbolizes a vast potential of images – a fact underscored by presentation in a museum where an inexhaustible repository of pictures counterbalances the chronological display of works by epochs and schools.

Although the title speaks of the "prehistory of images," what we in fact see are aquatic creatures, protozoa (early unicellular beings that foreshadow other forms of life), fungi (an intermediate stage between plant and animal), gold fish (symbol of domesticated and artifical fish) and finally Latimeria (one of the *history, the history of life, i.e. of evolution. Generally speaking, evolution could be described as transformation or more precisely as the transgression of medial boundaries (water-air). It is self-evident that we are terrestrial beings living on land with many other beings. Will it someday be equally self-evident for living beings to populate the new worlds in this pictorial medium? Pictures will be man's new habitat. We are forerunners of the new species, just as Latimeria are forerunners of ours. We are half body and half mind, extant and visible; when we show ourselves entirely, when we reveal ourselves, become visible, we will be all image. Visibility, self-exposure will be the precondition of this mutation. Pictures are testimony to such transformations. Pictures will be a stage in the evolution of living beings. Evolution as an all-embracing alche-*

mistic opus in order to place the idea of mutation in another context."[2]

Huber points out the significance of the primordial origins of the image and simultaneously projects its future development. He follows a tradition that originated with Paul Klee. Speaking at a lecture in Jena in 1924, Klee described this attitude as a transition from

Looking back does not, however, imply a negation of the present. Nor is the artist's desire to restore the balance of ecology mere nostalgia. It is, in fact, his overriding concern and, as such, embraces and expands the present!

Unlike the popular 19th century rendition of domesticated nature or earthly Edens with artistic boulders

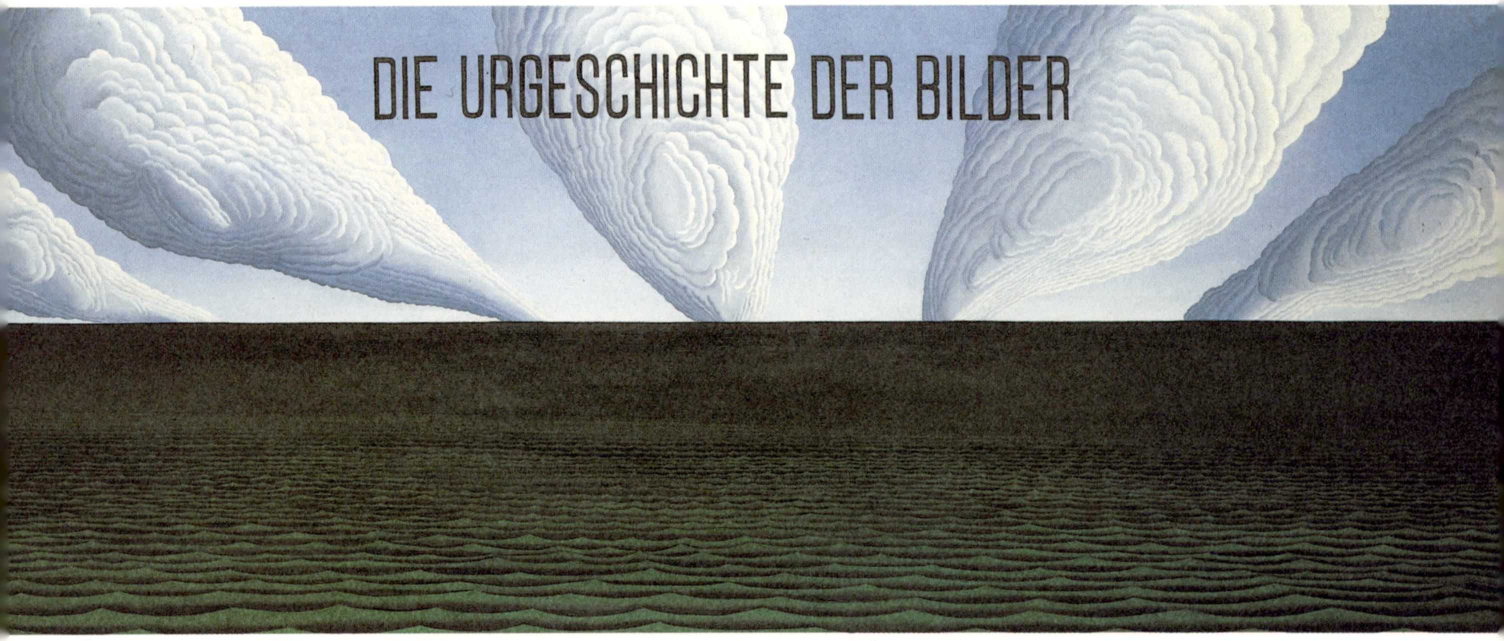

THOMAS HUBER, DIE URGESCHICHTE DER BILDER / *PREHISTORY OF IMAGES, 1987,*
ÖL AUF LEINWAND / *OIL ON CANVAS,* 120 x 300 cm / *47¼ x 118¹⁄₁₀".*

"the exemplary to the primary," in which those artists are called who have begun to explore "the secret source where the primal law feeds growth."[3]

Huber does not advocate a positivist theory of evolution; his painted wooden crates on chest-high pedestals suggest the fresh or saltwater aquariums one might see at a zoo or the showcases on display at a museum of natural history.

The propagation of a new genesis in terms of the ancient origin of images must be understood as a challenge or even as a chance to explore every image in terms of its own prehistory. This is not a logical-positivist process based on the notion of cause and effect. Instead, the origin of images is approached as a mysterious organism whose meaning goes beyond the confines of modern scientific research.

and grottoes, giant aquariums, and exotic gardens bordering on beautiful lakes, Huber's work is governed exclusively by the objective of liberating the image from its historical context and placing it within the larger framework of all-encompassing nature.[4]

(Translation: Catherine Schelbert)

NOTES:

1) Thomas Huber, REDE IN DER SCHULE, Vista Point Verlag GmbH, Cologne, 1987, p. 27. Cf. Catalog Thomas Huber, DIE URGESCHICHTE DER BILDER, Museum für Gegenwartskunst Basel (and other museums), Basel, 1987.

2) Thomas Huber in a letter to the author, October 2, 1987.

3) Paul Klee, lecture given on the occasion of an exhibition at the Jena Kunstverein on January 26, 1924, in: Jurg Spiller (ed.), DAS BILDNERISCHE DENKEN: SCHRIFTEN ZUR FORM- UND GESTALTUNGSLEHRE, Basel/Stuttgart, 1964, p. 93.

4) Werner Hofmann, DAS IRDISCHE PARADIES: MOTIVE UND IDEEN DES 19. JAHRHUNDERTS, Munich, 1974, p. 98.

INSERT

ROSEMARIE TROCKEL

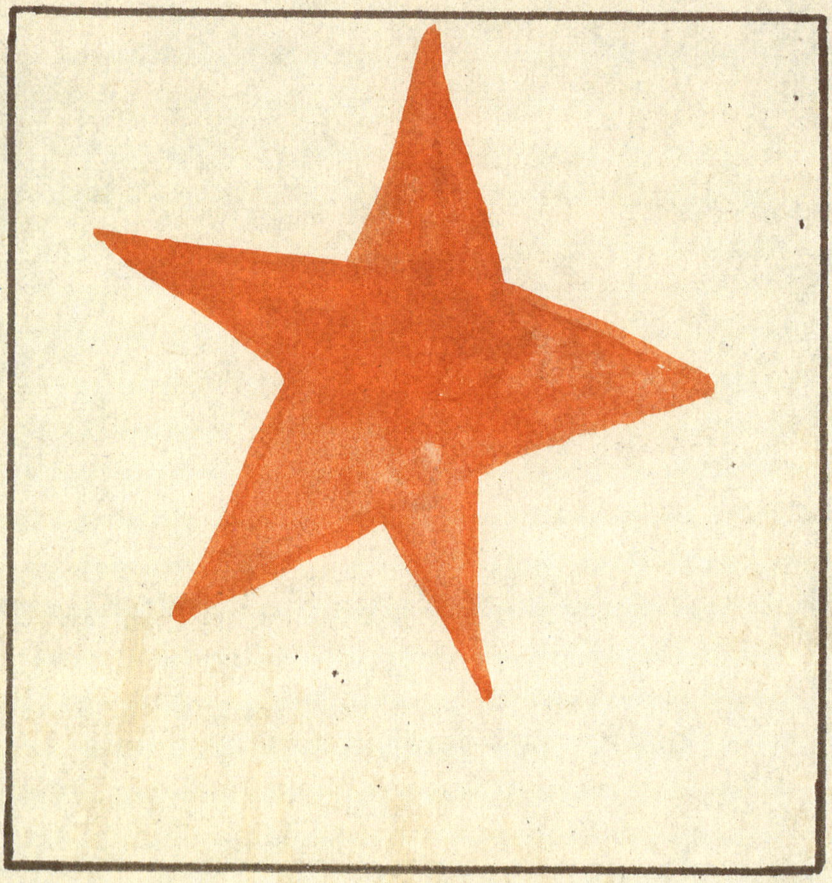

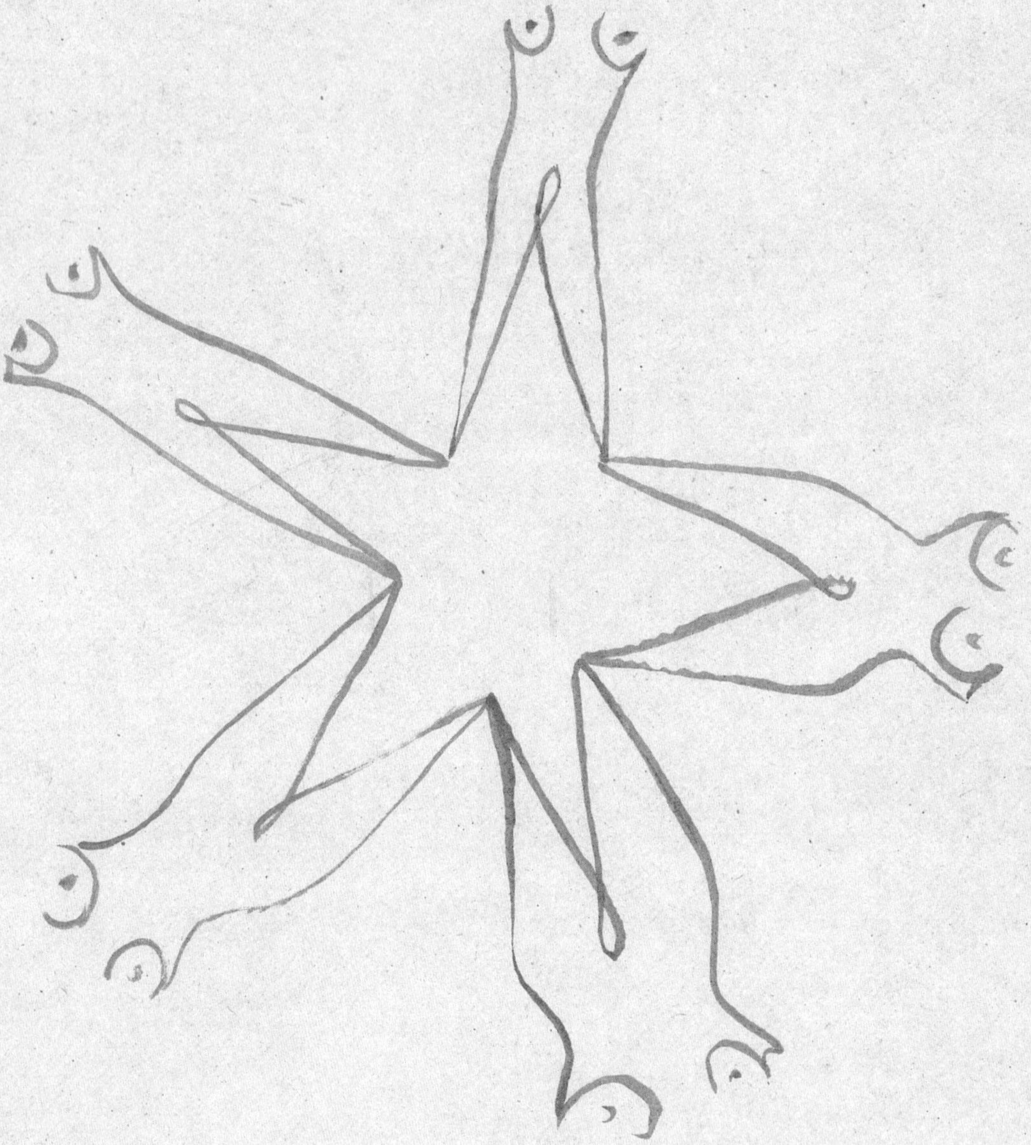

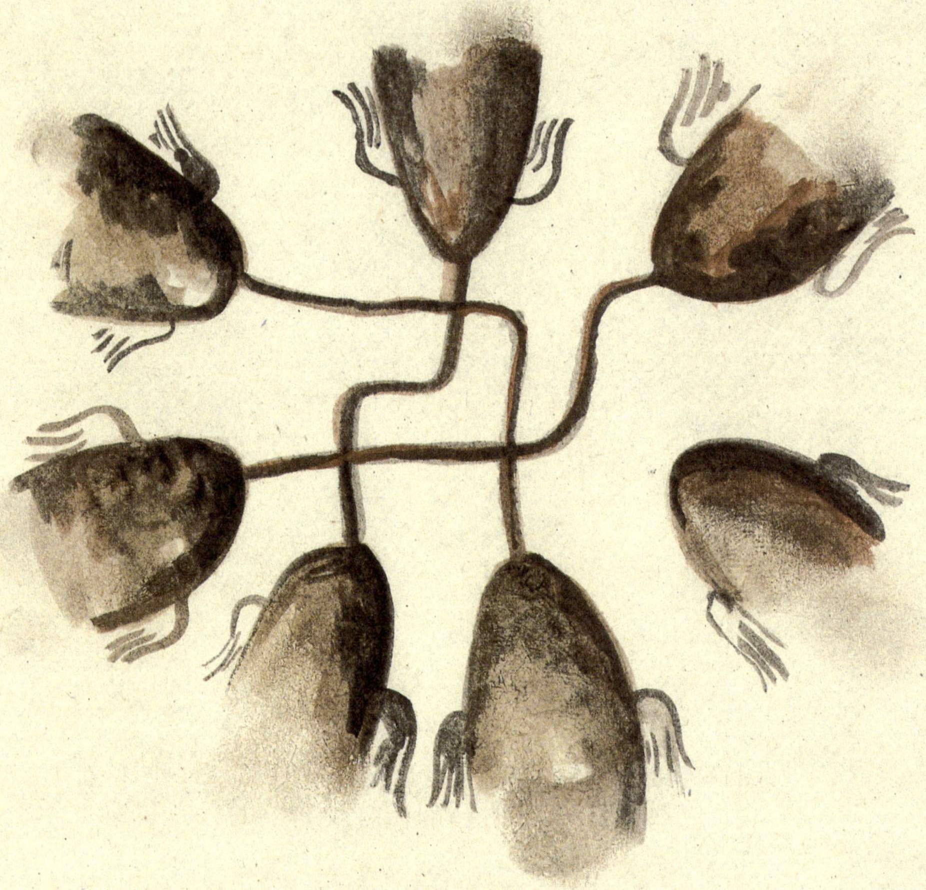

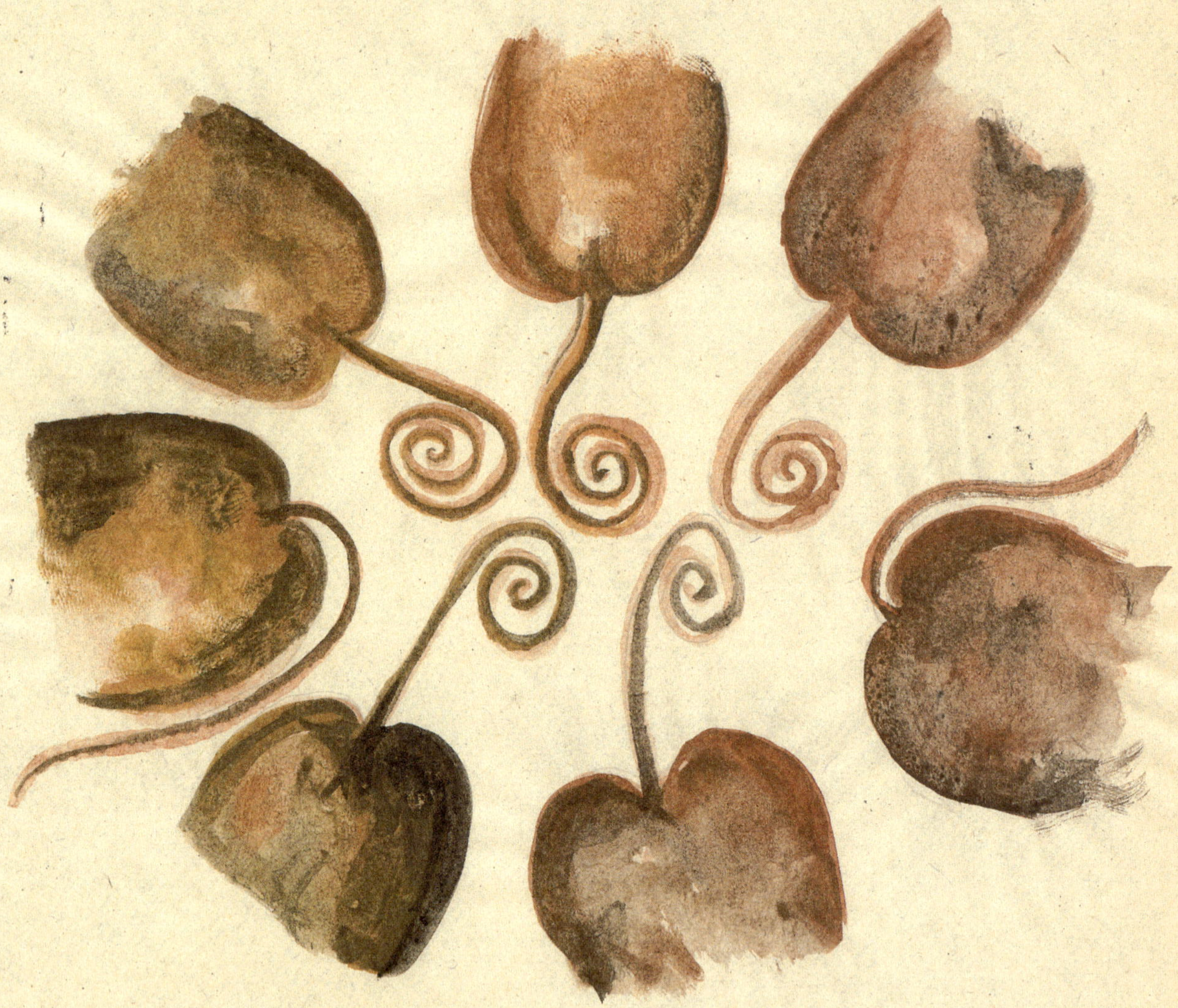

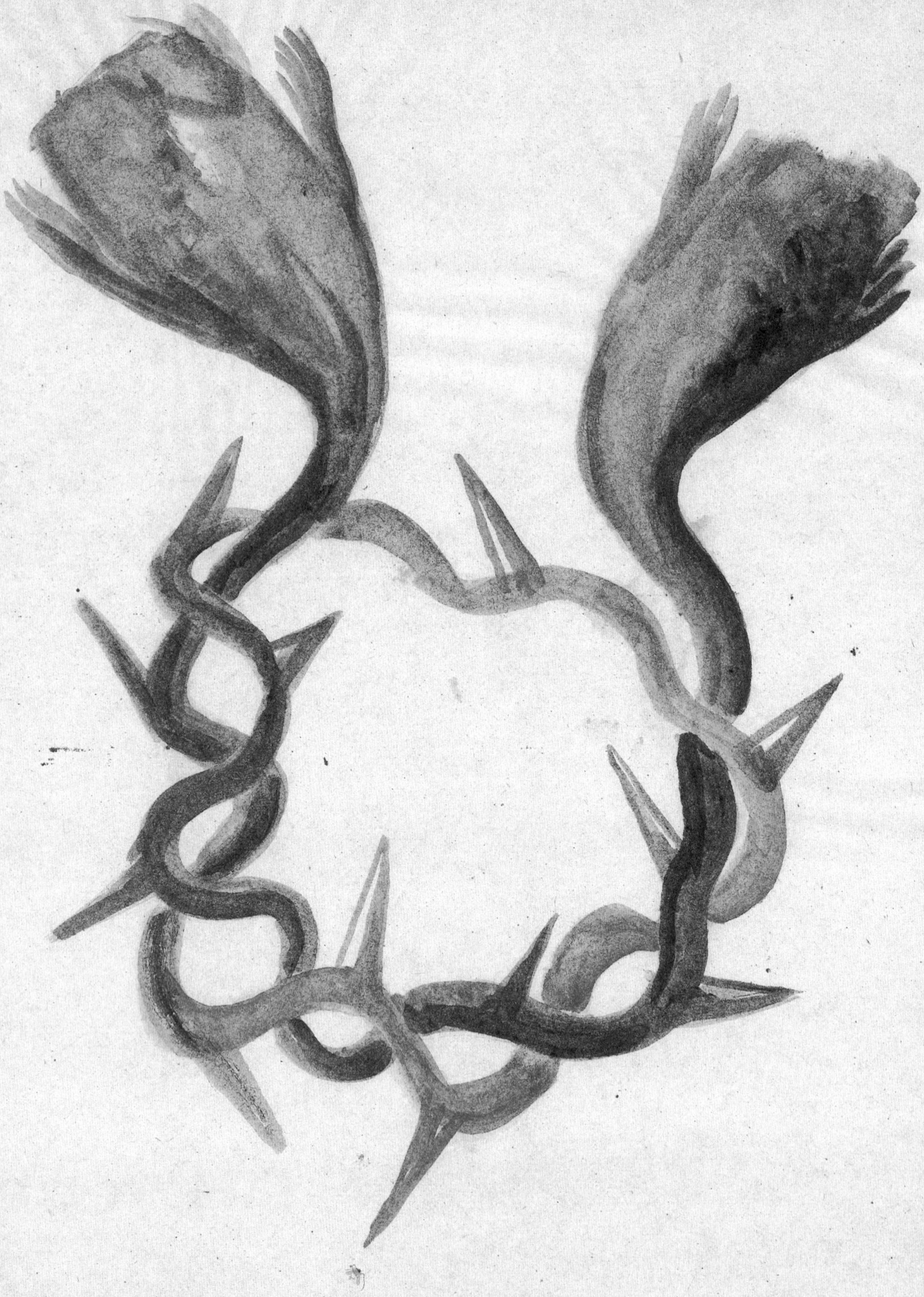

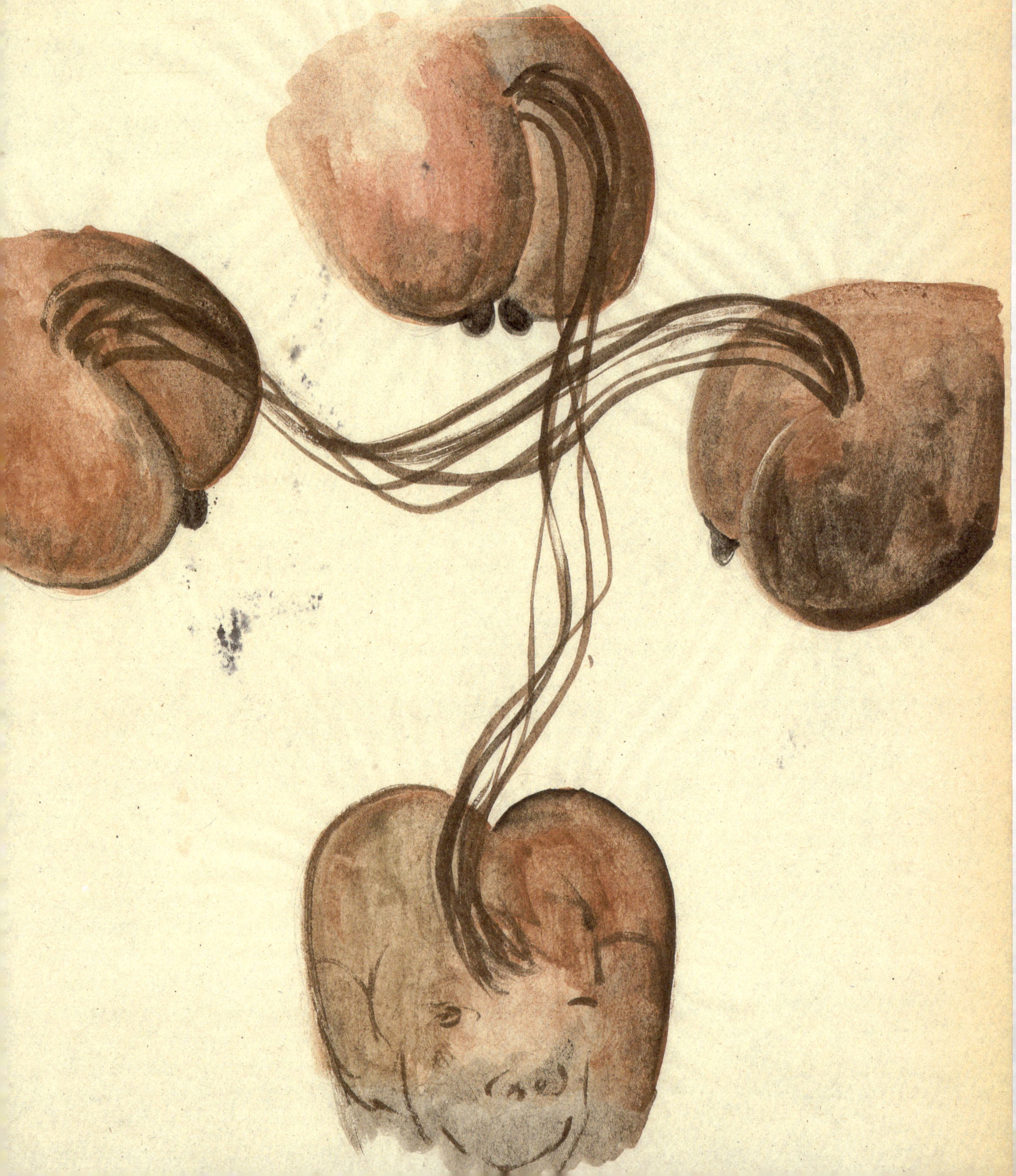

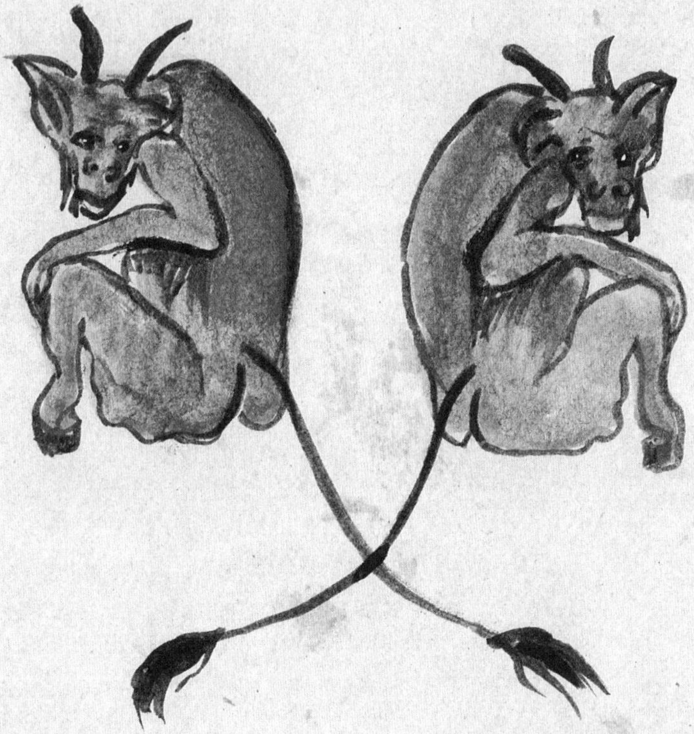

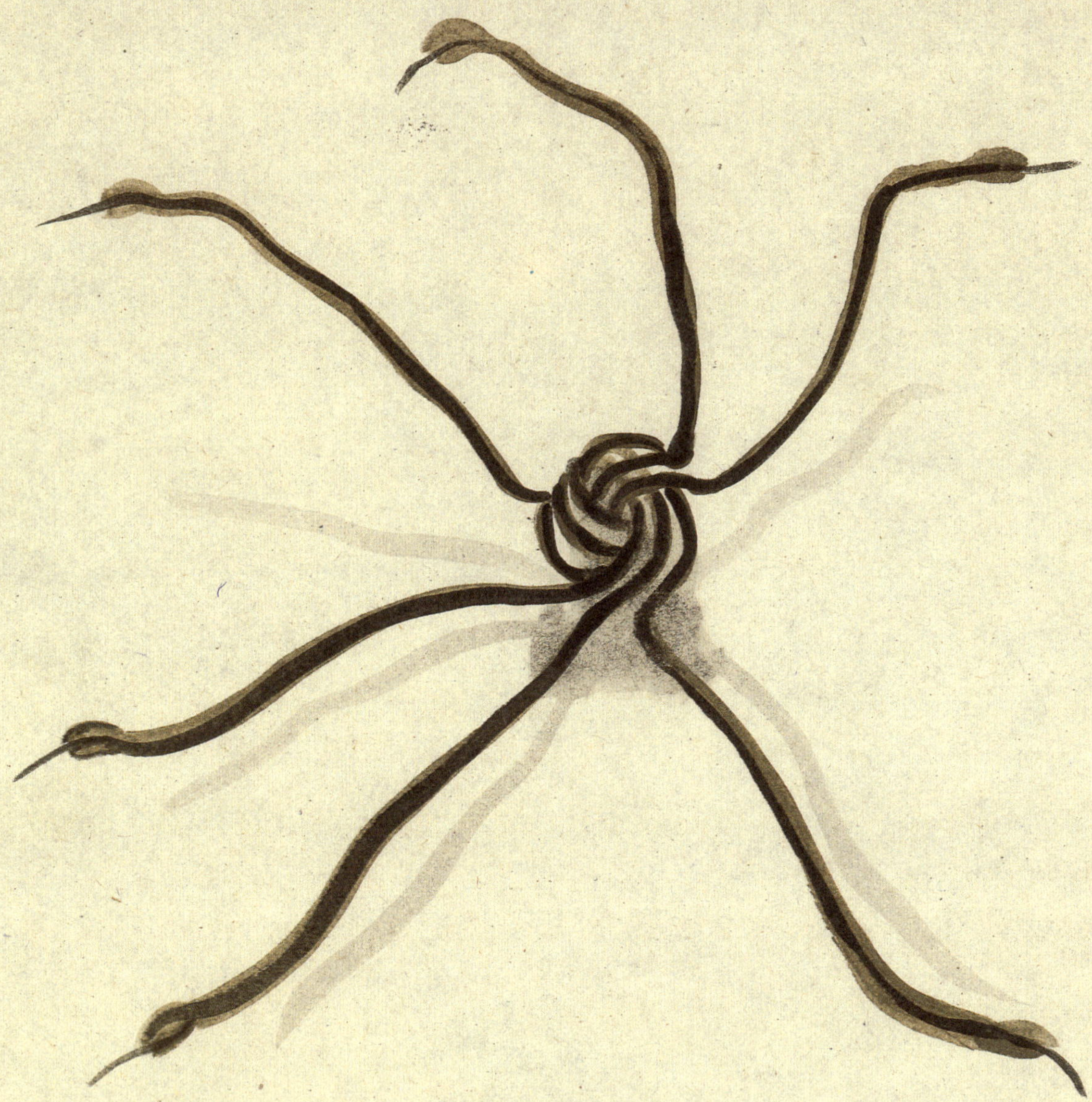

TWELVE NOTES ON THE PURSUIT OF EDEN

ROBERT DASH

1. Every incomparable time when buds break and seeds sprout inescapably reminds us of our first home, Eden. The garden is its most evocative sanctuary, a glad and utterly handsome vision of life. Eden is the most pertinacious memory of mankind, the least marred, most perfect reflection of the soul of our species, the only glass, kind to the face. That it perhaps exists only in that world between the dark and the light of morning, or *entre chien et loup*, or like the last dream of the night is of little issue. Everyone has been there, or feels so, it seems, which is why, when people see a beautiful garden, they call it Eden. Affirmatively. Unhesitatingly. This is Eden, they say. If you wish, call it permanent nostalgia. It is an iron vision of love and bread and shelter, the prelapsarian moment before pain, the moment before the moment that one came to know that all truth is mixed and perhaps random. If you wish, Eden is childhood.

2. Abstract in high degree, the inadvertent is at its core and from its bestrewment one learns to respect the roan, the random, the bird-sown, the volunteer, the stray colonizer, sifting through the planting like words of wit or wisdom but mostly like fall or splatter from brush or stick in endless serendipities. Eden and the everyday garden is not about gardens or Edens, however, but of life and giving. The lesson of the apple is that error, and transgression and the cold rain are the beginnings of wisdom, the start of real life. What we all had and lost was necessary to the broadness of our marred souls. If it is the place where we all want to be, it is because it remains the handsomest patch of the heart, our finest posture, a meadow that became a green trial with one judge and an ice-cold scapegoat. It is a privilege most pure, recreated through the simplest strategems of seed, trowel and shear, a kneeling, bowing, most humbling, lowering act in pursuit of a dream with the highest intention. It is probably the last public art, a secret shared by all. We would be in its original frame yet, were it not for our tinkering with an injunction that made little sense, were it not for our profoundly democratic aversion to the stupidity of power.

3. The fall of Eden said let us bend, bend, it is to be your finest act. The knee will lead to the heart, the heart to the hand and, be it by trowel or brush, your best works will be made by your wrist. Look at the earth. It shall be your first canvas. Before we gouged and tinted caves, celebrating the violence of the hunt, were there not always fruits falling and nuts and roots to be stored?

4. What we expected from Eden when we were in Eden is what we expect from the garden now, that it be a world entire to itself where stillness and beneficence reign, where one thing is like any other thing and all things are of equal importance, equal worth and weight, the small and the large, just like the elements of a painting, not one can be lost without the structure falling apart. Eden is a most proportionate place, as harmonious as the fit of a fiddle. I take paths out and put others in, move trees to make way for bushes, bushes to make way for grass, the world entirely green, as bright as a new sheet of paper, all of the garden's shapes reinforced through an endless program of incitement. Look at a meadow of grass in the still dawn and then, later, blowing in the rain and wind, and you will see what I mean.

5. Gardening and painting are the most beautiful ways to stumble. Whether the intention is high or low, precise or imprecise, the fine and the rough approach to gardening use the tool of time. One is never sure just how much of it has passed or just how much of it one uses on a daily basis, so smoothly is it all a part of living. While one sleeps, a long border is planted or a long horizontal painting is resolved, and one wakes to the vision of a long, meandering passageway through the garden, a place to read or rest

ROBERT DASH paints and gardens in Sagaponnack, Long Island, N.Y.

or admire the planting when the weather turns foul.

6. If I could make a school, it would be a school of poetry, painting and gardening. The best monitors of gardeners and of gardens are poetry and painting, and the making of poems returns similar courtesies to the studio. If "odors are the things to make the heartstrings crack" (Kipling) why then, the earth and the studio are memory's railsplitters unrolled like a sheet of intricate embroidery coiled on an old Chinese scroll. Like an occasion of the sky reflected in a pool, all fine work may be turned upside down and be as true.

7. Painting and gardening are acts of homage and celebration. They have simple tools and fewer principles. Their newest idea is that they have no ideas. They are experience piled up and up and one gets better by going at them over and over again. They need time to ripen their reinterpretations before they can pour over our landscape of neglect and indifference.

8. Love is the instigation of Eden and a fantasy equally powerful, in all of its repetitions painfully endured with promises as fragile and obscure as a gift left in the rain. Eden and love begin in the youth of the year and end frost-stricken and convulsed. The passions of romantic love are possessive and private but those of Eden constitute a world gift, an offering passed on and on because it has the more stable neutrality of righteous principle, one endowed with pilgrim possibilities, as alluring as the shy tints of a lime on a pewter plate. Those greens are as dull and as self-evident as a great and powerful moment in a fine painting which generally releases its d o n n é e slowly.

9. We are more in love with love and more in love with place than ever we will be in love with time. In the antiquity of the heart, after bread, roof, security, the garden as a paradise represents the ultimate finish and polish of a good life.

10. Now let us turn to the photographs of the garden, happily

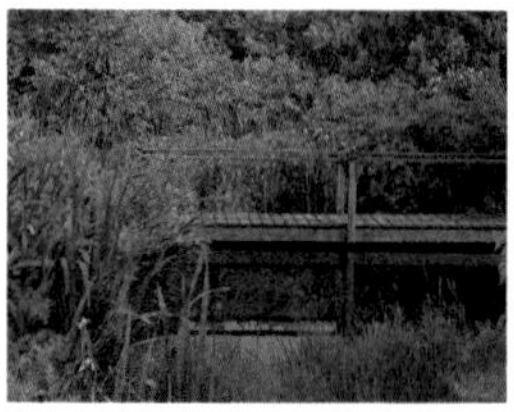

black and white. They are not illustrations, though. It is hard to make foliage seem real. Leaves can never be made of stone or steel, either. Far finer mineral matter is needed. One is dealing with a succession of moments piled up like a cathedral or a single beloved arm shining in the sky. A photograph of a garden is merely a way of detecting its privacies. For gardens to persevere they must be opened periodically and explored and even discussed, which is what we are doing here, are we not? I started my garden near the house and then moved it out to a hastily nailed fence at the edges of my property. The fence has now rotted away and the garden has met the fallen boards. They say it is Eden, those who visit it. Eden was in Mesopotamia, but place of origin never takes precedence over what one feels is true. The rainbow sorts us all and we come to see gold on our own doorstep. My garden has become part of me, my left hand, made by my right, under the light of the day. I would love to work at it by moonlight, love to make it a museum. It is small, but one may strive to express the genius of the place "writ in a very little" (Alexander Pope). If the little be writ intriguingly, size is of no matter. The air will do all of the painting. Life can flash from tableau to tableau, seem almost to complete itself in a continuum of shift and focus. But then perfections close in and then recede. Like pulse of seawater, or blood through the heart, we love and lose, make beauty, and all flowers fade.

11. Every field one plants is Eden and gardens too are this love. In the workings of both we celebrate the earth and all that it has ever held, all that it has given and will, ever, and we be wise with our custody. Of gardens we make, we can do so many brave things – we can make the wildness of the world border on the most strict, the better to reinforce the provocations of either. We can make the smallest things seem tall, confound blue with white, straighten curves, flatten columns, make new forms from old, throw foliage on foliage (the vine can be made to grow over the bush and vines can fall from trees so that they are no more than trellises). We can grow lilies above stones and have roses at water's edge, mix the prickled with the smooth, flower wood hyacinths below blueberries. We can make gardens where all distinctions are confounded, where the edible is left to blossom and the bloom comes to the table as food. It is an art, a wonderful art, everywhere as vibrant as any product of the studio and, although the forests, meadows and streams may illustrate great perfections, the art of gardening is hardly one of emulation and exactly as with painting and poetry, one gets better at it as one gets older.

12. It is all in the doing that one gets closer to Eden and no wild weather of the heart or sky will keep one from it. Indeed all such pain may be but nutrition.

PHOTOS OF ROBERT DASH'S GARDEN: MICK HALES

ZWÖLF ANMERKUNGEN AUF DER SUCHE NACH DEM GARTEN EDEN

ROBERT DASH

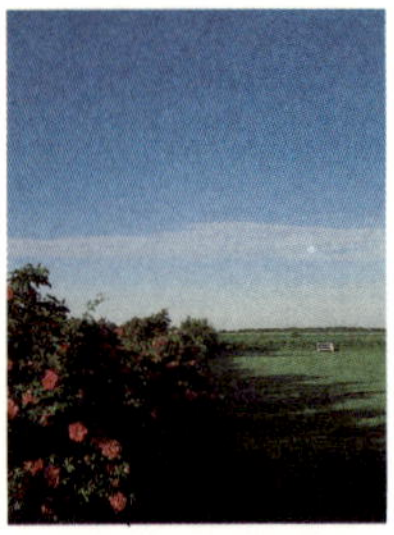

1. *Jedes unvergleichliche Mal, wenn Knospen sich entfalten und Samenkerne keimen, werden wir unvermeidlich an unser erstes Zuhause erinnert: an Eden. Der Garten ist sein evokativstes Heiligtum, eine heitere und äusserst schöne Vision des Lebens. Eden ist die hartnäckigste Erinnerung der Menschheit, die am wenigsten entstellte, vollkommenste Spiegelung der Seele unserer Spezies, der einzige unserem Gesicht wohlgesinnte Spiegel. Dass es vielleicht nur in jener Welt zwischen Finsternis und Morgengrauen, oder entre chien et loup, existiert, oder wie der letzte Traum der Nacht, ist unwichtig. Jedermann ist dort gewesen, so scheint es, oder glaubt es, und deshalb nennen die Leute, wenn sie einen schönen Garten erblicken, ihn Eden. Bestimmt, ohne zu zögern. Dies ist der Garten Eden, sagen sie; wenn du willst, nenne es permanente Nostalgie. Es ist wie eine eiserne Vision von Liebe und Brot und Geborgenheit, der Augenblick vor dem Schmerz des Sündenfalls, der Augenblick vor dem Augenblick, da man erfuhr, dass jegliche Wahrheit unrein und vielleicht zufällig ist. Wenn man will, ist Eden Kindheit.*

2. *Eden ist in hohem Masse abstrakt und das Unbeabsichtigte sein Kern. Durch ihre Streuung lernt man die Farbe des Rotschimmels zu achten, und das Zufällige, das Vogelgesäte, das Freiwillige, den vereinzelten Siedler, die alle durch das Bestellte streifen wie Worte des Witzes oder der Weisheit, aber meistens wie das Fallen oder Klecksen von Pinsel oder Stock in endlosen Gaben. Jedoch geht es bei Eden und dem alltäglichen Garten nicht um Gärten oder Edens, sondern es geht ums Leben und ums Geben. Die Lehre vom Apfel ist, dass Fehltritt und Sünde und kalter Regen die Anfänge der Weisheit sind, der Anfang des wahren Lebens. Das Paradies, das wir alle besassen und dann verloren haben, war nötig für die Grösse unserer beschädigten Seelen. Wenn es aber der Ort ist, in dem wir alle sein wollen, dann deshalb, weil es der hübscheste Fleck des Herzens bleibt, unsere edelste Haltung, eine Wiese, die zu einem grünen Gerichtsverfahren wurde und zu einem eiskalten Sündenbock. Es ist ein höchst reines Privileg, neu erschaffen durch die einfachsten Kunstgriffe von Samenkorn, Harke und Schere, zugleich ein kniender, beugender, sehr demütigender, erniedrigender Akt auf der Suche nach einem äusserst absichtsvollen Traum. Wahrscheinlich ist die letzte öffentliche Kunst ein von allen geteiltes Geheimnis. Wir befänden uns noch in Edens ursprünglichem Gefüge, hätten wir nicht mit einem Gebot herumgepfuscht, das uns sinnlos erschien, hätten wir nicht eine zutiefst demokratische Abneigung gegen die Dummheit der Macht gehegt.*

ROBERT DASH malt und gärtnert in Sagaponnack, Long Island, N.Y.

3. *Der Sündenfall von Eden besagt, beugen wir uns, unterwerfen wir uns, das wird unsere edelste Handlung sein. Das Knie wird zum Herzen führen, das Herz zur Hand und, geschehe es durch Harke oder Pinsel, deine besten Werke werden von deinem Handgelenk vollendet werden. Schau dir die Erde an. Sie wird deine erste Leinwand sein. Bevor wir Höhlen aushöhlten und einfärbten, um die Gewalt der Jagd zu feiern, hat es nicht immer schon fallende Früchte und Nüsse und Wurzeln zu verstauen gegeben?*

4. *Was wir von Eden erwarteten, als wir in Eden waren, das erwarten wir jetzt vom Garten: dass er eine Welt für sich sein möge, wo Stille und Wohlfahrt herrschen, wo ein Ding ist wie jedes andere und alle Dinge von gleicher Wichtigkeit sind, von gleichem Wert und Gewicht, das kleine und das grosse, ebenso wie die Elemente eines Gemäldes, nicht eines kann verlorengehen, ohne dass das Gefüge auseinanderbricht. Eden ist ein höchst proportionierter Ort, so harmonisch wie der Bau einer Violine. Ich nehme Wege heraus und lege andere an, versetze Bäume, um Platz für Büsche zu schaffen, Büsche, um Platz für Gras zu schaffen, die Welt ein einziges Grün, so hell wie ein neues Blatt Papier, alle Formen des Gartens werden durch ein unaufhörliches Programm des Anspornens bekräftigt. Betrachte eine Wiese in stiller Morgendämmerung und dann, später, von Wind und Regen erfasst, und du wirst sehen, was ich meine.*

5. *Gartenkunst und Malerei sind die schönste Art zu straucheln. Ob die Absicht hoch oder niedrig, präzis oder unpräzis ist; der zarte und der grobe Zugang*

zur Gärtnerei benutzt das Werkzeug der Zeit. Man ist niemals sicher, wieviel gerade vergangen ist oder wieviel genau man täglich benutzt, so fliessend ist all dies ein Teil des Lebens. Während man schläft, wird ein langes Randbeet bestellt oder ein langes, horizontales Bild vollendet, und man erwacht zur Vision einer langen, gewundenen Passage durch den Garten, ein Ort zum Lesen oder Rasten oder um das Pflanzenwerk zu bewundern, wenn das Wetter umschlägt.

6. Wenn ich eine Schule gründen könnte, wäre es eine Schule für Poesie, Malerei und Gärtnerei. Die besten Hüter von Gärtnern und Gärten sind Poesie und Malerei, und das Gedichtemachen bezeugt dem Atelier den gleichen höflichen Respekt. Wenn «Gerüche die Dinge sind, die Herzsaiten zum Zerspringen bringen» (Kipling), nun, dann spalten Erde und Atelier die Erinnerung, die entrollt ist wie ein Tuch kunstvoll gearbeiteter Stickerei einer alten chinesischen Schriftrolle. Wie der Augenblick einer Spiegelung des Himmels in einem Weiher, lässt sich jede gute Arbeit auf den Kopf stellen und ist dabei genauso wahr.

7. Malerei und Gärtnerei sind Akte der Huldigung und des Zelebrierens. Sie haben einfache Werkzeuge und weniger Prinzipien. Ihre neueste Idee ist, dass sie keine Ideen haben. Sie sind gehäufte Erfahrungen, und man wird besser, indem man das Malen und Gärtnern immer wieder anpackt. Sie brauchen Zeit, um ihre Re-Interpretationen reifen zu lassen, bevor sie sich über unsere Landschaft der Vernachlässigung und der Gleichgültigkeit ergiessen können.

8. Liebe ist der Antrieb Edens und ein gleichermassen machtvolles Phantasiegebilde, in all ihren schmerzvollen Wiederholungen, ertragen durch Versprechungen, so zerbrechlich und so dunkel wie ein im Regen liegengebliebenes Geschenk. Eden und Liebe fangen in der Jugend des Jahres an und hören frostgetroffen und erschüttert auf. Die Leidenschaften romantischer Liebe sind besitzgierig und privat, aber diejenigen Edens stellen ein Weltgeschenk dar, ein Opfer, immer wieder weitergereicht, weil es die stabilere Neutralität des gerechten Prinzips aufweist, ein Prinzip mit Pilger-Möglichkeiten, das so verführerisch ist wie die schüchternen Farbtöne einer Zitronelle auf einem Zinnteller. Derlei Grün ist so matt und so selbstverständlich wie ein grossartiger und machtvoller Augenblick in einem schönen Gemälde, das seine donnée *im allgemeinen zögernd freigibt.*

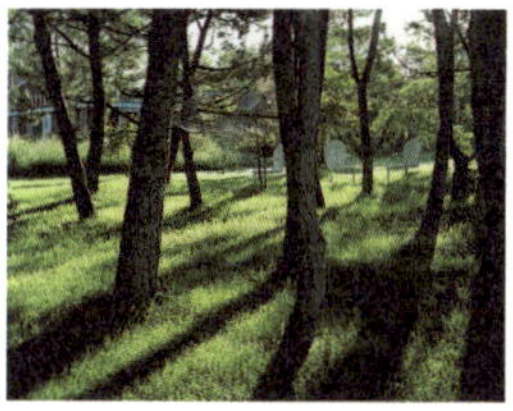

9. Wir sind mehr in Liebe verliebt und mehr in Örtlichkeit, als wir jemals in Zeit verliebt sein werden. In der Antike des Herzens bedeutet der Garten – nach Brot, Dach, Geborgenheit – auf paradiesische Art den höchsten Glanz und Schliff eines guten Lebens.

10. Wenden wir uns jetzt den Photographien vom Garten zu, glücklicherweise schwarzweiss. Wobei sie keine Illustrationen sind. Es ist schwer, Blätterwerk wie wirklich darzustellen, Blätter können auch nie aus Stein oder Stahl gemacht werden. Weitaus feinere anorganische Substanz wird benötigt. Man hat es mit einer Folge von Augenblicken zu tun, aufeinandergeschichtet wie eine Kathedrale oder ein einzelner geliebter Arm, der am Himmel strahlt. Eine Photographie von einem Garten ist lediglich eine Art, seine Verstecke zu entdecken. Um sich durchzusetzen, müssen Gärten regelmässig geöffnet und erforscht und sogar besprochen werden, was wir hier tun, oder etwa nicht? Ich fing meinen Garten nahe beim Haus an und verlegte ihn dann nach draussen, an einen hastig zusammengenagelten Zaun am Rande meines Grundstücks. Der Zaun ist mittlerweile morsch geworden, und der Garten ist mit den umgefallenen Brettern zusammengetroffen. Sie sagen, es sei Eden, diejenigen, die ihn besuchen. Eden lag in Mesopotamien, aber der Ursprungsort hat niemals Vorrang vor dem, was man als wahr empfindet. Der Regenbogen sortiert uns alle, und wir suchen das Gold vor unserer Türschwelle. Mein Garten ist ein Teil meiner selbst geworden, meine linke Hand, gemacht von meiner rechten unter dem Licht des Tages. Was gäbe ich darum, bei Mondlicht darin zu arbeiten, ihn zu einem Museum zu machen. Er ist klein, aber man kann bestrebt sein, die Atmosphäre des Ortes «in wenig Worte gefasst» (Alexander Pope) auszudrücken. Wenn das Wenige fesselnd geschrieben ist, spielt Grösse keine Rolle. Die Luft wird das ganze Malen übernehmen. Das Leben kann sich blitzartig von Tableaux zu Tableaux bewegen, scheint sich selbst zu vervollständigen in einem Kontinuum von Verschiebung und Konzentration. Aber dann tauchen Vollendungen auf und weichen wieder zurück. Wie der Puls des Meerwassers, oder durchs Herz pulsierendes Blut, wir lieben und verlieren, wir erzeugen Schönheit, und alle Blumen welken dahin.

11. Jedes Feld, das man bebaut, ist Eden, und auch Gärten sind diese Liebe. Bei der Bearbeitung beider feiern wir die Erde und alles das, was sie je geborgen, was sie gegeben hat und geben wird, immer wieder, und wir sollen weise mit unserer Obhut sein. Aus Gärten können wir so viele mutige Dinge machen – wir können die Wildheit der Welt an das Strenge grenzen lassen, um die Herausforderung beider besser zu verstärken. Wir können die kleinsten Dinge gross erscheinen lassen, Blau und Weiss mengen, Kurven geradebiegen, Säulen flach machen, aus alten Formen neue machen, Laub auf Laub werfen (die Klet-

terpflanze kann man über den Busch wachsen lassen, und Kletterpflanzen können von Bäumen fallen, so dass sie nicht mehr sind als Gitterwerk). Wir können Lilien über Steinen pflanzen und am Rand des Wassers Rosen haben, das Stachlige mit dem Glatten mischen, wilde Hyazinthen unter Heidelbeeren zum Blühen bringen. Wir können Gärten anlegen, wo alle Verschiedenheiten vermengt sind, wo das Essbare blühen darf und die Blüte als Nahrung auf den Tisch kommt. Es ist eine Kunst, eine wunderbare Kunst, durchaus so strahlend wie irgendein Produkt aus dem Atelier. Obwohl Wälder, Wiesen und Gewässer grosse Vollendungen darstellen können, ist die Kunst der Gärtnerei kaum eine des Nacheiferns. Genauso wie in der Malerei und der Poesie wird man besser, je älter man wird.

12. *Nur durch das Tätigsein kann man sich Eden nähern, und kein noch so stürmisches Wetter des Herzens oder des Himmels wird einen davon abhalten. Tatsächlich mag all solcher Schmerz nichts als Nahrung sein.*

(Übersetzung: Udo Breger)

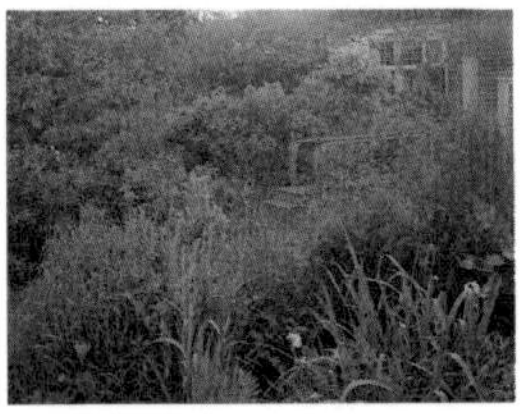

CUMULUS

. . FROM AMERICA

Our column "Cumulus" presents thoughts, personal perspectives and notable encounters, not in the sense of professional art criticism, but rather personal statements of professional endeavor. In each issue of Parkett "cumulus clouds" float in from America and Europe to all those interested in art.

Our contributors to this issue are Gary Garrels, a curator who has recently become Director of Programs of the Dia Art Foundation's new exhibition space at 22nd Street in New York, and Wolfgang Drechsler, curator at the Museum of Modern Art in Vienna.

GARY GARRELS

If there is a sense of frustration here, there also is hope. America still yearns to believe in promise, to realize a freedom of spirit, if not salvation, through good deeds and material bounty. "Materialism" and "transcendentalism" are nineteenth-century words but we cannot escape them. Whitman and Emerson are the cultural fathers of this distinctly American outlook and philosophy. Judd and Flavin are among its most recent progeny and probably its last potent

manifestations, thinking that the new can be unadorned and better, relying on self-experience and the innate qualities of materials to carry them forward.

The last eight years have been difficult ones. (I speak in advance of the end of the Reagan era, but it is an end we can feel, like a spring thaw when one goes outside without a coat and finds it is still cold despite the appearance of the sun.) Perhaps we are wiser, tempered by an increment of history with a weight we feel, lived and not just perceived as a prepared text. There is a sense of the human condition bounded by the past, constrained by what has been learned rather than by what is unknown. Perhaps this explains in part our fascination now with Europe.

How precise can we be in our understanding of Beuys? His words and objects are filled with the ballast of World War II, the last war fought in Europe but only its latest. Layers of felt are stacked like a geology of desire and loss, cut by humanity's ravaging past. The inscription which accompanies the iron blocks of the DOUBLE FOND reads: "The great weight of these iron blocks makes it more difficult for me to escape from this hell."

The myth of America since its discovery by European explorers has been that of the Edenic garden. We escape time not by its endless repetition but by its absence. The war did not physically touch us; cities and countryside remain unscarred. We did not feel the pain so directly. And again Europeans came to America as refuge. Mondrian was made welcome, provided a home (here acknowledgement, now eulogy to Harry Holtzman), BROADWAY BOOGIE-WOOGIE, his legacy, our accolade, a celebration of the openness and energy, the directness of America, embodied by New York. It is a crucial painting for us.

BROADWAY BOOGIE-WOOGIE hangs in a gallery at The Museum of Modern Art devoted to Mondrian, enshrined as an icon of Modernism. What does it mean to look at a painting repeatedly? One of the possibilities of living in New York is to have a membership card to The Museum of Modern Art, to walk in and spend time with one picture and then to leave, and to do this as often as one wants. But this, too, is a weight, sometimes it seems too much for the institution, if not for us, to bear.

The state of museums as form-givers to the present, rather than just caretakers, is generally disappointing both in Europe and America, but more so in America. We must find ways to get beyond convenient understanding and stagnant complacency. The task it seems to me is to be no less responsible than the artists who teach us something we did not know before.

Back to the frontier. The canyons grow deeper here; sometimes the darkness is so deep the romance flickers and is gone. New York's grid until recently was open, holes and cracks as much a part of its structure as its relentlessness. These now are almost filled in, swollen shut. It is a critical if not dangerous situation. To survive is to be successful. The "official" closing of the American frontier was declared in 1890 by Frederick Jackson Turner. It seems now the wave has returned to the shore, a one-hundred-year journey to close the urban frontier. Warhol articulates all sides of this landscape if one bothers to get past the words. Fifteen minutes is less adequate now than it was twenty years ago. We cannot avoid a reckoning with the consequences of civilization, history made rather than immanent, but still we do not believe it is closed.

Wenn hierzulande ein Gefühl der Frustration in der Luft liegt, so gibt es doch auch Anlass zur Hoffnung. Amerika glaubt noch immer gerne daran, dass geistige Freiheit, wenn nicht gar das Seelenheil, durch gute Taten und materielle Grosszügigkeit zu verwirklichen seien. «Materialismus» und «Transzendentalismus» sind Begriffe des 19. Jahrhunderts, aber wir können uns trotzdem nicht von ihnen lossagen. Whitman und Emerson sind die geistigen Väter dieser typisch amerikanischen Haltung und

GARY GARRELS

Anschauung. Zu ihren jüngsten Vertretern gehören Judd und Flavin, mit denen sich diese Sicht wahrscheinlich zum letzten Mal auf überzeugende Weise manifestiert. Sie glauben, dass das Neue ungeschmückt und besser sein könne, weil sie ganz auf ihre eigene Erfahrung und die vorgegebenen Qualitäten des Materials setzen.

Die letzten acht Jahre waren schwierig. (Ich sage dies im Hinblick auf das Ende der Reagan-Ära – doch angesichts dieses Endes erleben wir Ähnliches wie bei Tauwetter im Frühling, wenn wir ohne Mantel hinausgehen und, obwohl die Sonne sichtbar ist, noch immer Kälte empfinden.) Vielleicht sind wir klüger geworden, gemässigt durch einen Zuwachs an Geschichte, deren Last wir fühlen, weil sie gelebt wurde und nicht bloss verstanden wie ein vorbereiteter Text. Wir spüren, dass unser Sein durch die Vergan-

In der Rubrik «Cumulus» sollen Meinungen, persönliche Rückblicke, denkwürdige Begegnungen rapportiert werden – nicht im Sinne einer professionellen Kunstkritik, sondern als persönliche Darstellung einer berufsmässigen Auseinandersetzung. In jeder Ausgabe von Parkett peilt eine «Cumulus»-Wolke aus Amerika und eine aus Europa den interessierten Kunstfreund an.

Die Beiträge dieser Ausgabe stammen von Gary Garrels, Kurator und Director of Programs der neu eröffneten Ausstellungsräume der Dia Art Foundation an New Yorks 22. Strasse, und Wolfgang Drechsler, Kurator am Museum moderner Kunst in Wien.

genheit begrenzt wird und dass wir heute durch das Gelernte viel mehr eingeschränkt sind als früher durch das Unbekannte. Möglicherweise liegt darin zum Teil unsere Faszination für Europa.

Wie genau können wir Beuys verstehen? Seine Worte und Objekte sind angefüllt mit dem Ballast des Zweiten Weltkrieges, dem jüngsten der vielen in Europa ausgetragenen Kriege. Filzschichten liegen gleich einer Geologie von Sehnsucht und Verlust übereinander, durch die zerstörerische Vergangenheit der Menschheit entzweigeschnitten. Der Merksatz zu den eisernen Blöcken des DOUBLE FOND lautet: «Die Eisenklötze sind deshalb so schwer, dass ich mich nicht leichtfertig aus dieser Hölle entferne.»

Seit seiner Entdeckung durch europäische Forschungsreisende haftet Amerika der Mythos vom Garten Eden an. Durch die Abwesenheit des Zeitrades und nicht durch sein endloses Weiterdrehen werden wir uns befreien. Der Krieg hat uns nicht physisch betroffen; unsere Städte und Landschaften tragen keine Narben. Wir haben den Schmerz nicht so direkt zu spüren bekommen. Und wieder suchten die Europäer Amerika als Zufluchtsort auf. Mondrian wurde willkommen geheissen, man bot ihm ein Heim (an dieser Stelle gebührt Harry Holtzman Anerkennung). Mit seinem Vermächtnis, dem BROADWAY-BOOGIE-WOOGIE, schenkte Mondrian uns ein Loblied auf die Offenheit und Energie, auf die Direktheit Amerikas, die von New York verkörpert wird. Es ist ein entscheidendes Bild für uns.

Der BROADWAY-BOOGIE-WOOGIE hängt in einer Mondrian gewidmeten Abteilung des Museums of Modern Art und wird gleich einer Ikone des Modernismus verwahrt. Was bedeutet es nun, ein Bild immer wieder zu betrachten? Eine der Möglichkeiten, die das Leben in New York bietet, besteht darin, Besitzer einer Mitgliedkarte des Museum of Modern Art zu werden, dorthin zu gehen, eine Weile vor einem Bild zu verbringen, um dann wieder zu gehen. Und das kann man tun, sooft es einem gefällt. Aber auch dies ist eine Last, und zuweilen macht es den Anschein, als ob es zuviel würde – vielleicht nicht für uns, doch zumindest für die Institution.

Die Rolle der Museen als Formgeber der Gegenwart und nicht bloss als Verwalter ist im allgemeinen enttäuschend, sowohl in Europa als auch – hier jedoch in vermehrtem Masse – in Amerika. Wir müssen Mittel und Wege finden, die über bequeme Erkenntnisse und träge Selbstzufriedenheit hinausführen. Meiner Meinung nach wäre es unsere Aufgabe, nicht weniger Verantwortung zu tragen als die Künstler, die uns etwas lehren, das wir vorher nicht wussten.

Back to the frontier. Die Abgründe unserer Cañons werden immer tiefer, und zuweilen wird die Dunkelheit so gross, dass alle Romantik ins Wanken gerät und schliesslich ganz verschwindet. New Yorks Rasterplan war bis vor kurzem noch offen und die Schlupflöcher und Ritzen darin genauso Teil seiner Struktur wie ein unbarmherziger Druck. Diese Löcher sind mittlerweile aber fast ausgefüllt und zugeschwollen. Wir befinden uns in einer kritischen, ja gefährlichen Situation. Überleben heisst erfolgreich sein. «Offiziell» wurde die amerikanische Siedlungsgrenze im Jahre 1890 von Frederick Jackson Turner für geschlossen erklärt. Nun scheint die Welle nach einer hundert Jahre dauernden Reise endlich ans Ufer zurückgekommen zu sein. Der verbliebene Raum ist aufgefüllt. Warhol beleuchtet alle Seiten dieser geographischen und psychologischen Landschaft, falls man sich die Mühe macht, hinter seine Worte zu kommen. Fünfzehn Minuten sind heute weniger angemessen als vor zwanzig Jahren. Es wird unvermeidlich sein, dass wir uns für die Konsequenzen der Zivilisation verantworten müssen; Geschichte ist nicht gottgegeben – wir haben sie gemacht. Aber wir wollen noch immer nicht glauben, dass die Grenze erreicht ist.

CUMULUS

... VON EUROPA

WOLFGANG DRECHSLER

Nach Jahrzehnten des Unbeachtetseins darf sich die österreichische Kunstszene seit einigen Jahren zunehmender Aufmerksamkeit erfreuen. Von Venedig über Wien bis Paris und New York – Grossausstellungen österreichischer Kunst und Kultur der Jahrhundertwende wurden zu viel bejubelten Publikumsmagneten. Die internationalen Auktionshäuser melden Versteigerungsrekorde für Arbeiten von Klimt und Schiele – und auch die zweite und dritte Künstlergarnitur erzielte bei einer Sonderauktion in London Rekordpreise, die noch vor kurzem für völlig unrealistisch gehalten wurden (und die auch heute noch in Österreich selbst kaum zu erzielen wären). Doch nicht nur «Wien um 1900» hat eine Aufwertung erfahren, die internationalen Medien und Ausstellungsmacher entdecken auch immer öfter die österreichische Kunst der Gegenwart. Ausstellungen wie «Junge Künstler in Österreich» (Luzern, Bonn, 1982), «Arte austriaca 1960/84» (Bologna 1984), «Weltpunkt Wien» (Strassburg 1985), um nur einige zu nennen, mussten zwar noch von Österreichern initiiert und zum Teil im Zuge von Austauschgeschäften realisiert werden, genauso wie die Retrospektiven Attersees (Frankfurt, Aarau, Aachen, Wilhelmshaven 1983), Lassnigs (Düsseldorf, Nürnberg 1985), Brus' (München, Düsseldorf 1986) und Kocherscheidts (Karlsruhe, Eindhoven 1988). Parallel dazu gab es aber auch ein selbständiges Umdenken der jenseits der Grenze beheimateten Museumsleute, wie etwa die Ausstellungen «Körperzeichen. Österreich» (Winterthur 1982), Rainer (München, Bern 1977, Berlin, Baden-Baden, Bonn 1980/81), Nitsch, Brus (Eindhoven 1983, 1984), «Rennweg», (Turin 1985) und Pichler (Frankfurt 1987) beweisen. Für die nähere Zukunft sind weitere Expositionen geplant, so in Lausanne und Düsseldorf. Auch die Kunstzeitschriften haben sich bereits massiv des Themas angenommen, z.B. «art» (1986) und jüngst erst «Kunstforum». In fast jeder grösseren Überblicksausstellung sind heute Österreicher vertreten, auf den Kunstmessen sind Österreichs Galerien nicht zu übersehen. (Die Exporthilfe, die von der Bundeswirtschaftskammer jedem Messeteilnehmer im Ausland gewährt wird, kommt auch Kunsthändlern zugute und hat sich als eine der besten Arten der Kunstsubvention erwiesen.)

Alles scheint in Ordnung. Auch die Museen melden steigende Besucherzahlen (in letzter Zeit wieder etwas rückläufig), die Bundesregierung hat kürzlich ein Sonderfinanzierungsprogramm für die dringendsten Sanierungsmassnahmen der Bundesmuseen beschlossen (allerdings erst nachdem einige Schäden, deren mögliches Auftreten seit etlichen Jahren gemeldet wurde, tatsächlich entstanden sind), bei der von den Politikern und Medien sogenannten «Jahrhundertchance» eines neuen Museumszentrums wurde in den letzten Wochen die erste Phase des Architektenwettbewerbs abgeschlossen. (Wie das Ganze dann bezahlt werden kann, fragt sich jedoch nicht nur der Finanzminister, der es sich jedenfalls, wie er öffentlich bekundete, nicht vorstellen kann.)

Ist somit wirklich alles in Ordnung? Die zunehmende Akzeptanz der österreichischen Kunst im Ausland ist sicherlich begrüssenswert, sie ist notwendig und war längst fällig. Sie birgt aber auch Gefahren in sich, und zwar für die österreichische Kunstszene selbst. Die verstärkte Aufmerksamkeit von aussen könnte den hier ohnehin vorhandenen Hang zu einer austrozentrischen Haltung noch zementieren. Der Nationalstolz erhält neue Nahrung, der Blick über die engen Grenzen bleibt weiter getrübt. (Nicht zufällig trägt der Österreich gewidmete Band des Kunstforums den Titel «Insel Austria».) Wie alles in Österreich hat auch dies seine Tradition. Die rege und erfolgreiche Sammeltätigkeit des Kaiserhauses erfuhr spätestens in der Mitte des 19. Jahrhunderts eine beträchtliche Einschränkung. Gerade zu der Zeit, in der diese Kunstsammlungen in Form des Kunsthistorischen Museums eine neue, der Öffentlichkeit zugängliche Heimstadt gefunden haben, wurde der Gegenwartskunst, besonders der internationalen, wenig Gegenliebe entgegengebracht. Diese offizielle Ignoranz stand

mit der privaten in Einklang, auch die Privatsammlungen orientierten sich weitgehend an der Vergangenheit, besonders der eigenen. Unzufrieden mit dieser Situation waren eigentlich nur einige wenige Künstler, was 1897 mit zur Gründung der Wiener Secession geführt hat. Doch auch deren Öffnungsversuchen war nur geringer Erfolg beschieden. Aus den grossen internationalen Secessions-Ausstellungen fanden nur wenige Werke ausländischer Künstler ihren Weg in staatliche Sammlungen. Und dann überwiegend nur deshalb, weil sie von der Secession dem Staat geschenkt wurden (Van Gogh, Segantini), um dadurch den Aufbau einer modernen Sammlung zu erzwingen. Auch von privater Seite wurde nur wenig gekauft, am meisten noch vom gebildeten Grossbürgertum jüdischer Herkunft.

So kann es nicht verwundern, dass Werke der internationalen klassischen Moderne in Österreich kaum anzutreffen sind. Schenkungen und Leihgaben, von denen die amerikanischen und auch schweizerischen Museen (die ja überwiegend auch nicht selbst rechtzeitig gekauft haben) heute einen Teil ihres Ruhms und ihrer Anziehungskraft beziehen, fehlen. Spätestens 1938 haben diese Werke (meist zusammen mit ihren Besitzern) Österreich verlassen müssen. Doch die historische Dimension, die zwei Weltkriege und die ökonomisch sicherlich nicht leichte Zeit dazwischen, erklärt noch nicht alles. Auch Deutschland war davon unmittelbar betroffen, und trotzdem konnten die Kämpfer gegen die «Entartete Kunst» in den dortigen Museen wesentlich reichere Feldzüge starten als bei uns. (Eine vorzügliche Ausstellungsserie mit gutrecherchierten Katalogen bringt dies gerade jetzt in Düsseldorf wieder in Erinnerung.) Der Zyniker würde sagen, wir haben Glück gehabt, was man nicht hat, kann einem auch nicht genommen werden.

Aber auch nach dem Krieg, als die Deutschen versuchten, die brutal geschlagenen Lücken wieder zu schliessen, gab es in Österreich lange fast kein Interesse. Erst 1962 wurde das Museum des 20. Jahrhunderts eröffnet und dessen Leiter, Werner Hofmann, ein einigermassen ausreichendes Budget zur Verfügung gestellt (zumindest in den ersten Jahren, bald musste er drastische Kürzungen in Kauf nehmen), womit um die wenigen schon vorhandenen Werke eine kleine, aber zum überwiegenden Teil exzellente Sammlung aufgebaut werden konnte. Mangelndes Geld schuf aber in der Folge neue Lücken, die Sammlung wuchs – gerade im internationalen Bereich – nur in kleinen Schritten, was allerdings die Öffentlichkeit und die zuständigen Politiker nicht weiter gestört hat. Heute noch ist der Kreis der wirklich Interessierten äusserst klein. Eine Aktion wie in Basel, wo die Bevölkerung für den Ankauf einiger Werke Picassos votiert hat, wäre in Wien unmöglich. Erfolgversprechender wäre ein Volksbegehren zur Abschaffung der Museen moderner Kunst, für das Kunsthistorische wären eher Stimmen zu bekommen, es gehört zumindest zum Bildungsgut, auch wenn man selten hingeht. Denn die erfreulichen Besucherzahlen sind kaum auf ein gestiegenes Interesse der Österreicher an bildender Kunst zurückzuführen, sondern (auch wenn konkrete Statistiken fehlen, wird jeder Museumskassier dies bestätigen können) auf das Anwachsen des Städtetourismus. So war es auch nicht verwunderlich, dass fast ausschliesslich die Wiener Hoteliervereinigung gegen die wegen Personalmangels für den heurigen Winter notwendige, zum Teil kräftige Kürzung der Öffnungszeiten bei einigen Museen protestiert hat. (Diese Vereinigung hat auch schon durch eine Finanzspritze den bereits für Herbst – die Hauptsaison der Kunsttouristen – drohenden Kollaps aufgeschoben.)

Das gestörte Verhältnis des Österreichers zur internationalen Moderne kann auch anhand des Engagements des Ehepaares Ludwig studiert werden. Anfänglich (1978/79) wurden die Leihgaben der deutschen Grosssammler und die damit verbundene Erweiterung des Museums des 20. Jahrhunderts zum Museum moderner Kunst mit dem Haupthaus im Palais Liechtenstein von den Medien überwiegend freudig begrüsst. Mit der Zeit mehrten sich aber die negativen Stimmen, besonders als es um die – dann doch realisierte – Ludwig-Stiftung gegangen ist. Dabei wurde nicht nur die ausländische Einmischung in österreichische Angelegenheiten angegriffen (die Hälfte der Stiftungsratsmitglieder wird von den Ludwigs nominiert, was nur von Vorteil sein kann, denn ein Franz Meyer, der ehemalige Direktor des Basler Kunstmuseums, dürfte doch etwas mehr Ahnung vom internationalen Kunstgeschehen haben als noch so verdienstvolle österreichische Minister und Sektionschefs), sondern auch die durch Ludwig nach Wien gekommenen Kunstwerke selbst. So wurde in der auflagenstärksten Tageszeitung die Frage gestellt, was z.B. die amerikanische Pop-Art mit Österreich zu tun haben sollte, besser wäre es doch, sich auf die österreichische Kunst der Jahrhundertwende zu konzentrieren. Dabei kommt die Ludwig-Stiftung nicht nur den Museen zugute, sondern auch indirekt der gesamten Kunstszene. Durch sie werden die jährlich für Ankäufe zur Verfügung stehenden Mittel mehr als verdoppelt, was im Vergleich zur deutschen, schweizerischen oder französischen Situation immer noch gering ist. Ein grosser Teil davon fliesst in die öster-

reichischen Galerien, die dadurch auch ermuntert werden, mehr internationale Kunst zu zeigen. Denn die privaten Käufer, sofern es sie grösseren Kalibers überhaupt gibt, bevorzugen weiterhin vorwiegend heimische Kost. Eine Ausstellung Rainers, Attersees oder Anzingers ist heute für eine Galerie keinerlei Risiko, der finanzielle Erfolg ist garantiert. Anders ist die Situation etwa bei Mario Merz, Disler oder Büttner, auch wenn deren Preise denen der obengenannten entsprechen oder sogar darunter liegen. Hier müssen Verkäufe ins Ausland (vor allem an den Kunstmessen) helfen, ehrgeizigere Programme und Informationsarbeit zu finanzieren.

Die Situation im öffentlichen Ausstellungswesen ist ähnlich. Eine umfassende Retrospektive Gerhard Richters hatte wesentlich weniger Besucher als die Maria Lassnigs, Harald Szeemanns Wiederaufführung seiner Zürcher Skulpturenausstellung nur etwas mehr als die Hälfte von «Hacken im Eis», einer Gruppenausstellung von fünf jungen österreichischen Malern, die zur selben Zeit gezeigt worden ist.

Das unterschiedliche Interesse an heimischer und fremder Kunst hat sich auch jüngst wieder gezeigt. Martin Disler wurde vom Museum moderner Kunst eingeladen, eine Ausstellung im barokken Festsaal des Palais Liechtenstein zu realisieren. Nach langen Diskussionen und Überlegungen entschied er sich, erstmals ausschliesslich plastische Arbeiten zu zeigen, wobei die Auseinandersetzung mit der übernommenen Aufgabe die Entwicklung dieser Plastiken nicht unwesentlich mitbestimmt hat. Resultat war wirklich Neues und zwar zum Teil aus der Wiener Situation Entwickeltes. Pressekonferenz wie Vernissage waren dann nicht nur für den Künstler, sondern auch für mich, als dem für die Ausstellung Verantwortlichen, eine grosse Enttäuschung. Wenig Journalisten, wenig Besucher (die aus dem Ausland angereisten und die heimischen hielten sich beinahe die Waage). Manche Journalisten sind dann später gekommen, die Presseberichte sind gar nicht so schlecht, nur der staatliche Monopolbetrieb ORF hat weder im Hörfunk noch im Fernsehen darüber berichtet. Gerade dort sitzen aber Kritiker, die dem Museum mangelnde internationale Ausstellungstätigkeit vorwerfen. Auch die Galeristen und Galeristinnen, die ins selbe Horn stossen, haben diese Ausstellung nicht gesehen. (Die Vorwürfe sind im erwähnten Band des Kunstforums nachzulesen.) Einige Tage später wurde die Ausstellung «Hans Hollein» eröffnet – die Kunstszene war fast vollständig versammelt, der Aufwand des ORF war dementsprechend. Nicht zufällig ist die wichtigste Neuerung des gerade im TV eingeführten neuen Programmschemas ein täglicher Gesellschaftsspiegel. Dafür wurde die aktuelle Kulturberichterstattung am anderen Kanal durch die Sportnachrichten konkurrenziert und die einzige manchmal unbequeme und kontroverse Sendung, der Club 2, in die spätere Nacht verschoben und personell entschärft.

Die engagierte Arbeit für die internationale moderne Kunst wird in Österreich mit Frustrationen bezahlt. Und trotzdem lebt die Szene. Zwar haben die etablierten Galerien gleichsam eine Aufnahmesperre verhängt, doch fast monatlich werden neue eröffnet, noch mutige und auch dem Fremden aufgeschlossene. Für den Interessierten wird es bald schwierig, den Überblick zu bewahren. Doch nur diese Konfrontation und der intensive Kontakt zur internationalen Kunstszene, wie er sich in solchen Projekten wie in dem mit Martin Disler niederschlägt, helfen die tägliche Ignoranz und Selbstbeweihräucherung zu ertragen.

After having been ignored for decades, the Austrian art scene has picked up considerably in the past few years. From Venice via Vienna to Paris and New York – megashows of Austrian art and culture have drawn record crowds and won international acclaim. Auction houses report record sales of works by Klimt and Schiele. At a special auction in London, second and third rate paintings went for prices that had till then been considered utterly unrealistic (and

WOLFGANG DRECHSLER

probably still are in Austria). Not only has "Vienna in 1900" been upvalued, the international media and exhibition makers have also discovered Austria's contemporary artists. It is true that exhibitions like "Junge Künstler in Österreich" (Luzern, Bonn, 1982), "Arte austriaca 1960/84" (Bologna, 1984) and "Weltpunkt Wien" (Strassburg, 1985), to name only a few, were initiated by Austrians and in some cases made possible through exchange agreements, such as the retrospectives of work by Attersee (Frankfurt, Aarau, Aachen, Wilhelmshaven, 1983), Lassnig (Düsseldorf, Nuremberg, 1985), Brus (Munich, Düsseldorf, 1986) and Kocherscheidt (Karlsruhe, Eindhoven, 1988). However, there has also been an independent upsurge of curatorial interest beyond the borders of Austria, as

evidenced by such events as "Körperzeichen. Österreich" (Winterthur, 1982), Rainer (Munich, Bern, 1977; Berlin, Baden-Baden, Bonn, 1980/81), Nitsch, Brus (Eindhoven, 1983, 1984), "Rennweg", (Turin, 1985) and Pichler (Frankfurt, 1987). And more exhibitions are forthcoming, for instance, in Lausanne and Düsseldorf. Austria's revival is reflected in art magazines as well, e.g. "art" (1986) and just recently "Kunstforum". Virtually every major survey exhibition today includes Austrian artists and Austrian galleries are not to be overlooked at art fairs. (The federal government provides export funding for anyone who participates in foreign fairs, including art fairs, which has turned out to be an excellent means of subsidizing art.)

Everything seems to be in order. On the whole museum attendance is increasing despite a slight drop in numbers at the moment; the federal government has just set up a special program to finance the most urgent repairs of the country's museums (but only after threats of serious damage, which have been regularly reported for years, had finally taken their toll); and an architectural competition is underway for a new museum complex or, as the media and politicians call it, the "chance of the century." (A lot of people are wondering how the whole thing is supposed to be financed including the minister of finance; he certainly doesn't know, as he has publicly stated himself.)

So is everything really in order? Growing acceptance of Austrian art abroad is certainly encouraging; it is necessary and long overdue. But it also holds certain dangers, especially for the Austrian art scene itself. It could aggravate the existing inclination towards an austro-centric attitude. It could feed national pride and exacerbate the murky view across narrow borders. (Interestingly enough, the issue of "Kunstforum" on Austrian art has been titled "Insel [Island] Austria.")

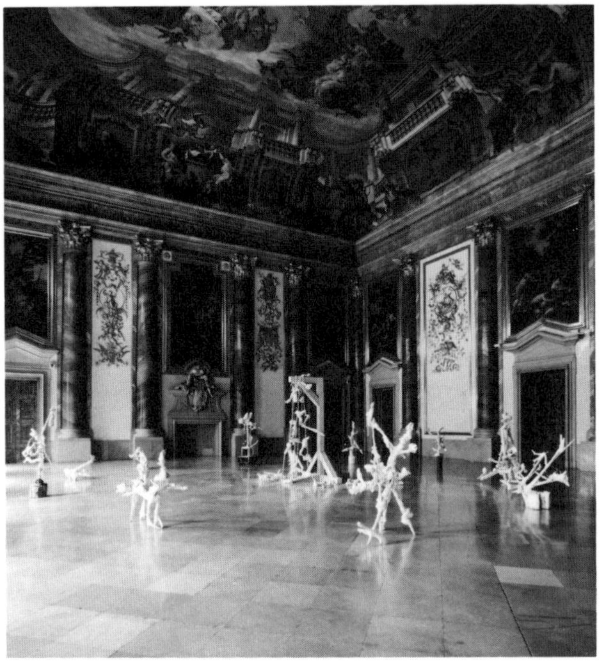

MARTIN DISLER, DAS GEDRÄNGE DER GÖTTER, DER WUCHER DES MENSCHEN / *SCRAMBLING GODS, MUSHROOMING MAN, 1987,* MUSEUM FÜR MODERNE KUNST, PALAIS LICHTENSTEIN WIEN.

Like everything else in Austria, this attitude rests on tradition. Austrian emperors were able to give uncontrolled vent to their keen and successful interest in collecting until well into the 19th century. Just at the time when these collections were made accessible to the public through the newly instituted art museum, there was precious little love left over for contemporary and especially international art. Official and private ignorance went hand in hand, since the attention of private collectors was also focused on the past, their own in particular. The only people dissatisfied with this situation were a few artists, who founded the Viennese Secession in 1897. Their efforts to broaden horizons were only moderately successful. Very few works by foreign artists made their way from the Secession's international exhibitions into the state collections, and those that did were for the most part donated by the Secession (Van Gogh, Segantini) in an attempt to force the museum to build up a collection of modern art. Nor did private collectors do much buying with the exception of the cultivated Jewish bourgeoisie.

It is no wonder, therefore, that international classical modern art is poorly represented in Austria's museums. Besides, they did not receive the donations and loans which have significantly enhanced the fame and appeal of American and Swiss museums today (most of which also failed to buy in time). By 1938 at the latest these works (most of them with their owners) had to leave Austria. However, the blame does not rest only on historical considerations, i.e. the two world wars and the weak economy between them. Germany was, after all, directly affected and yet the enemies of "degenerate art" in Germany managed to launch considerably more successful campaigns in German museums. (This is borne

out by a series of excellent shows with well-researched catalogs that has been mounted in Düsseldorf.) Cynics would say that we were lucky; you can't be deprived of something you never had.

But after the war as well, when the Germans tried to fill the viciously gaping holes, Austria showed a singular lack of interest. The Museum of the 20th Century was not opened until 1962 with a more or less adequate budget for its director, Werner Hofmann – at least in the early years. (He later had to make do with drastic cutbacks.) Hofmann managed to build up a small but excellent collection around the few works that had already been acquired. Lack of funding has now created new gaps and the collection, particularly of international work, has only grown in small steps – not that this seems to bother the public or the responsible politicians. The circle of genuinely interested people is still extremely small. The public in Basel voted to appropriate funds for the purchase of works by Picasso. This would have been impossible in Austria. A referendum to close down the museums of modern art would probably have a greater chance of success; Austrians would at most vote for museums of old art, which do, after all, belong to their cultural heritage even if they rarely go to them. The gratifying increase in museum goers is not due to a growing interest in art among Austrians but rather to the rise in foreign tourists (as any museum cashier will tell you although there are no statistics on the subject). And naturally, only the Viennese Hotel Association protested when it was announced that some of the museums would have to cut down visiting hours this winter because of a shortage in personnel. (This association also provided the financial shot in the arm to ward off impending collapse this fall, i.e. high season for art tourists.)

The poor attitude of the Austrians towards international modern art is further demonstrated by their reception of the Ludwigs. Originally (1978/79), the Ludwig loans and the attendant extension of the Museum of the 20th Century to a museum of modern art with headquarters in the Palais Liechtenstein was enthusiastically welcomed by the media. But gradually a negative chorus rose in crescendo against the idea of a Ludwig Foundation. The media attacked not only what they considered foreign interference in domestic affairs, but even the artworks brought to Austria by the Ludwigs. (Half of the foundation's board was nominated by the Ludwigs, which is all too the good, since a man like Franz Meyer, former director of the Museum of Art in Basel, may just possibly be better informed about developments in international art than the most illustrious Austrian ministers and secretaries.) The country's biggest daily wanted to know, for instance, what American pop-art has to do with Austria, declaring that it would be better to concentrate on fin-de-siècle Austrian art. No one seems to appreciate the fact that the Ludwig Foundation not only benefits museums but, indirectly, the entire art scene through funds that more than double the annual acquisitions budget (although it still can't compete with the situation in Germany, Switzerland or France). A major portion goes to Austrian galleries, giving them the incentive to show more international art. Private buyers, inasmuch as there are any big ones left, still prefer domestic fare. There is no risk involved in mounting a Rainer, Attersee or Anzinger exhibition; financial success is assured. Not so when Mario Merz, Disler or Büttner are on view, even though their works go for the same or even lower prices. Sales abroad (especially at art fairs) have to help finance more ambitious programs and promotion.

The situation in public art institutions is similar. A comprehensive Gerhard Richter retrospective did not attract nearly as many visitors as the Maria Lassnig show and Harald Szeemann's reconstruction of his Zurich sculpture exhibition attracted little more than half as many people as "Hacken im Eis" ("Hacking the Ice"), a group show of five young Austrian painters on view at the same time.

The disparity between interest in local and foreign art was recently underscored once again. The Museum of Modern Art had invited Martin Disler to mount an exhibition in the baroque ballroom of the Palais Liechtenstein. After considerable discussion and forethought, he finally decided to show only sculptures, for the first time. His involvement with the given situation exerted no small influence on their development, yielding entirely new work and, in some cases, specific responses to the situation in Vienna. The press conference as well as the opening were a great disappointment to the artist and to me as curator of the exhibition. Few journalists, few visitors (there were hardly more local people than there were visitors from abroad). Some journalists did show up later and press coverage was not bad at all. Only ORF, the state radio and television monopoly, serenely ignored the show. Yet ORF voices are the loudest in criticism of the museum for its neglect of international exhibitions. Gallery owners, who voice the same complaint, did not even attend the show. (The accusations can be studied in full in the above-mentioned issue of "Kunstforum"). A few days later at the opening of the "Hans Hollein" exhibition, the entire art world showed up and ORF naturally rose to the occasion. It is no accident that a daily social mirror happens to be the most important innovation in the new t.v. program that has just been announced. Coverage of cultural events on the other channel now has to compete with sport news, while Club 2, the only critical and controversial cultural program, has been relegated to a late evening hour with tempered moderation.

In Austria, commitment to international modern art is rewarded with frustration (no

wonder Werner Hofmann escaped to Hamburg after major pioneering achievements here). Nonetheless, the art scene is very much alive. Despite a virtual boycott imposed by the established galleries, there is hope in the buoyant new galleries opening almost monthly – so many, in fact, that it is almost impossible to keep track of them. But this kind of confrontation and in-depth contact with the international art scene (the Martin Disler project is a case in point) is the only means of surviving the daily confrontation with rampant ignorance and lofty conceit.

(Translation: Catherine Schelbert)

BALKON

NANCY PRINCENTHAL

THE WHITE CUBE DISSOLVES

A little over ten years ago, Brian O'Doherty wrote a series of essays for *Artforum* called "Inside the White Cube." These essays have recently been published in book form, providing a happy occasion for reconsidering his ideas about the ideology of exhibition spaces and practices, and for reflecting on how these conditions have changed since 1976.

Broadly addressing the history of modernism and its dénouement, O'Doherty suggested that the flattening of pictorial space was bound in an ultimately reciprocal relationship to the purification of the exhibition space. "We have reached a point where we see not the art but the *space* first," he wrote. "The mystique of the shallow plane... had been transferred to the context of art." In the Minimal and Conceptual art of the sixties and seventies, O'Doherty saw potent challenges to the politics of the gallery system – challenges that, in a 1986 afterword, he finds have proven abortive. As he sees it (and it's hard to argue with him), "the gallery space has again become the unchallenged arena of discourse."

But that's not the end of the story; the more things stay the same, the more they change. And even within the timeframe of O'Doherty's remarkably fresh and bountifully perceptive tale, there were plot developments – geographical rather than architectural – that he chose not to follow. By the late seventies, Soho, a community whose appeal was symbolic as well as economic, had indisputably become the "white cube"'s international capital. Originally zoned for light manufacturing, Soho stood for *work*, for the studio/residence of a demarginalized artist and the consumption of a deluxurified product. Miscellaneous goods from local textile wholesale houses and from office supply stores, along with construction materials and hardware, became a part of the art made there, contributing to its argument by association. Similarly, the galleries that located in Soho took (temporary) cover under the aegis

NANCY PRINCENTHAL is a free-lance writer living in New York and an associate editor of "The Print Collector's Newsletter."

of light industry. If art could not escape commerce altogether in the deserts of the southwest or in the alternative institutions of the outer boroughs, it need not restrict itself to the uptown grazing grounds of the rich.

The shift of the commercial network to the East Village involved many things, some paradoxical; one of them was a rejection of the manufacturing esthetic. Art was not work, it was play (the Fun Gallery, now defunct). The artist's place was not under a hardhat on the scaffolds of an enlightened culture, it was back in the margins of society, expressing, perhaps cynically, perhaps not, personal visions and esthetic cogitations. Again, living and exhibiting spaces were neighbors, alongside a developed entertainment sector – a parody of prewar Europe's convivial cabarets and cramped ateliers, working class in locale if nothing else. While the nonfigurative work of the early Soho years valued above all the articulation of space (it is worth recalling that the leitmotif, or maybe the central narrative, of the seventies was real estate speculation), the work associated with the East Village favored local color and street smarts, cultural maneuvering rather than spatial manipulation.

Now, evidently, that's over too. Many East Village galleries have moved to Soho, where the shopping mall is the new development model. Of course, the Soho that these galleries grace is no longer industrial; it is one of New York's most exclusive retail and residential districts. Not coincidentally, analysis of consumerism has become a sine qua non for both artists and critics. Meanwhile, the unsaleable installation work that alternative spaces were largely established to support has evolved in significant measure from an art of resistance to one of public service, in the form of architectural amenities. And museums are bent on nothing if not expansion; mass appeal is the prevailing motive of presentation, as mass media is of art. In short, the distinction between the display of art and that of other commodities has become confused. The white cube survives but, in the vast echo chamber where culture now plays, its distinctive resonance is lost.

NANCY PRINCENTHAL

DER WEISSE WÜRFEL LÖST SICH AUF

Vor gut zehn Jahren verfasste Brian O'Doherty für die Zeitschrift «Artforum» eine Aufsatzreihe mit dem Titel «Inside the White Cube». Diese Artikel liegen nun seit kurzem als Buch vor. Damit bietet sich eine gute Gelegenheit, seine Ansichten zur Ideologie des Ausstellungsraums und der Ausstellungspraktiken noch einmal zu überdenken und sich zugleich den Wandel zu vergegenwärtigen, dem diese Bedingungen seit 1976 unterworfen waren.

Bezogen auf die Geschichte des Modernismus und dessen Ende erkennt O'Doherty zwischen der Verflachung des Bildraums und der Purifizierung des Ausstellungsraums eine durchaus wechselseitige Beziehung. «Wir haben einen Punkt erreicht, an dem wir nicht zuerst die Kunst, sondern den

NANCY PRINCENTHAL ist freiberufliche Autorin und Redaktorin bei «The Print Collector's Newsletter». Sie lebt in New York.

Raum sehen», schrieb er. «Das Mysterium der flachen Ebene ... wurde auf den Kunst-Kontext übertragen.» In der Minimal Art und Konzeptkunst der 60er und 70er Jahre sah O'Doherty eine zwingende Herausforderung an die Politik des Galeriesystems – eine Herausforderung, die er 1986 in einem Nachwort als fehlgeschlagen wertet. Nach seiner Ansicht (und die ist ihm nicht leicht zu widerlegen) ist «der Galerie-Raum wieder zur unangefochtenen Arena des Diskurses» geworden.

Aber damit ist die Geschichte noch nicht zu Ende. Je mehr die Dinge bleiben, was sie sind, desto mehr wandeln sie sich. Doch selbst innerhalb jenes Zeitraums, in dem sich O'Dohertys bemerkenswert unbedarfte und grosszügige Wahrnehmungsgeschichte abspielt, sind Positionen entstanden – geographischer eher denn architektonischer Art –, die er geflissentlich übergeht. Gegen Ende der 70er Jahre war Soho, ein Areal von symbolischer wie wirtschaftlicher Anziehungskraft, zweifellos zur internationalen Metropole des «White Cube» (des «Weissen Würfels») geworden. Soho, ursprünglich Standort der Kleinfabrikation, stand für Arbeit, war Arbeits- und Wohnort des entmarginalisierten Künstlers und Schauplatz für den Konsum eines nicht länger luxuriösen Produkts. Die verschiedensten Waren aus dem hier ansässigen Textil-Grosshandel und aus den Geschäften für Büromaterial sowie Baumaterialien und Eisenwaren fanden Eingang in die Kunst, ja wurden in dieser Verbindung Teil der künstlerischen Aussage. Und auch die Galerien in Soho hängten sich (zeitweise) an die Kleinfabrikation an. Auch wenn die Kunst sich in Soho, d.h. im unwirtlichen Südwesten Manhattans, und in den Alternativ-Einrichtungen der Aussenbezirke nicht generell dem Kommerz zu entziehen vermochte, so musste sie sich geographisch nicht gleich ganz auf das Uptown-Territorium der Reichen beschränken.

Die darauffolgende Verlagerung des Geschäftslebens ins East Village hatte viele – zum Teil paradoxe – Auswirkungen: eine davon war das Eindämmen der Kleinfabrikations-Ästhetik. Kunst war nicht Arbeit, sondern Spiel (siehe die inzwischen nicht mehr existierende Fun Gallery). Der Platz des Künstlers war nicht unter dem Sturzhelm auf dem Gerüst einer aufgeklärten Kultur, sondern wieder am Rande der Gesellschaft, wo er – mag sein mit, vielleicht aber auch ohne Zynismus – private Visionen und ästhetische Reflexionen zum besten gab. Wohn- und Ausstellungsraum waren nun wieder vereint, Seite an Seite mit einem ausgeprägten Unterhaltungssektor – ein Abklatsch des amüsanten Cabarets und beengter Ateliers im Vorkriegs-Europa; und wenn auch nur dies: Arbeitermilieu am Tatort allemal. Während es bei der ungegenständlichen Arbeit der Anfangsjahre in Soho um die Betonung des Raums ging (wir sollten uns daran erinnern, dass das Leitmotiv oder vielleicht das Hauptthema der siebziger Jahre die Immobilien-Spekulation war), favorisierte die Arbeit im East Village Lokalkolorit und Lokalmatadore, eher kulturelle Manövertaktik denn Manipulation des Raumes.

Doch auch das ist inzwischen offensichtlich vorbei. Viele Galerien sind vom East Village nach Soho gezogen, wo die Einkaufsstrasse nun das grosse Entwicklungsvorbild ist. Das Soho, das diese Galerien zieren, hat natürlich nichts mehr mit Fabrikation zu tun, sondern ist zu einem der exklusivsten New Yorker Einkaufs- und Wohngebiete geworden. Nicht von ungefähr ist inzwischen die Analyse des Konsumentenverhaltens für Künstler und Kritiker ein sine qua non. Unterdessen haben sich die unverkäuflichen Installationen, zu deren Präsentation die «alternative spaces» ja vor allem gedacht waren, in beträchtlichem Masse von einer Kunst des Widerstands zur öffentlichen Dienstleistung in Form von architektonischen Artigkeiten entwickelt. Und Museen sind nur noch auf ihre Erweiterung erpicht. Anziehung der Massen – das ist der Angelpunkt für jedwede Ausstellungstätigkeit, grad so wie es die Massenmedien für die Kunst sind. Kurz gesagt, Kunst bietet sich so zur Schau wie sich Waren zum Kauf anbieten. Der weisse Würfel überlebt, doch im grossen Echoraum, in dem Kultur sich nun abspielt, hat er seinen spezifischen Klang verloren.

(Übersetzung: Elisabeth Brockmann)

Entschwinden

Alle Zeichen sind in Bewegung, heute . . .
alles ist da wie ein Berg von Angst . . .
der gute Geschmack hofft, dass man Stellung bezieht,
auswählt . . . er ist der grösste Feind der Malerei.
Wir erleben jetzt den Abschluss eines Zyklus, der den Zustand
des Erstaunens der Form vergessen hat. Aber die Malerei
hat längst den Ort angekündet, wo die Form regiert.
Daher bleibe man in diesem, den Beziehungen nach aussen
verschlossenen Territorium, um im Innern der Dinge
die Form wiederzufinden, um einzutauchen . . . zu schweben . . .
zu entschwinden !
um eine Ebene zu finden, . . . ein Zeichen, das markiert.

Disappearing

Today all signs are on the move . . . all things
are present like a mass of fear . . .
taste hopes that one will take sides, chooses . . . but this
is the first enemy of painting.
I think what we experience now, is like the conclusion of a
cycle that has forgotten the form's state of wonder.
But for some time now painting has already anticipated where
form reigns.
Therefore, it is necessary to stay in this territory closed to any
relationship with the exterior, to find the form again within
things, to sink . . . to float . . . to disappear!
to find again a level, . . . a sign that leaves a mark.

AUS / FROM:
ENZO CUCCHI SPARIRE (ENTSCHWINDEN / DISAPPEARING)
PETER BLUM EDITION, NEW YORK, 1987 ERHÄLTLICH BEI / AVAILABLE FROM:
PARKETT VERLAG AG, QUELLENSTRASSE 27, CH-8005 ZÜRICH

GILBERT & GEORGE

SONNABEND 420 WEST BROADWAY NEW YORK

HAIM STEINBACH

SONNABEND 420 WEST BROADWAY NEW YORK
JAY GORNEY 100 GREEN STREET NEW YORK

October 24 – December 19, 1987

ENZO CUCCHI

GALERIE BEYELER

Bäumleingasse 9, CH-4001 Basel, Tel. 061/23 54 12

Robert Mangold

31 October-26 November 1987, Large Gallery

Tony Smith: 'Maze'

7-26 November, Small Gallery

Changing Group Exhibition

1-24 December, Small Gallery

Michael Hurson

1-24 December, Large Gallery

Changing Group Exhibition

7-30 January 1988

Paula Cooper 155 Wooster N.Y. 212 674.0766

SIGMAR POLKE

FEBRUARY

DAVID SALLE

MARCH

BRICE MARDEN

APRIL

MARY BOONE

MICHAEL WERNER

417 WEST BROADWAY, NEW YORK 10012

CY TWOMBLY

JANNIS KOUNELLIS

DECEMBER 1987

CHRISTIAN STEIN 15 VIA LAZZARETTO 20124 MILANO (02) 670 47 54

Galerie Hans Mayer

Grabbeplatz 2
4000 Düsseldorf
Telefon (02 11) 13 21 35

Fictions

A Selection of Pictures from the 18th, 19th & 20th Centuries

Curated by Douglas Blau

November 17 - December 24
Illustrated catalog available.

KENT FINE ART
41 East 57 Street
New York 10022
(212) 980-9696

CURT MARCUS GALLERY
578 Broadway
New York 10012
(212) 226-3200

GALLERIA GIORGIO PERSANO

Torino piazza Vittorio Veneto 9 tel. (011) 835527-830886

Joseph Kosuth

December

GALERIE NÄCHST ST. STEPHAN
ROSEMARIE SCHWARZWÄLDER

JOHN ARMLEDER
HELMUT FEDERLE
FRANZ GRAF
IMI KNOEBEL
GERHARD MERZ
GERWALD ROCKENSCHAUB
NIELE TORONI

GRÜNANGERGASSE 1/2 1010 WIEN/AUSTRIA, TEL. 0222/512 12 66

ETTORE SPALLETTI

DECEMBER 11-JANUARY 8

ULAY & MARINA ABROMOVIC

JANUARY 15-FEBRUARY 13

CHARLES RAY

FEBRUARY 19-MARCH 19

JEAN BERNIER

51 MARASLI STR., GR-106 76 ATHENS, GREECE
TEL. 723 56 57

RICHARD LONG

JANUARY 1988

ULRICH RÜCKRIEM

FEBRUARY 1988

JANNIS KOUNELLIS RICHARD SERRA ANTONI TAPIES

MARCH 1988

34 rue des archives 75004 paris téléphone (1) 42 72 09 10

baudoin lebon

jean clareboudt

november 8 – december 7

dubuffet

december (with galerie de france)

GALERIE CROUSEL – ROBELIN

BAMA

1987–1988

GÜNTHER FÖRG

KEN LUM – LOUISE LAWLER – JENNY HOLZER

MARIA NORDMAN

JOCHEN GERZ

BERNARD FRIZE

TONY CRAGG

SIGMAR POLKE

MARTIN DISLER

GEORGE BRECHT

MARIE-FRANCOISE POUTAYS

THOMAS RUFF

40, RUE QUINCAMPOIX, 75004 PARIS (331) 42 77 38 87

ARCO '88

THE CONTEMPORARY ART FAIR IN MADRID
FEBRUARY 11-16, 1988

FRONTLINE ZURICH

LES SOIES

FABRIC FRONTLINE ZURICH AG, DIENERSTRASSE 16/18, CH-8004 ZURICH,
TELEFON 01/241 64 55, TELEX 814 368, TELEFAX 242 20 02

E X H I B I T I O N S

B A S E L

BEYELER	Bäumleingasse 9, Basel	*LANDSCHAFTEN UND HORIZONTE*	*16.10.–19.12.87*
	Tel. 061/23 54 12	von Monet bis Rothko	
		ENZO CUCCHI	24.10.–19.12.87
STAMPA	Spalenberg 2, Basel	*BRICE MARDEN*	*Dez.–10.1.88*
		Etchings to Rexroth	
		ROSEMARIE TROCKEL	*Jan./Feb./März 88*
		JOSEF FELIX MÜLLER	
		GENERAL IDEA	

B E R N

MICHÈLE ZELLER	Kramgasse 20, Bern	*JOHANNA HESS-DAHM, Schmuck*	*3.–22.11.87*
	Tel. 031/22 93 88	*SCHMUCK FÜR MÄNNER*	*3.12.–22.1.88*
		MARGRETH DAEPP, Installation, Objekte	*28.1.–27.2.88*

G E N È V E

ERIC FRANCK	15, route de Florissant, Genève	*ALIGHIERO E BOETTI*	*9.11.–2.1.88*
	Tel. 022/47 08 09	*Oeuvres récentes*	
HALLE SUD GENÈVE	1, place de l'Ile, Genève	*PHILIPPE DELÉGLISE*	*bis Anfang Dez. 88*
	Tel. 022/28 46 20	*«Prix Placette»*	
DANIEL VARENNE	15, chemin de Sierne, Genève	*IMPRESSIONISTS &*	
	Tel. 022/84 15 93/84 15 97	*20th CENTURY MASTERS*	

S T. G A L L E N

WILMA LOCK	Schmiedgasse 15, St. Gallen	*Zehn mal Eins*	*4.11.–9.1.88*
	Tel. 071/22 62 52	*10 Künstler – 10 Arbeiten*	
		FRANZ WEST	*16.1.–5.3.88*
		JÜRGEN PARTENHEIMER	*19.3–7.5.88*

ZÜRICH

THOMAS AMMANN FINE ART	Restelbergstr. 97, Zürich	*IMPRESSIONISTS*	*by appoint-*
	P.O. Box 116, Tel. 01/252 90 52	*and 20th CENTURY MASTERS*	*ment only*
BRUNO BISCHOFBERGER	Utoquai 29, Zürich	*JIRI GEORG DOKOUPIL, Zodiac*	*21.11.–9.1.88*
	Tel. 01/69 40 20	*ENZO CUCCHI, new paintings*	*16.1.–13.2.88*
ELISABETH KAUFMANN ZÜRICH	Quellenstr. 27, Zürich	*URS LÜTHI*	*Dez. 87*
	Tel. 01/42 29 97	*IRENE GRUNDEL*	*Jan. 88*
		MIRIAM CAHN	*ab. 20.2.88*
MAEGHT LELONG ZÜRICH	Predigerplatz 10/12, Zürich	*HENRI MICHAUX*	*Dez./Jan. 88*
	Tel. 01/251 11 20	*peinture, ecriture*	
MAURER AG	Münstergasse 14/18, Zürich	*WILHELM JAEGER*	*Nov./Dez. 87*
	Tel. 01/47 85 00	*MARIANNE EIGENHEER*	*Jan./Feb. 88*
		LES GAMBIS	*März/April 88*
SCHLÉGL	Minervastr. 119, Zürich	*JOHANNES ITEN*	*21.11.–Ende Dez. 87*
	Tel. 01/251 49 63	*WILLY MEYER-OSBURG*	*Jan.–Mitte Feb. 88*
STORRER GALLERY ZURICH	Scheuchzerstr. 25, Zürich	*GEORGES AUTARD*	*Dez.–Feb. 88*
	Tel. 01/362 73 14		
TURSKE & TURSKE	Seefeldstr. 225, Zürich	*BOYLE FAMILY*	*Nov. 87*
	Tel. 01/55 97 70	*ALOIS MOSBACHER, Zeichnungen*	*Nov. 87*
		MAGDALENA ABAKANOWICZ	*Dez.87/Jan. 88*
		Inkarnationen	
		KIMBER SMITH, Arbeiten auf Papier	*Feb. 88*
ANNEMARIE VERNA	Scheuchzerstr. 35, Eingang	*DON JUDD NEW YORK*	*21.11.–Feb. 88*
	Turnersteig, Zürich		
	Tel. 01/361 90 70		
SUSAN WYSS	Dienerstr. 16, Zürich	*WERNER BÜTTNER*	*Nov./Jan. 88*
	Tel. 01/242 87 24	*GEORG HEROLD*	*Feb./März 88*
BOB GYSIN	Oberdorfstr. 113, Dübendorf	*ADRIAN SCHIESS*	*20.11.–16.1.88*
	Tel. 01/821 52 66		

BISHER ERSCHIENENE NUMMERN

BACK ISSUES

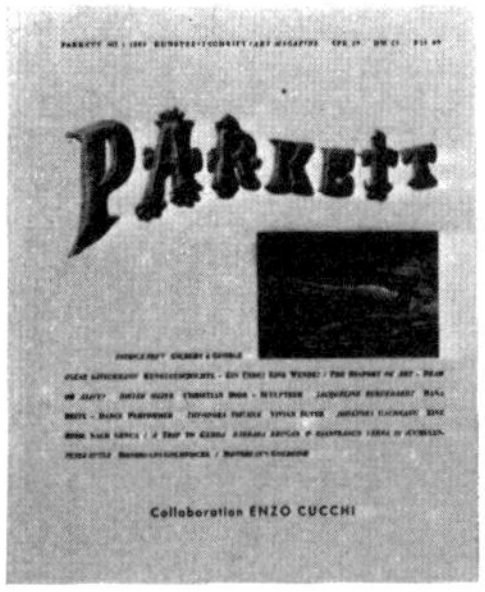

NO. 1

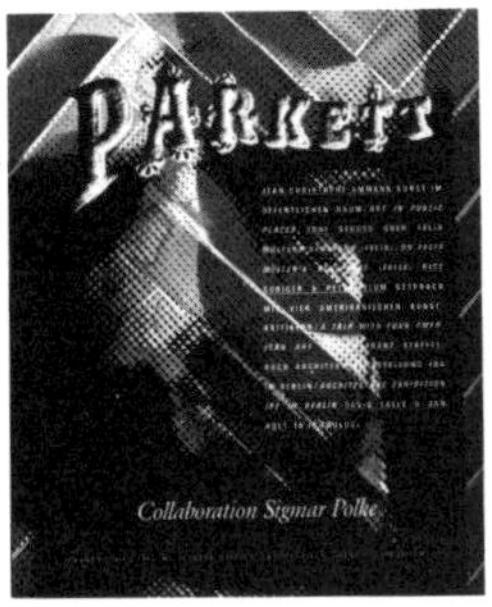

NO. 2

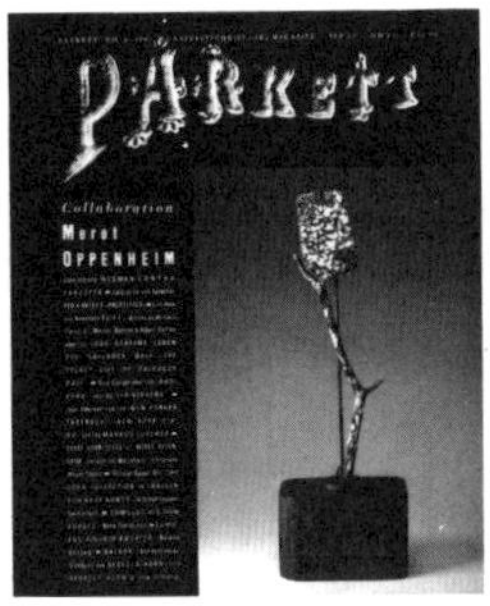

NO. 4

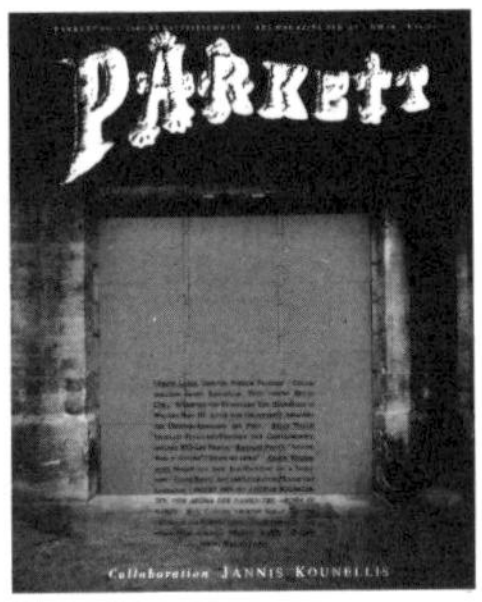

NO. 6

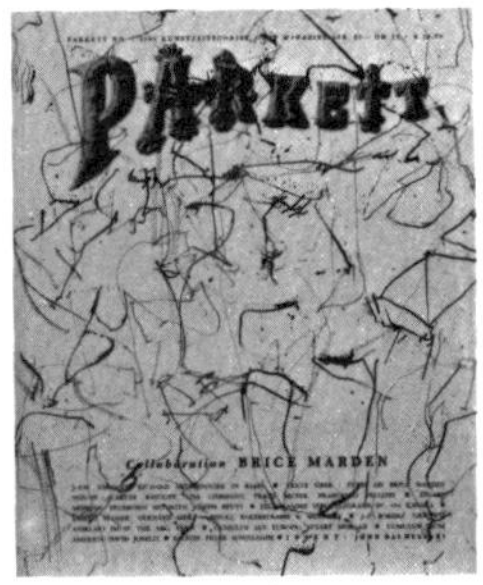

NO. 7

NOS. 1, 2, 4, 6, 7 SIND VERGRIFFEN / *NOS. 1, 2, 4, 6, 7 ARE OUT OF PRINT*

NO. 3

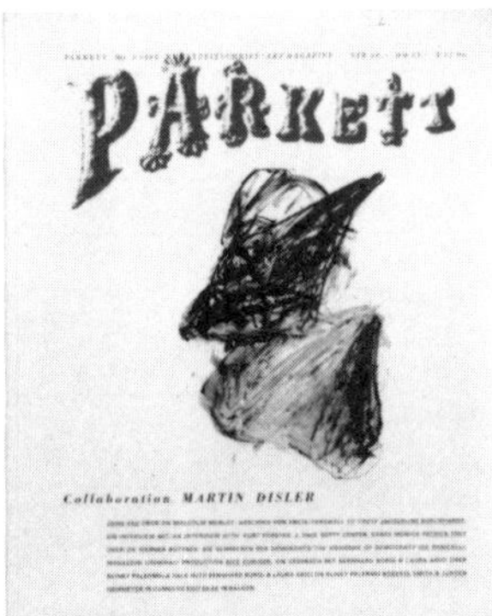

COLLABORATION · MARTIN DISLER
TEXTE VON / *TEXTS BY: DEMOSTHENES DAVVETAS, MARTIN DISLER, BICE CURIGER, MONICA DE CARDENAS, ANNA TILROE*
JOHN YAU ÜBER / *ON:* **MALCOLM MORLEY: ABSCHIED VON KRETA / *FAREWELL TO CRETE***
JACQUELINE BURCKHARDT: **EIN INTERVIEW MIT / *AN INTERVIEW WITH:* KURT FORSTER, J. PAUL GETTY CENTER, SANTA MONICA**
PATRICK FREY ÜBER / *ON:* **DIE SCHRECKEN DER DEMOKRATIE / *THE HORRORS OF DEMOCRACY***
IDA PANICELLI: ***MAGAZZINI CRIMINALI PRODUCTION***
BICE CURIGER: **EIN GESPRÄCH MIT BERNHARD BÜRGI & LAURA ARICI ÜBER BLINKY PALERMO / *A TALK WITH BERNHARD BÜRGI & LAURA ARICI ON BLINKY PALERMO***
CUMULUS: *ROBERTA SMITH & JÜRGEN HOHMEYER*
BALKON: *EDIT DEAK*

NO. 5

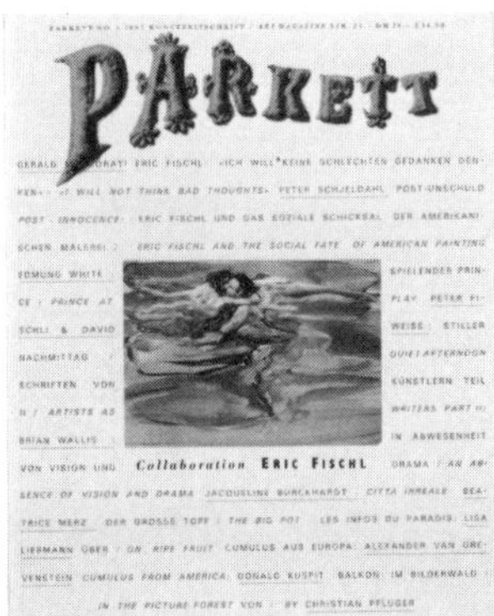

COLLABORATION · ERIC FISCHL
TEXTE VON / *TEXTS BY: GERALD MARZORATI, PETER SCHJELDAHL*
EDMUND WHITE: **SPIELENDER PRINCE / *PRINCE AT PLAY***
PETER FISCHLI & DAVID WEISS: **STILLER NACHMITTAG / *QUIET AFTERNOON***
BRIAN WALLIS: **IN ABWESENHEIT VON VISION UND DRAMA / *AN ABSENCE OF VISION AND DRAMA***
JACQUELINE BURCKHARDT: **CITTÀ IRREALE,** ÜBER / *ON:* ***MARIO MERZ***
BEATRICE MERZ: **DER GROSSE TOPF / *THE BIG POT***
LISA LIEBMANN ÜBER / *ON:* ***RIPE FRUIT***
ALEXANDER VAN GREVENSTEIN & DONALD KUSPIT IN: ***CUMULUS***
CHRISTIAN PFLUGER: **IM BILDERWALD / *IN THE PICTURE-FOREST***
CUMULUS AUS EUROPA: *ALEXANDER VAN GREVENSTEIN*
CUMULUS FROM AMERICA: *DONALD KUSPIT*
BALKON: CHRISTIAN PFLUGER: IM BILDERWALD / *IN THE PICTURE FOREST*

NO. 8

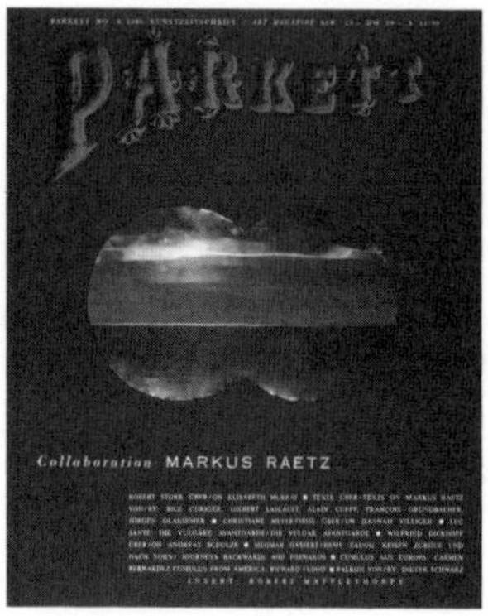

COLLABORATION · MARKUS RAETZ
TEXTE VON / *TEXTS BY: BICE CURIGER, GILBERT LASCAULT, ALAIN CUEFF, FRANÇOIS GRUNDBACHER, JÜRGEN GLAESEMER*
R. STORR ÜBER / *ON:* **ELISABETH MURRAY**
CH. MEYER-THOSS ÜBER / *ON:* **HANNAH VILLIGER**
LUC SANTE: **DIE VULGÄRE AVANTGARDE / *THE VULGAR AVANTGARDE***
W. DICKHOFF ÜBER / *ON:* **ANDREAS SCHULZE**
S. GASSERT / R. ZAUGG: **REISEN ZURÜCK UND NACH VORN / *JOURNEYS BACKWARDS AND FORWARDS***
CUMULUS AUS EUROPA: *CARMEN BERNÁRDEZ*
CUMULUS FROM AMERICA: *RICHARD FLOOD*
BALKON VON / *BY:* **DIETER SCHWARZ**
INSERT: ROBERT MAPPLETHORPE

NO. 9

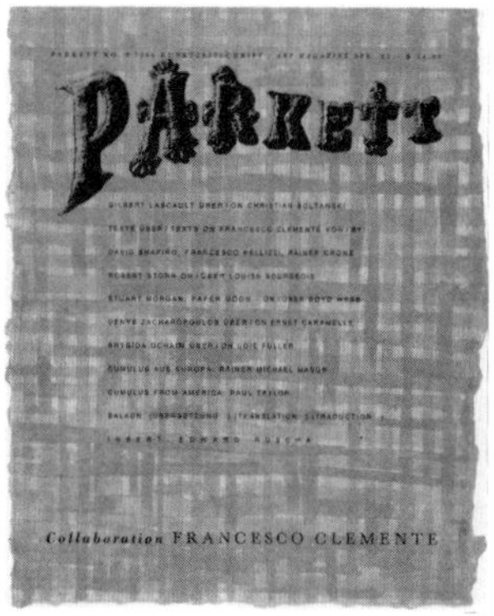

COLLABORATION FRANCESCO CLEMENTE TEXTE VON / *TEXTS BY: DAVID SHAPIRO, FRANCESCO PELLIZZI, RAINER CRONE, GILBERT LASCAULT* ÜBER / *ON:* **CHRISTIAN BOLTANSKI**
ROBERT STORR ON / ÜBER: **LOUISE BOURGEOIS**
STUART MORGAN: **PAPER MOON –**
ON / ÜBER: **BOYD WEBB** *DENYS ZACHAROPOULOS* ÜBER / *ON:* **ERNST CARAMELLE** *BRYGIDA OCHAIM* ÜBER / *ON:* **LOÏE FULLER**
CUMULUS AUS EUROPA: *RAINER MICHAEL MASON*
CUMULUS FROM AMERICA: *PAUL TAYLOR*
BALKON: (ÜBERSETZUNG:) *(TRANSLATION:) (TRADUCTION:)*
INSERT: EDWARD RUSCHA

NO. 10

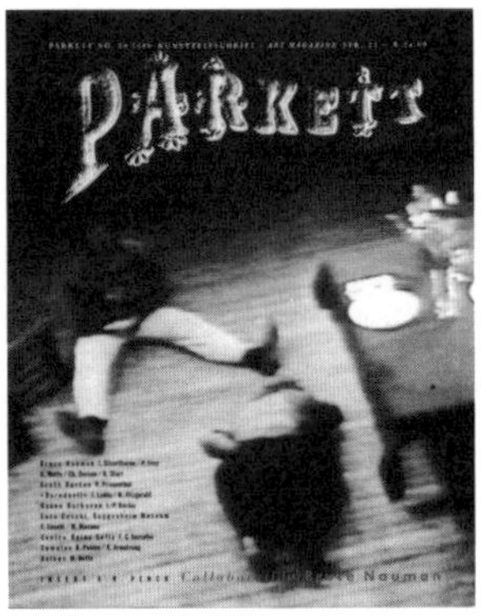

COLLABORATION BRUCE NAUMAN TEXTE VON / *TEXTS BY: JEANNE SILVERTHORNE, PATRICK FREY, REIN WOLFS, CHRIS DERCON, ROBERT STORR*
NANCY PRINCENTHAL ÜBER / *ON:* **SCOTT BURTON**
JEAN-PIERRE BORDAZ ÜBER / *ON:* **HANNE DARBOVEN**
MARIO DIACONO ÜBER / *ON:* **ENZO CUCCHI** IM / *AT THE* **GUGGENHEIM-MUSEUM, NEW YORK 1986**
INSERT: A.R. PENCK
FRANCISCO CALVO SERRALLER ÜBER / *ON:* **CENTRO REINA SOFIA, MADRID**
CUMULUS AUS EUROPA: *ANNELIE POHLEN*
CUMULUS FROM AMERICA: *RICHARD ARMSTRONG*
BALKON: MARIO BOTTA IM GESPRÄCH MIT / *MARIO BOTTA IN CONVERSATION WITH BICE CURIGER*

NO. 11

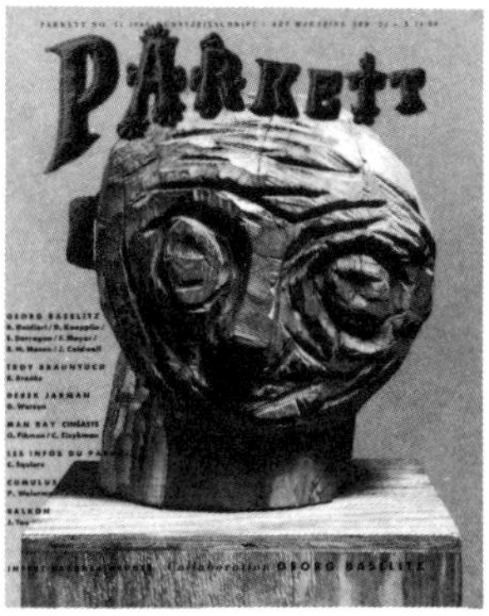

COLLABORATION GEORG BASELITZ TEXTE VON / *TEXTS BY: REMO GUIDIERI, DIETER KOEPPLIN, ERIC DARRAGON, RAINER MICHAEL MASON,* FRANZ MEYER, JOHN CALDWELL
ROSETTA BROOKS ÜBER / *ON:* **TROY BRAUNTUCH**
GRAY WATSON ÜBER / *ON:* **DEREK JARMAN**
GUY FIHMAN & CLAUDINE EIZYKMAN: **MAN RAY – FILM-MAKER**
INSERT: BARBARA KRUGER
CAROL SQUIERS: ***PHOTO OPPORTUNITY*/PHOTO GELEGENHEITEN**
CUMULUS AUS EUROPA: *PETER WEIERMAIR*
CUMULUS FROM AMERICA: *JEANNE SILVERTHORNE*
BALKON: *JOHN YAU*

NO. 12

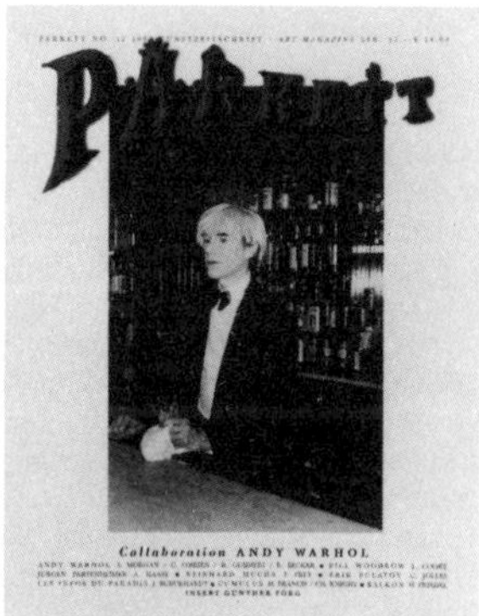

COLLABORATION · ANDY WARHOL
TEXTE VON / *TEXTS BY: STUART MORGAN, GLENN O'BRIEN, REMO GUIDIERI, ROBERT BECKER,*
LYNNE COOKE ÜBER / *ON:* **BILL WOODROW,**
CLAUDIA JOLLES ÜBER / *ON:* **ERIK BULATOW "IDU" ICH GEHE / *I'M GOING***
AMINE HAASE ÜBER / *ON:* **JÜRGEN PARTENHEIMER**
PATRICK FREY ÜBER / *ON:* **REINHARD MUCHA**
INSERT: GÜNTHER FÖRG
JACQUELINE BURCKHARDT ÜBER / *ON:* **SKULPTUR PROJEKTE MÜNSTER 1987 / *SCULPTURE PROJECTS MÜNSTER 1987***
CUMULUS AUS EUROPA: *MARK FRANCIS*
CUMULUS FROM AMERICA: *CHRISTOPHER KNIGHT*
BALKON: *OTTO KÜNZLI,* «KETTE» / *"CHAIN"*

NO. 13

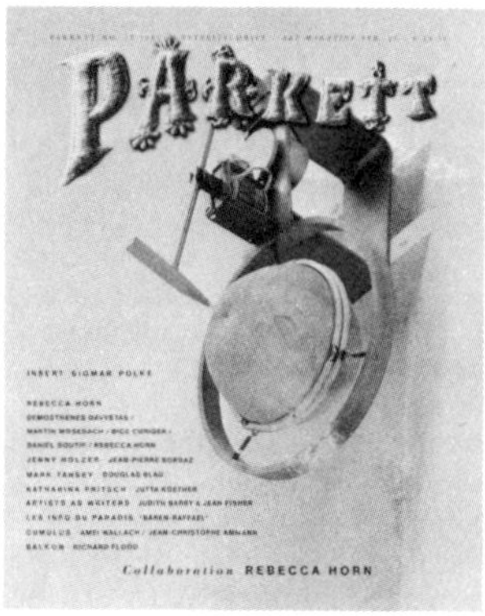

COLLABORATION · REBECCA HORN
TEXTE VON / *TEXTS BY: REBECCA HORN, BICE CURIGER, DEMOSTHENES DAVVETAS, MARTIN MOSEBACH, DANIEL SOUTIF*
ALAIN CUEFF ÜBER / *ON:* **ALIGHIERO E BOETTI**
JEAN-PIERRE BORDAZ ÜBER / *ON:* **JENNY HOLZER**
DOUGLAS BLAU ÜBER / *ON:* **MARK TANSEY "CONVERSATION"**
JUTTA KOETHER ÜBER / *ON:* **KATHARINA FRITSCH "ELEPHANT"**
SCHRIFTEN VON KÜNSTLERN / *ARTISTS AS WRITERS:*
JEAN FISHER: DER VAMPIR DES TEXTES / *THE VAMPIRE OF THE TEXT*
JUDITH BARRY: CHOROS / (VAMPRY...)
INSERT: SIGMAR POLKE
INFOS DU PARADIS: *"BÄREN-RAFFAEL"*
CUMULUS AUS EUROPA: *JEAN CHRISTOPHE AMMANN*
CUMULUS FROM AMERICA: *AMEI WALLACH*
BALKON: *RICHARD FLOOD, ROMANCE LANGUAGE* / DAS ABENTEUER SPRACHE

VORSCHAU / *PREVIEW:*

NO. 15 FEBRUAR / *FEBRUARY 1988* *Collaboration* MARIO MERZ

VORZUGSAUSGABEN / *DELUXE EDITIONS*

Jede Nummer der Zeitschrift entsteht in Collaboration mit einem Künstler, der eigens für die Leser von PARKETT einen Originalbeitrag gestaltet. Dieses Werk ist in der gesamten Auflage abgebildet und zusätzlich als limitierte und signierte Vorzugsausgabe erhältlich.

Each issue of the magazine is created in collaboration with an artist, who contributes an original work specially made for the readers of PARKETT. The work is reproduced in the regular edition. It is also available in a signed and limited Deluxe Edition.

ENZO CUCCHI

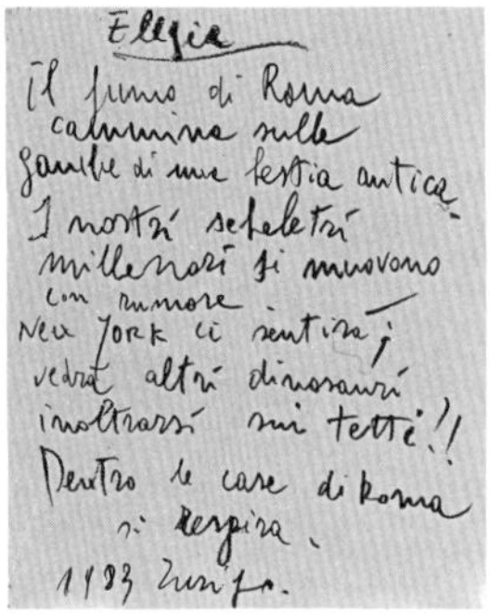

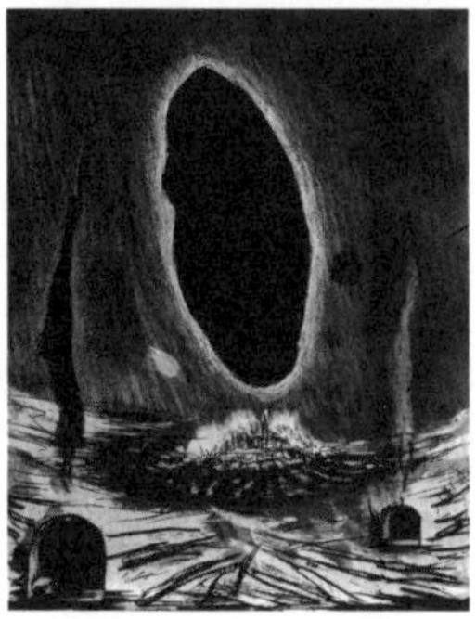

«ELEGIE UND RADIERUNG»
Aquatinta, ed. 80. Vorzugsausgabe Nr. 1 ist vergriffen.
"ELEGY AND ETCHING"
Aquatint ed. 80. Deluxe Edition no. 1 is sold out.

SIGMAR POLKE

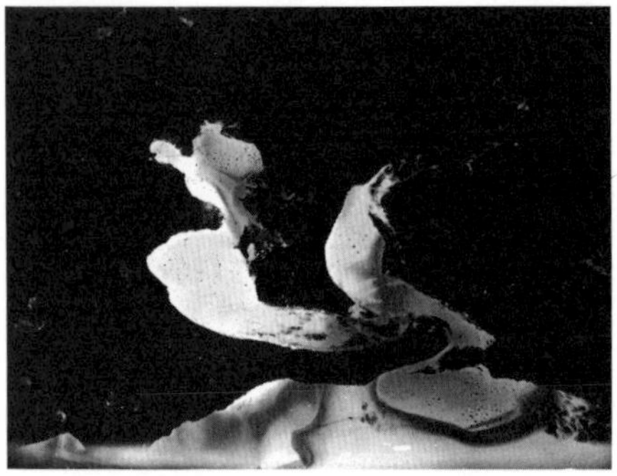

«DESASTRES UND ANDERE BARE WUNDER»
60 Unikat-Photos. Vorzugsausgabe Nr. 2 ist vergriffen.
60 unique photographs. Deluxe Edition no. 2 is sold out.

MARTIN DISLER

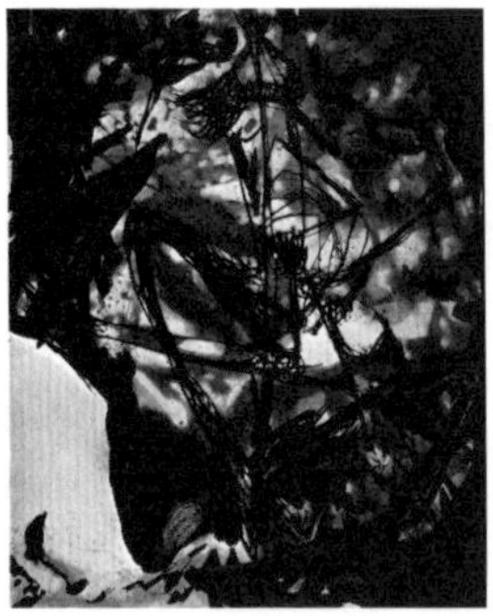

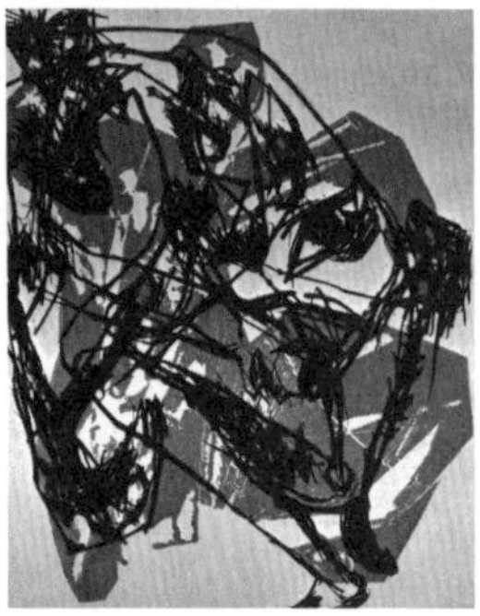

"IN THE EROTIC SPACE OF A HEAD"
Kaltnadel und Aquatinta, ed. 50. Die Ausgabe ist vergriffen.
Drypoint and aquatint, ed. 50. The edition is sold out.

"LITTLE RED PUSHER"
Lederschnitt und Kaltnadel, ed. 50. Die Ausgabe ist vergriffen.
Leathercut and drypoint, ed. 50. The edition is sold out.

MERET OPPENHEIM

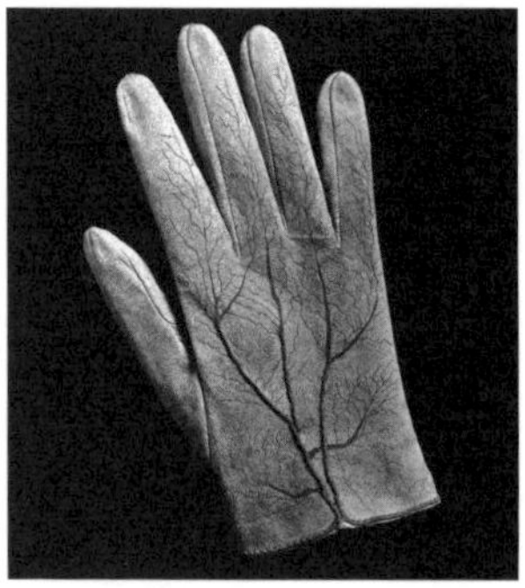

«HANDSCHUH»
Ziegenwildleder, von Hand passepoiliert und mit Siebdruck versehen, ed. 150 Paare.
Vorzugsausgabe Nr. 4 ist vergriffen.
"GLOVE"
Goat suede with silk-screen and hand-stitched, ed. 150 pairs.
Deluxe Edition no. 4 is sold out.

ERIC FISCHL

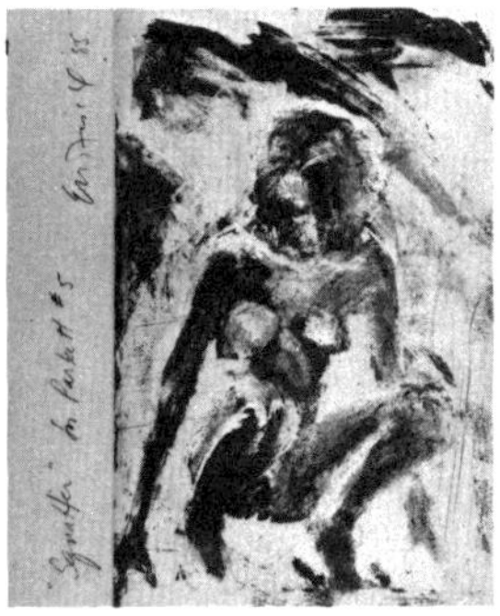

«KAUERNDE»
Aquatinta und Aussprengverfahren ed. 100.
Vorzugsausgabe Nr. 5 ist vergriffen.
"SQUATTER"
Aquatint and sugar lift ed. 100.
Deluxe Edition no. 5 is sold out.

JANNIS KOUNELLIS

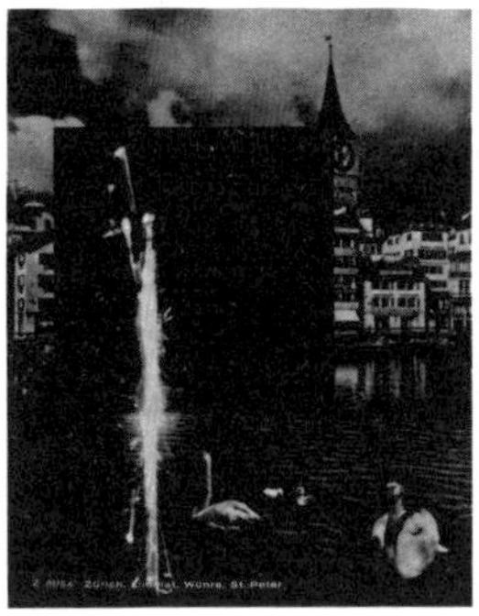

«OHNE TITEL»
Photoätzung, Aquatinta und Schabtechnik
auf Zerkall-Bütten, ed. 80. Vorzugsausgabe Nr. 6 sFr. 750.–.
"UNTITLED"
Photo-etching, aquatint and scraping, on Zerkall-Vellum, ed. 80.
Deluxe Edition no. 6 $ 300.00.

BRICE MARDEN

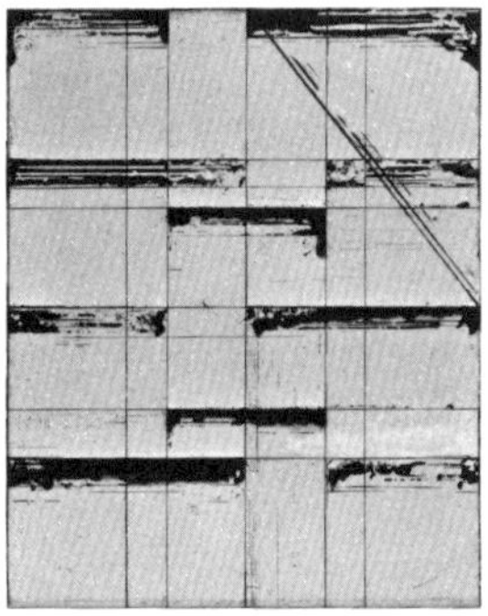

«RADIERUNG FÜR PARKETT»
Aussprengverfahren und Aquatinta
auf Rives BFK., ed. 100. Vorzugsausgabe Nr. 7 sFr. 650.–.
"ETCHING FOR PARKETT"
Sugar lift and aquatint on Rives BFK., ed. 100.
Deluxe Edition no. 7 $ 300.00.

MARKUS RAETZ

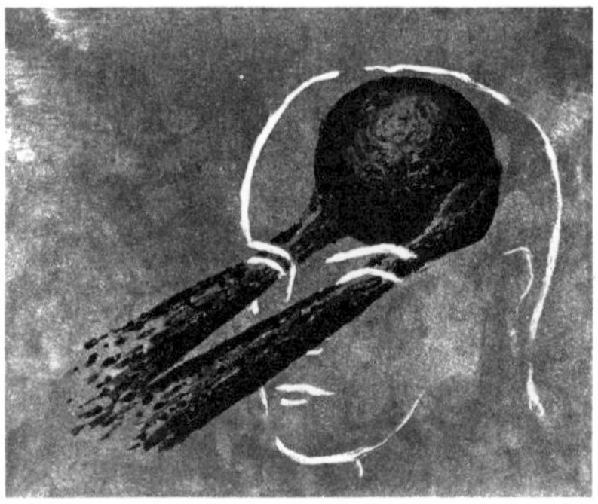

«OHNE TITEL»
Aquatinta und Aussprengtechnik auf Zerkall-
Bütten, ed. 100. Vorzugsausgabe Nr. 8 sFr. 550.–.
"UNTITLED"
Aquatint and sugar lift on Zerkall-Vellum,
ed. 100. Deluxe Edition no. 8 $ 270.00.

FRANCESCO CLEMENTE

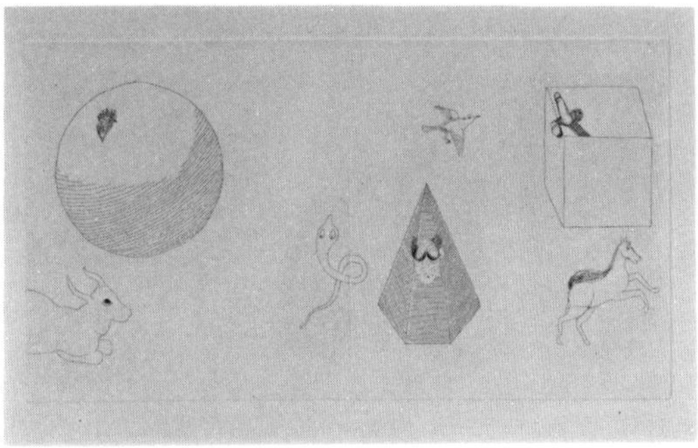

«VERSÖHNUNG»
Kaltnadel-Radierung, ed. 100.
Vorzugsausgabe Nr. 9 sFr. 700.–.
"RECONCILIATION"
Drypoint etching, ed. 100.
Deluxe Edition no. 9 $ 350.00.

BRUCE NAUMAN

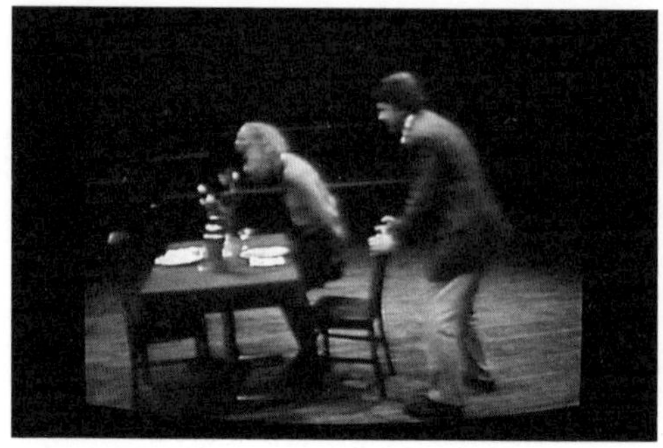

«GEWALTTÄTIGER ZWISCHENFALL – MANN/FRAU SEGMENT»
Video-Tape von 30 Min. (Dauer einer Sequenz: 28 Sek.),
erhältlich auf U-matic- oder VHS-Kassetten, NTSC-
oder PAL-TV-Standard, Farbe und Ton.
Ed. 200, numeriert und signiert. Vorzugsausgabe Nr. 10 sFr. 400.–.
"VIOLENT INCIDENT – MAN/WOMAN SEGMENT"
Videotape of 30 min. (time of one sequence: 28 sec.), available on
U-matic- or VHS-cassettes, NTSC- or PAL-tv-standard, color and sound.
Ed. 200, numbered and signed. Deluxe Edition no. 10 $ 250.00.

GEORG BASELITZ

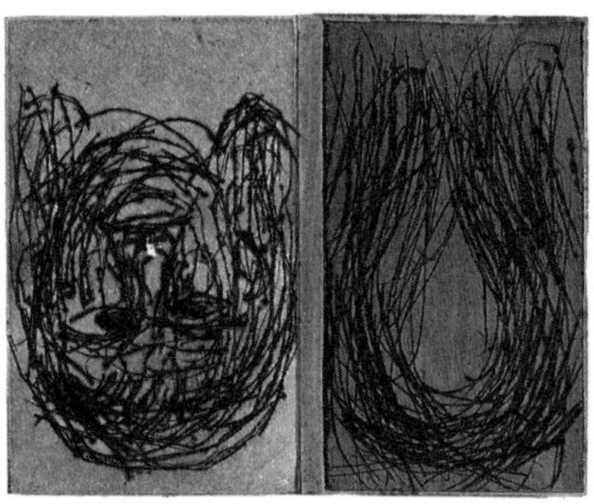

«GESICHT UND TRÄNE»
Kaltnadel-Radierung auf schabloniertem, englisch-rotem
Grund von zwei Platten auf Zerkall Werkdruck 145 g.
Linke Platte: 12,7 x 8,1 cm
Rechte Platte: 12,3 x 7,2 cm
Ed. 60. Vorzugsausgabe Nr. 11 ist vergriffen.
"FACE AND TEARDROP"
Drypoint etching on stenciled english-red ground of two plates
on Zerkall book paper 145 g.
Left plate: 12,7 x 8,1 cm / 5 x 3 1/5"
Right plate: 12,3 x 7,2 cm / 4 4/5 x 2 4/5"
Ed. 60. Deluxe Edition no. 11 is sold out.

ANDY WARHOL

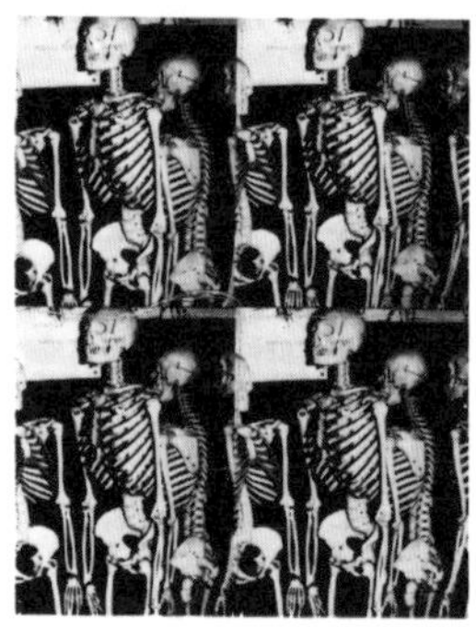

«PHOTO EDITION FÜR PARKETT, 1987»
Ed. 120 numerierte, signierte Exemplare,
24,6 x 19,6 cm, maschinengenäht,
in Pergamentpapiertasche der Vorzugsausgabe
von Parkett beigefügt.
Vorzugsausgabe Nr. 12 ist vergriffen.
"PHOTO EDITION FOR PARKETT, 1987"
Ed. 120 numbered and signed copies,
24.6 x 19.6 cm / 9.6 x 7.7", machine-sewn
and inserted in a parchment cover in the
deluxe edition of Parkett.
Deluxe Edition no. 12 is sold out.

REBECCA HORN

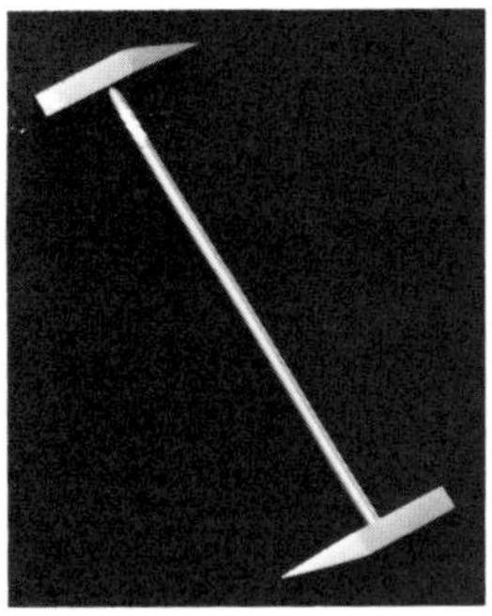

«DER DOPPELGÄNGER»
Hämmerchen, Messing versilbert,
25,2 x 8,2 x 0,7 cm, eingelegt in
signierte und numerierte Schachtel. Ed. 99.
Vorzugsausgabe Nr. 13 sFr. 660.–
«DER DOPPELGÄNGER» ("THE DOUBLE")
little silver-plated brass hammer,
9¾ x 3⅙ x ¼", placed in a
signed and numbered box. Ed. 99.
Deluxe Edition no. 13 $ 440.00.

GILBERT & GEORGE

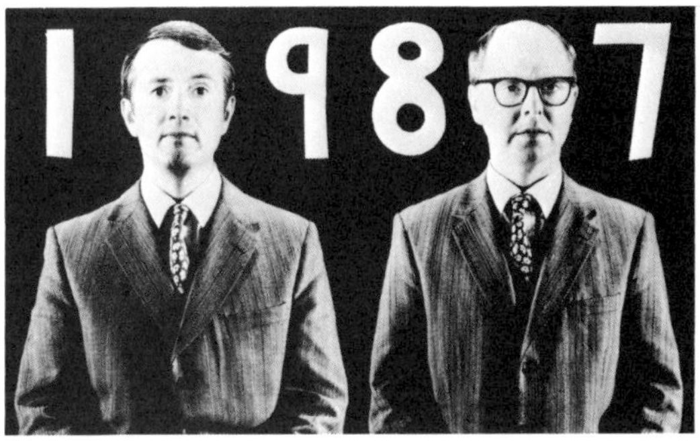

«1987»
Photo Edition, auf Karton aufgezogen,
in der Mitte faltbar. 25,5 x 42 cm. Ed. 200.
Vorzugsausgabe Nr. 14 sFr. 440.–.
"1987"
Photo edition mounted on cardboard
and folded in the middle. 10 x 16½". Ed. 200.
Deluxe Edition no. 14 $ 300.00.

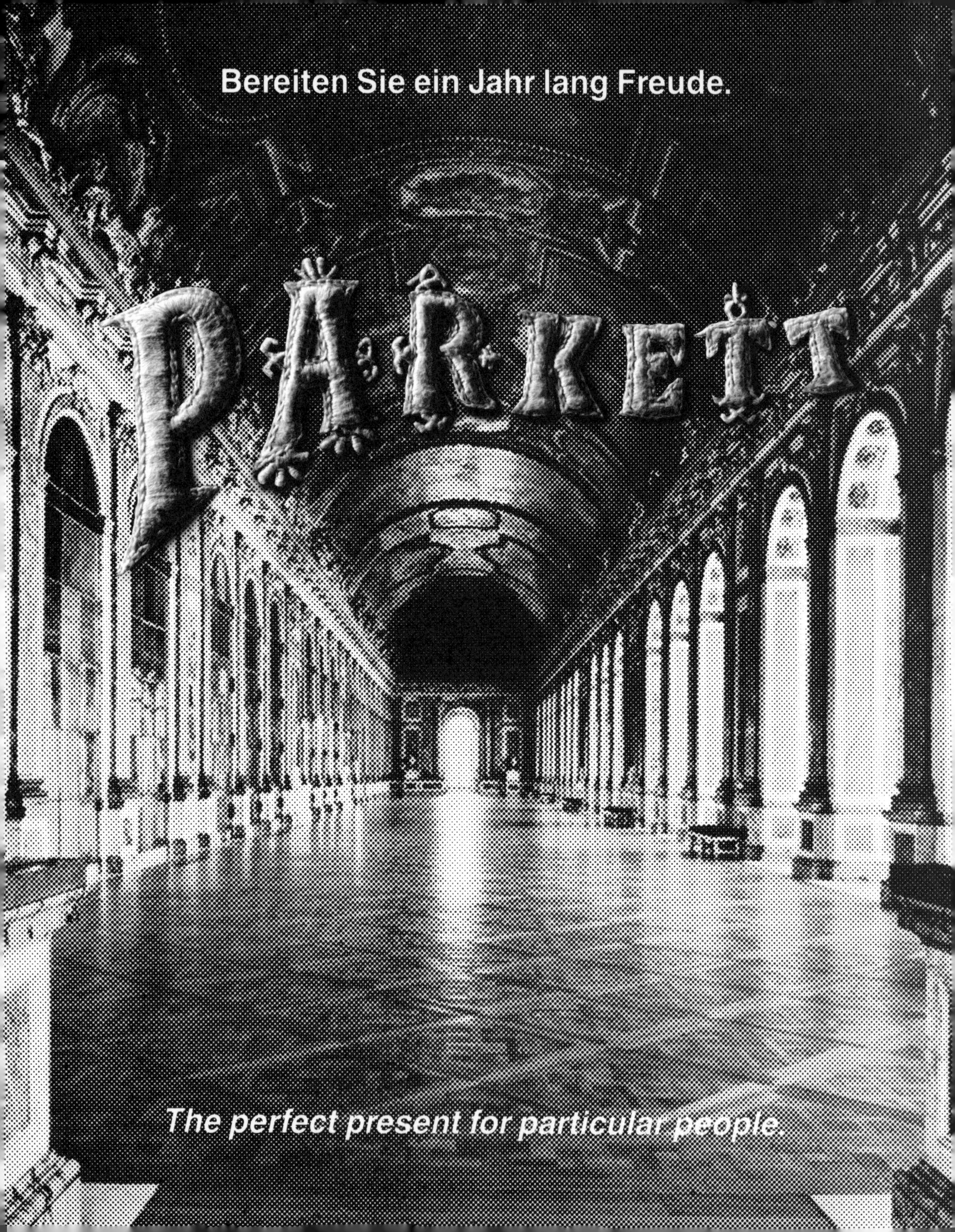
Bereiten Sie ein Jahr lang Freude.
PARKETT
The perfect present for particular people.

VERTRIEB / *DISTRIBUTION* AUSKUNFT UND ABONNEMENTS / *INFORMATION AND SUBSCRIPTIONS:*
«PARKETT»-VERLAG AG, QUELLENSTRASSE 27, CH-8005 ZÜRICH / SWITZERLAND, TEL. 01/42 81 40 ***PARKETT,** 14, WEST 10TH STREET, NEW YORK, N.Y. 10011, PHONE 212/475-0227*

SCHWEIZ
IM AUSGEWÄHLTEN BUCH-,
ZEITSCHRIFTEN- UND KUNSTHANDEL
ALLER GRÖSSEREN STÄDTE

DEUTSCHLAND
BERLIN
BÜCHERBOGEN, AM SAVIGNYPLATZ,
1000 BERLIN 12
GALERIE 2000, KNESEBECKSTR. 56–58,
1000 BERLIN 15
BREMEN
ANTIQUARIAT,
BEIM STEINERNEN KREUZ 1,
2800 BREMEN
BUCHLADEN BETTINA WASSMANN
AM WALL 164,
2800 BREMEN
DARMSTADT
GEORG BÜCHNER,
LAUTESCHLÄGERSTR. 18,
6100 DARMSTADT
DÜSSELDORF
M. + R. FRICKE, POSTSTR. 3,
4000 DÜSSELDORF
SCHWAN & BÖGER, KÖNIGSALLEE 14–16,
4000 DÜSSELDORF
FRANKFURT
LAND IN SICHT, ROTTECKSTR. 13,
6000 FRANKFURT
PETER NAACHER, STEINWEG 3,
6000 FRANKFURT
HAMBURG
H. VON DER HÖH, GROSSE BLEICHEN 21,
2000 HAMBURG
SAUTTER UND LACKMANN,
KLOSTERSTERN 8,
2000 HAMBURG
HANNOVER
BUCHHANDLUNG
IM SPRENGELMUSEUM,
KURT-SCHWITTERS-PLATZ,
3000 HANNOVER 1
HEIDELBERG
KUNSTHANDLUNG
W. WELKER, HAUPTSTR. 106,
6900 HEIDELBERG 1
KÖLN
WALTHER KÖNIG, EHRENSTR. 4,
5000 KÖLN 1
K. BITTNER, ALBERTUSSTR. 6,
5000 KÖLN 1
MÜNCHEN
ILKA KÖNIG, AM KOSTTOR 1,
8000 MÜNCHEN 1
H. GOLZ, TÜRKENSTR. 54,
8000 MÜNCHEN 40
SAARBRÜCKEN
BUCHHANDLUNG
AM ST. JOHANNER MARKT,
ST. JOHANNER MARKT 13,
6600 SAARBRÜCKEN
TÜBINGEN
HUGO FRICK,
NAUKLERSTR. 7,
7400 TÜBINGEN 1
STUTTGART
GALERIE VALENTIEN, KÖNIGSBAU,
7000 STUTTGART 1

OESTERREICH
GRAZ
BUCHHANDLUNG GALERIE
VERLAG DROSCHL,
BISCHOFPLATZ 1,
8010 GRAZ
INNSBRUCK
WAGNERSCHE
UNIVERSITÄTSBUCHHANDLUNG,
MUSEUMSTR. 4,
6021 INNSBRUCK
WIEN
JUDITH ORTNER,
SONNENFELSGASSE 8,
1010 WIEN
SHAKESPEARE & COMPANY
BOOKSELLERS,
STEINGASSE 2,
1010 WIEN

HOLLAND
ARNHEM
BRAND & BRAND & HENDRIKS,
LOOIERSTRAAT 14,
6811 AX ARNHEM
AMSTERDAM
ART BOOK, PRINSENGRACHT 645,
1046 HV AMSTERDAM
ATHENAEUM NIEUWSCENTRUM,
SPUI 14–16,
1012 XA AMSTERDAM
PREMSELA, VAN BAERLESTRAAT 78,
1071 BB AMSTERDAM

BELGIQUE
BRUXELLES
POST-SCRIPTUM,
37 RUE DES ÈPERONNIERS,
1000 BRUXELLES
GENT
COPYRIGHT, JAKOBIJNENSTRAAT 8,
9000 GENT

ESPAÑA
BARCELONA
METRÒNOM,
CARRER DE LA FUSSINA 9,
08003 BARCELONA
MADRID
LIBROS ARGENSOLA,
ARGENSOLA 20,
28004 MADRID

FRANCE
PARIS
LA HUNE, 170 BLVD ST-GERMAIN,
75008 PARIS
«FLAMMARION 4»
LIBRAIRIE DU CENTRE
GEORGES POMPIDOU,
PLATEAU BEAUBOURG,
75004 PARIS
BORDEAUX
LIBRAIRIE DU
MUSÉE CAPC
ENTREPÔT LAINÉ
33000 BORDEAUX

ITALIA
MILANO
MILANO LIBRI,
VIA G.VERDI 2,
20121 MILANO
ROMA
CENTRO DI
GALLERIA NAZIONALE D'ARTE MODERNA,
VIA DELLE BELLE ARTI 131,
00196 ROMA
FELTRINELLI,
VIA DEL BABUINO 41,
00187 ROMA
GALLERIA PRIMO PIANO,
VIA PANISPERNA 203,
00184 ROMA

PORTUGAL
LISBOA
COMICOS ESPAÇO INTER-MEDIA,
RUA TENENTE RAUL CASCAIS 1B,
1200 LISBOA

SVERIGE
STOCKHOLM
VENNERGREN & WILLIAM,
NORDENFLYCHTSVÄGEN 70,
10425 STOCKHOLM

GREAT BRITAIN
DISTRIBUTOR
NIGEL GREENWOOD BOOKS,
4, NEW BURLINGTON STREET,
LONDON, W1
LONDON
ARTS COUNCIL, BOOKSHOP,
8 LONG ACRE COVENT GARDEN,
LONDON WC2 9L6
NIGEL GREENWOOD,
4, NEW BURLINGTON STREET,
LONDON W1
THE TATE GALLERY, MILLBANK,
LONDON SW1 P4 RS

USA
DISTRIBUTORS
B. DE BOER INC.,
113 EAST CENTRE STREET,
NUTLEY N.J. 07110
ARTINFORM,
2237 SECOND AVENUE,
SEATTLE, WASHINGTON 98121
BOSTON
MUSEUM OF FINE ARTS BOSTON,
465 HUNTINGTON AVE.,
BOSTON, MASS. 02115
BERKELEY
MOE'S BOOKS,
2476 TELEGRAPH,
BERKELEY, CA 94704
CAMBRIDGE
MANDRAKE BOOK STORE,
8 STORY STREET,
CAMBRIDGE, MA 02138
CHICAGO
MUSEUM OF CONTEMPORARY ART,
237 EAST ONTARIO ST.,
CHICAGO, Ill. 60611
LOS ANGELES
ART CATALOGUES,
625 N. ALMONT DR.,
LOS ANGELES, CA 90069
NEW YORK
BOOKS AND COMPANY,
939 MADISON AVE.,
NEW YORK, NY 10021
JAAP RIETMANN,
134 SPRING STREET,
NEW YORK, NY 10012
UNTITLED II INC.,
680 BROADWAY,
NEW YORK, NY 10012
SAN FRANCISCO
SAN FRANCISCO MUSEUM
OF MODERN ART
BOOKSHOP,
VAN NESS AVE. AT MCALLISTER ST.,
SAN FRANCISCO, CA 94102
SANTA MONICA
HENNESSEY + INGALLS BOOKS,
1254 SANTA MONICA MALL,
SANTA MONICA, CA 90401
WASHINGTON
NATIONAL GALLERY,
6TH STREET
AND CONSTITUTION AVENUE NW
WASHINGTON D.C. 20565

CANADA
MONTREAL
ARTEXTE,
3575 ST. LAURENT,
MONTREAL
TORONTO
ART METROPOLE,
217 RICHMOND STR. W.,
TORONTO

AUSTRALIA
THE ARTS BOOKSHOP,
1067 HIGH STREET,
ARMADALE, VICTORIA 3143

JAPAN
TOKIO
EUROPA ART GMBH,
CHERRY-HEIGHTS 102,
17–26, SHOAN 1 CHOME, SUGINAMI-KU,
TOKYO 167

MUSEE D'ART MODERNE
MUSEUM OF MODERN ART
KUNST MUSEUM

Concerning
the

SALE
OF A KILOGRAM OF FINE GOLD
IN THE
INGOT

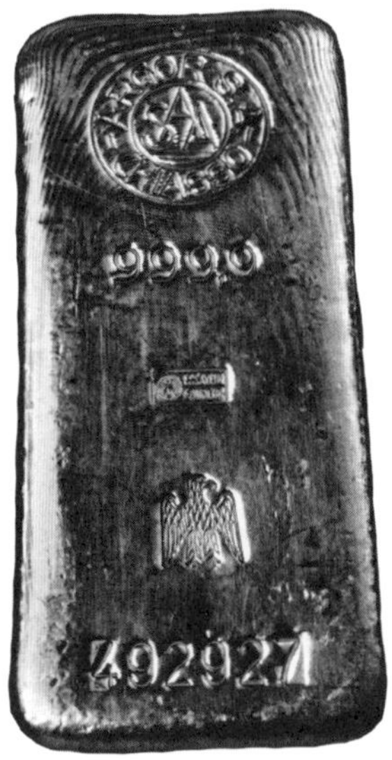

PROPOSED BY THE FINANCIAL
SECTION OF THE DEPARTMENT
OF EAGLES

PLATANENSTRASSE 7
4000 DÜSSELDORF
TELEFON 0211/68 59 08

KONRAD FISCHER

MUTTER-EY-STRASSE 5
4000 DÜSSELDORF
TELEFON 0211/32 41 05